CISCO

WI

Course Booklet

CCNA Exploration

LAN Switching and Wireless

Version 4.0

ciscopress.com

Cisco | Networking Academy
Mind Wide Open

CCNA Exploration Course Booklet LAN Switching and Wireless, Version 4.0

Cisco Networking Academy

Copyright© 2010 Cisco Systems, Inc.

Published by:
Cisco Press
800 East 96th Street
Indianapolis, IN 46240 USA

Printed in the United States of America

First Printing   September 2009

Library of Congress Cataloging-in-Publication Data is available upon request

ISBN-13: 978-1-58713-254-4

ISBN-10: 1-58713-254-0

Publisher
Paul Boger

Associate Publisher
Dave Dusthimer

Cisco Representative
Erik Ullanderson

Cisco Press Program Manager
Anand Sundaram

Executive Editor
Mary Beth Ray

Managing Editor
Patrick Kanouse

Project Editor
Bethany Wall

Editorial Assistant
Vanessa Evans

Cover Designer
Louisa Adair

Composition
Mark Shirar

Warning and Disclaimer

This book is part of the Cisco Networking Academy® series from Cisco Press. The products in this series support and complement the Cisco Networking Academy curriculum. If you are using this book outside the Networking Academy, then you are not preparing with a Cisco trained and authorized Networking Academy provider.

For more information on the Cisco Networking Academy or to locate a Networking Academy, Please visit www.cisco.com/edu.

ılıılıı
CISCO.

Trademark Acknowledgments

All terms mentioned in this book that are known to be trademarks or service marks have been appropriately capitalized. Cisco Press or Cisco Systems, Inc., cannot attest to the accuracy of this information. Use of a term in this book should not be regarded as affecting the validity of any trademark or service mark.

Feedback Information

At Cisco Press, our goal is to create in-depth technical books of the highest quality and value. Each book is crafted with care and precision, undergoing rigorous development that involves the unique expertise of members from the professional technical community.

Readers' feedback is a natural continuation of this process. If you have any comments regarding how we could improve the quality of this book, or otherwise alter it to better suit your needs, you can contact us through email at feedback@ciscopress.com. Please make sure to include the book title and ISBN in your message.

We greatly appreciate your assistance.

CISCO

Americas Headquarters
Cisco Systems, Inc.
San Jose, CA

Asia Pacific Headquarters
Cisco Systems (USA) Pte. Ltd.
Singapore

Europe Headquarters
Cisco Systems International BV
Amsterdam, The Netherlands

Cisco has more than 200 offices worldwide. Addresses, phone numbers, and fax numbers are listed on the Cisco Website at **www.cisco.com/go/offices**.

CCDE, CCENT, Cisco Eos, Cisco HealthPresence, the Cisco logo, Cisco Lumin, Cisco Nexus, Cisco StadiumVision, Cisco TelePresence, Cisco WebEx, DCE, and Welcome to the Human Network are trademarks; Changing the Way We Work, Live, Play, and Learn and Cisco Store are service marks; and Access Registrar, Aironet, AsyncOS, Bringing the Meeting To You, Catalyst, CCDA, CCDP, CCIE, CCIP, CCNA, CCNP, CCSP, CCVP, Cisco, the Cisco Certified Internetwork Expert logo, Cisco IOS, Cisco Press, Cisco Systems, Cisco Systems Capital, the Cisco Systems logo, Cisco Unity, Collaboration Without Limitation, EtherFast, EtherSwitch, Event Center, Fast Step, Follow Me Browsing, FormShare, GigaDrive, HomeLink, Internet Quotient, IOS, iPhone, iQuick Study, IronPort, the IronPort logo, LightStream, Linksys, MediaTone, MeetingPlace, MeetingPlace Chime Sound, MGX, Networkers, Networking Academy, Network Registrar, PCNow, PIX, PowerPanels, ProConnect, ScriptShare, SenderBase, SMARTnet, Spectrum Expert, StackWise, The Fastest Way to Increase Your Internet Quotient, TransPath, WebEx, and the WebEx logo are registered trademarks of Cisco Systems, Inc. and/or its affiliates in the United States and certain other countries.

All other trademarks mentioned in this document or website are the property of their respective owners. The use of the word partner does not imply a partnership relationship between Cisco and any other company. (0812R)

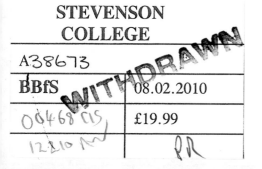

Contents at a Glance

Contents

Command Syntax Conventions

The conventions used to present command syntax in this book are the same conventions used in the IOS Command Reference. The Command Reference describes these conventions as follows:

- **Boldface** indicates commands and keywords that are entered literally as shown. In actual configuration examples and output (not general command syntax), boldface indicates commands that are manually input by the user (such as a **show** command).

- *Italic* indicates arguments for which you supply actual values.

- Vertical bars (|) separate alternative, mutually exclusive elements.

- Square brackets ([ ]) indicate an optional element.

- Braces ({ }) indicate a required choice.

- Braces within brackets ([{ }]) indicate a required choice within an optional element.

About this Course Booklet

Your Cisco Networking Academy Course Booklet is designed as a study resource you can easily read, highlight, and review on the go, wherever the Internet is not available or practical:

- The text is extracted directly, word-for-word, from the online course so you can highlight important points and take notes in the "Your Chapter Notes" section.

- Headings with the exact page correlations provide a quick reference to the online course for your classroom discussions and exam preparation.

- An icon system directs you to the online curriculum to take full advantage of the images, labs, Packet Tracer activities, and dynamic Flash-based activities embedded within the Networking Academy online course interface.

The Course Booklet is a basic, economical paper-based resource to help you succeed with the Cisco Networking Academy online course.

Welcome

Welcome to the CCNA Exploration LAN Switching and Wireless course. The goal is to develop an understanding of how switches are interconnected and configured to provide network access to LAN users. This course also teaches how to integrate wireless devices into a LAN. The specific skills covered in each chapter are described at the start of each chapter.

More than just information

This computer-based learning environment is an important part of the overall course experience for students and instructors in the Networking Academy. These online course materials are designed to be used along with several other instructional tools and activities. These include:

- Class presentation, discussion, and practice with your instructor
- Hands-on labs that use networking equipment within the Networking Academy classroom
- Online scored assessments and a matching grade book
- Packet Tracer simulation tool
- Additional software for classroom activities

A global community

When you participate in the Networking Academy, you are joining a global community linked by common goals and technologies. Schools, colleges, universities and other entities in over 160 countries participate in the program. You can see an interactive network map of the global Networking Academy community at http://www.academynetspace.com.

The material in this course encompasses a broad range of technologies that facilitate how people work, live, play, and learn by communicating with voice, video, and other data. Networking and the Internet affect people differently in different parts of the world. Although we have worked with instructors from around the world to create these materials, it is important that you work with your instructor and fellow students to make the material in this course applicable to your local situation.

Keep in Touch

These online instructional materials, as well as the rest of the course tools, are part of the larger Networking Academy. The portal for the program is located at http://cisco.netacad.net. There you will obtain access to the other tools in the program such as the assessment server and student grade book), as well as informational updates and other relevant links.

Mind Wide Open®

An important goal in education is to enrich you, the student, by expanding what you know and can do. It is important to realize, however, that the instructional materials and the instructor can only facilitate the process. You must make the commitment yourself to learn new skills. Below are a few suggestions to help you learn and grow.

1. Take notes. Professionals in the networking field often keep Engineering Journals in which they write down the things they observe and learn. Taking notes is an important way to help your understanding grow over time.

2. Think about it. The course provides information both to change what you know and what you can do. As you go through the course, ask yourself what makes sense and what doesn't. Stop and ask questions when you are confused. Try to find out more about topics that interest you. If you are not sure why something is being taught, consider asking your instructor or a friend. Think about how the different parts of the course fit together.

3. Practice. Learning new skills requires practice. We believe this is so important to e-learning that we have a special name for it. We call it e-doing. It is very important that you complete the activities in the online instructional materials and that you also complete the hands-on labs and Packet Tracer® activities.

4. Practice again. Have you ever thought that you knew how to do something and then, when it was time to show it on a test or at work, you discovered that you really hadn't mastered it? Just like learning any new skill like a sport, game, or language, learning a professional skill requires patience and repeated practice before you can say you have truly learned it. The online instructional materials in this course provide opportunities for repeated practice for many skills. Take full advantage of them. You can also work with your instructor to extend Packet Tracer, and other tools, for additional practice as needed.

5. Teach it. Teaching a friend or colleague is often a good way to reinforce your own learning. To teach well, you will have to work through details that you may have overlooked on your first reading. Conversations about the course material with fellow students, colleagues, and the instructor can help solidify your understanding of networking concepts.

6. Make changes as you go. The course is designed to provide feedback through interactive activities and quizzes, the online assessment system, and through interactions with your instructor. You can use this feedback to better understand where your strengths and weaknesses are. If there is an area that you are having trouble with, focus on studying or practicing more in that area. Seek additional feedback from your instructor and other students.

Explore the world of networking

This version of the course includes a special tool called Packet Tracer 4.1®. Packet Tracer is a networking learning tool that supports a wide range of physical and logical simulations. It also provides visualization tools to help you to understand the internal workings of a network.

The Packet Tracer activities included in the course consist of network simulations, games, activities, and challenges that provide a broad range of learning experiences.

Create your own worlds

You can also use Packet Tracer to create your own experiments and networking scenarios. We hope that, over time, you consider using Packet Tracer – not only for experiencing the activities included in the course, but also to become an author, explorer, and experimenter.

The online course materials have embedded Packet Tracer activities that will launch on computers running Windows® operating systems, if Packet Tracer is installed. This integration may also work on other operating systems using Windows emulation.

Course Overview

The primary focus of this course is on LAN switching and wireless LANs. The goal is to develop an understanding of how a switch communicates with other switches and routers in a small- or medium-sized business network to implement VLAN segmentation.

This course focuses on Layer 2 switching protocols and concepts used to improve redundancy, propagate VLAN information, and secure the portion of the network where most users access network services.

Switching technologies are relatively straightforward to implement; however, as with routing, the underlying protocols and algorithms are often quite complicated. This course will go to great lengths to explain the underlying processes of the common Layer 2 switching technologies. The better the underlying concepts are understood, the easier it is to implement, verify, and troubleshoot the switching technologies.

Each switching concept will be introduced within the context of a single topology for each chapter. The individual chapter topologies will be used to explain protocol operations as well as providing a setting for the implementation of the various switching technologies.

The labs and Packet Tracer activities used in this course are designed to help you develop an understanding of how to configure switching operations while reinforcing the concepts learned in each chapter.

Chapter 1 LAN Design — In Chapter 1, you learn the fundamental aspects of designing local area networks. In particular, hierarchical network design utilizing the core-distribution-access layer model is introduced and referenced throughout the remainder of the course.

Chapter 2 Basic Switch Concepts and Configuration — Chapter 2 introduces switch forwarding methods, symmetric and asymmetric switching, memory buffering, and Layer 2 and Layer 3 switching. You are introduced to navigating the Cisco IOS CLI on a Catalyst 2960 and performing an initial switch configuration. An integral role of a switch administrator is to maintain a secure network; to this end, you learn to configure various passwords on the switch as well as SSH to mitigate common security attacks.

Chapter 3 VLANs — Chapter 3 presents the types of VLANs used in modern switched networks. It is important to understand the role of the default VLAN, user/data VLANs, native VLANs, the management VLAN, and voice VLANs. VLAN trunks with IEEE 802.1Q tagging facilitate inter-switch communication with multiple VLANs. You learn to configure, verify, and troubleshoot VLANs and trunks using the Cisco IOS CLI.

Chapter 4 VTP — VTP is used to exchange VLAN information across trunk links, reducing VLAN administration and configuration errors. VTP allows you to create a VLAN once within a VTP domain and have that VLAN propagated to all other switches in the VTP domain. VTP pruning limits the unnecessary propagation of VLAN traffic across a LAN by determining which trunk ports forward which VLAN traffic. You learn to configure, verify, and troubleshoot VTP implementations.

Chapter 5 STP — STP makes it possible to implement redundant physical links in a switched LAN by creating a logical loop-free Layer 2 topology. By default Cisco switches implement STP in a per-VLAN fashion. The configuration of STP is fairly straightforward, but the underlying processes are quite complicated. IEEE 802.1D defined the original implementation of spanning-tree protocol. IEEE 802.1w defined an improved implementation of spanning tree called rapid spanning tree protocol. RSTP convergence time is approximately five times faster than convergence with 802.1D. RSTP introduces several new concepts, such as link types, edge ports, alternate ports, backup ports, and the discarding state. You will learn to configure both the original IEEE 802.1D implementation of STP as well as the newer IEEE 802.1w implementation of spanning tree.

Chapter 6 Inter-VLAN Routing — Inter-VLAN routing is the process of routing traffic between different VLANs. You learn the various methods of inter-VLAN routing. You learn to implement inter-VLAN routing in the router-on-a-stick topology, where a trunk link connects a Layer 2 switch to a router configured with logical subinterfaces paired in a one-to-one fashion with VLANs.

Chapter 7 Basic Wireless Concepts and Configuration — Wireless LAN standards are evolving for voice and video traffic, with newer standards being supported with quality of service. An access point connects to the wired LAN provides a basic service set to client stations that associate to it. SSIDs and MAC filtering are inherently insecure methods of securing a WLAN. Enterprise solutions such as WPA2 and 802.1x authentication enable very secure wireless LAN access. End users have to configure a wireless NIC on their client stations which communicates with and associates to a wireless access point. When configuring a wireless LAN, you should ensure that the devices have the latest firmware so that they can support the most stringent security options.

CHAPTER 1

LAN Design

Chapter Introduction

Refer to
Figure
in online course

For the small- and medium-sized business, communicating digitally using *data*, voice, and video is critical to business survival. Consequently, a properly designed *LAN* is a fundamental requirement for doing business today. You must be able to recognize a well-designed LAN and select the appropriate *devices* to support the *network* specifications of a small- or medium-sized business.

In this chapter, you will begin exploring the *switched LAN* architecture and some of the principles that are used to design a hierarchical network. You will learn about converged networks. You will also learn how to select the correct *switch* for a hierarchal network and which Cisco switches are best suited for each network layer. The activities and labs confirm and reinforce your learning.

1.1 Switched LAN Architecture

1.1.1 The Hierarchical Network Model

Refer to
Figure
in online course

When building a LAN that satisfies the needs of a small- or medium-sized business, your plan is more likely to be successful if a hierarchical design model is used. Compared to other network designs, a hierarchical network is easier to manage and expand, and problems are solved more quickly.

Hierarchical network design involves dividing the network into discrete layers. Each layer provides specific functions that define its role within the overall network. By separating the various functions that exist on a network, the network design becomes modular, which facilitates scalability and performance. The typical hierarchical design model is broken up in to three layers: access, distribution, and core. An example of a three-layer hierarchical network design is displayed in the figure.

Access Layer

The access layer interfaces with end devices, such as PCs, printers, and IP phones, to provide access to the rest of the network. The access layer can include *routers*, switches, *bridges*, hubs, and wireless access points (*AP*). The main purpose of the access layer is to provide a means of connecting devices to the network and controlling which devices are allowed to communicate on the network.

Roll over the ACCESS button in the figure.

Distribution Layer

The distribution layer aggregates the data received from the access layer switches before it is transmitted to the core layer for routing to its final destination. The distribution layer controls the *flow* of network traffic using policies and delineates *broadcast domains* by performing *routing* functions between virtual LANs (*VLANs*) defined at the access layer. VLANs allow you to *segment* the traffic on a switch into separate *subnetworks*. For example, in a university you might separate traffic according to faculty, students, and guests. Distribution layer switches are typically high-performance devices that have high availability and *redundancy* to ensure reliability. You will learn more about VLANs, broadcast domains, and inter-VLAN routing later in this course.

Roll over the DISTRIBUTION button in the figure.

Core Layer

The core layer of the hierarchical design is the high-speed *backbone* of the *internetwork*. The core layer is critical for interconnectivity between distribution layer devices, so it is important for the core to be highly available and redundant. The core area can also connect to *Internet* resources. The core aggregates the traffic from all the distribution layer devices, so it must be capable of *forwarding* large amounts of data quickly.

Roll over the CORE button in the figure.

Note: In smaller networks, it is not unusual to implement a **collapsed core** model, where the distribution layer and core layer are combined into one layer.

A Hierarchical Network in a Medium-Sized Business

Refer to **Figure** in online course

Let us look at the hierarchical network model applied to a business. In the figure, the access, distribution, and core layers are separated into a well-defined hierarchy. This logical representation makes it easy to see which switches perform which function. It is much harder to see these hierarchical layers when the network is installed in a business.

Click the Physical Layout button in the figure.

The figure shows two floors of a building. The user computers and network devices that need network access are on one floor. The resources, such as *e-mail servers* and database servers, are located on another floor. To ensure that each floor has access to the network, access layer and distribution switches are installed in the *wiring closets* of each floor and connected to each of the devices needing network access. The figure shows a small rack of switches. The access layer switch and distribution layer switch are stacked one on top of each other in the wiring closet.

Although the core and other distribution layer switches are not shown, you can see how the physical layout of a network differs from the logical layout of a network.

Benefits of a Hierarchical Network

Refer to **Figure** in online course

There are many benefits associated with hierarchical network designs.

Scalability

Hierarchical networks scale very well. The modularity of the design allows you to replicate design elements as the network grows. Because each instance of the module is consistent, expansion is easy to plan and implement. For example, if your design model consists of two distribution layer switches for every 10 access layer switches, you can continue to add access layer switches until you have 10 access layer switches cross-connected to the two distribution layer switches before you need to add additional distribution layer switches to the network *topology*. Also, as you add more distribution layer switches to accommodate the load from the access layer switches, you can add additional core layer switches to handle the additional load on the core.

Redundancy

As a network grows, availability becomes more important. You can dramatically increase availability through easy redundant implementations with hierarchical networks. Access layer switches are connected to two different distribution layer switches to ensure path redundancy. If one of the distribution layer switches fails, the access layer switch can switch to the other distribution layer switch. Additionally, distribution layer switches are connected to two or more core layer switches to ensure path availability if a core switch fails. The only layer where redundancy is limited is at the access layer. Typically, end node devices, such as PCs, printers, and IP phones, do not have the ability to connect to multiple access layer switches for redundancy. If an access layer switch fails, just the devices connected to that one switch would be affected by the outage. The rest of the network would continue to function unaffected.

Performance

Communication performance is enhanced by avoiding the transmission of data through low-performing, intermediary switches. Data is sent through aggregated switch *port* links from the access layer to the distribution layer at near wire speed in most cases. The distribution layer then uses its high performance switching capabilities to forward the traffic up to the core, where it is routed to its final destination. Because the core and distribution layers perform their operations at very high speeds, there is less contention for network *bandwidth*. As a result, properly designed hierarchical networks can achieve near wire speed between all devices.

Security

Security is improved and easier to manage. Access layer switches can be configured with various port security options that provide control over which devices are allowed to connect to the network. You also have the flexibility to use more advanced security policies at the distribution layer. You may apply access control policies that define which communication *protocols* are deployed on your network and where they are permitted to go. For example, if you want to limit the use of HTTP to a specific user community connected at the access layer, you could apply a policy that blocks HTTP traffic at the distribution layer. Restricting traffic based on higher layer protocols, such as IP and HTTP, requires that your switches are able to process policies at that layer. Some access layer switches support Layer 3 functionality, but it is usually the job of the distribution layer switches to process Layer 3 data, because they can process it much more efficiently.

Manageability

Manageability is relatively simple on a hierarchical network. Each layer of the hierarchical design performs specific functions that are consistent throughout that layer. Therefore, if you need to change the functionality of an access layer switch, you could repeat that change across all access layer switches in the network because they presumably perform the same functions at their layer. Deployment of new switches is also simplified because switch configurations can be copied between devices with very few modifications. Consistency between the switches at each layer allows for rapid recovery and simplified troubleshooting. In some special situations, there could be configuration inconsistencies between devices, so you should ensure that configurations are well documented so that you can compare them before deployment.

Maintainability

Because hierarchical networks are modular in nature and scale very easily, they are easy to maintain. With other network topology designs, manageability becomes increasingly complicated as the network grows. Also, in some network design models, there is a finite limit to how large the network can grow before it becomes too complicated and expensive to maintain. In the hierarchical design model, switch functions are defined at each layer, making the selection of the correct switch easier. Adding switches to one layer does not necessarily mean there will not be a bottleneck or other limitation at another layer. For a *full mesh* network topology to achieve maximum performance, all switches need to be high-performance switches, because each switch needs to be capable of performing all the functions on the network. In the hierarchical model, switch functions are different at each layer. You can save money by using less expensive access layer switches at the lowest layer, and spend more on the distribution and core layer switches to achieve high performance on the network.

1.1.2 Principles of Hierarchical Network Design

Refer to
Figure
in online course

Hierarchical Network Design Principles

Just because a network seems to have a hierarchical design does not mean that the network is well designed. These simple guidelines will help you differentiate between well-designed and poorly designed hierarchical networks. This section is not intended to provide you with all the skills and knowledge you need to design a hierarchical network, but it offers you an opportunity to begin to practice your skills by transforming a flat network topology into a hierarchical network topology.

Network Diameter

When designing a hierarchical network topology, the first thing to consider is network diameter. Diameter is usually a measure of distance, but in this case, we are using the term to measure the number of devices. Network diameter is the number of devices that a *packet* has to cross before it reaches its destination. Keeping the network diameter low ensures low and predictable *latency* between devices.

Roll over the Network Diameter button in the figure.

In the figure, PC1 communicates with PC3. There could be up to six interconnected switches between PC1 and PC3. In this case, the network diameter is 6. Each switch in the path introduces some degree of latency. Network device latency is the time spent by a device as it processes a packet or *frame*. Each switch has to determine the destination *MAC address* of the frame, check its MAC address table, and forward the frame out the appropriate port. Even though that entire process happens in a fraction of a second, the time adds up when the frame has to cross many switches.

In the three-layer hierarchical model, Layer 2 segmentation at the distribution layer practically eliminates network diameter as an issue. In a hierarchical network, network diameter is always going to be a predictable number of hops between the source and destination devices.

Bandwidth Aggregation

Each layer in the hierarchical network model is a possible candidate for bandwidth aggregation. Bandwidth aggregation is the practice of considering the specific bandwidth requirements of each part of the hierarchy. After bandwidth requirements of the network are known, *links* between specific switches can be aggregated, which is called link aggregation. Link aggregation allows multiple switch port links to be combined so as to achieve higher *throughput* between switches. Cisco has a proprietary link aggregation technology called EtherChannel, which allows multiple *Ethernet* links to be consolidated. A discussion of EtherChannel is beyond the scope of this course. To learn more, visit: http://www.cisco.com/en/US/tech/tk389/tk213/tsd_technology_support_protocol_home.html.

Roll over the Bandwidth Aggregation button in the figure.

In the figure, computers PC1 and PC3 require a significant amount of bandwidth because they are used for developing weather simulations. The network manager has determined that the access layer switches S1, S3, and S5 require increased bandwidth. Following up the hierarchy, these access layer switches connect to the distribution switches D1, D2, and D4. The distribution switches connect to core layer switches C1 and C2. Notice how specific links on specific ports in each switch are aggregated. In this way, increased bandwidth is provided for in a targeted, specific part of the network. Note that in this figure, aggregated links are indicated by two dotted lines with an oval tying them together. In other figures, aggregated links are represented by a single, dotted line with an oval.

Redundancy

Redundancy is one part of creating a highly available network. Redundancy can be provided in a number of ways. For example, you can double up the network connections between devices, or you can double the devices themselves. This chapter explores how to employ redundant network paths between switches. A discussion on doubling up network devices and employing special network protocols to ensure high availability is beyond the scope of this course. For an interesting discussion on high availability, visit: http://www.cisco.com/en/US/products/ps6550/products_ios_technology_home.html.

Implementing redundant links can be expensive. Imagine if every switch in each layer of the network hierarchy had a connection to every switch at the next layer. It is unlikely that you will be able to implement redundancy at the access layer because of the cost and limited features in the end devices, but you can build redundancy into the distribution and core layers of the network.

Roll over the Redundant Links button in the figure.

In the figure, redundant links are shown at the distribution layer and core layer. At the distribution layer, there are two distribution layer switches, the minimum required to support redundancy at this layer. The access layer switches, S1, S3, S4, and S6, are cross-connected to the distribution layer switches. This protects your network if one of the distribution switches fails. In case of a failure, the access layer switch adjusts its transmission path and forwards the traffic through the other distribution switch.

Some network failure scenarios can never be prevented, for example, if the power goes out in the entire city, or the entire building is demolished because of an earthquake. Redundancy does not attempt to address these types of disasters.

Start at the Access Layer

Imagine that a new network design is required. Design requirements, such as the level of performance or redundancy necessary, are determined by the business goals of the organization. Once the design requirements are documented, the designer can begin selecting the equipment and infrastructure to implement the design.

When you start the equipment selection at the access layer, you can ensure that you accommodate all network devices needing access to the network. After you have all end devices accounted for, you have a better idea of how many access layer switches you need. The number of access layer switches, and the estimated traffic that each generates, helps you to determine how many distribution layer switches are required to achieve the performance and redundancy needed for the network. After you have determined the number of distribution layer switches, you can identify how many core switches are required to maintain the performance of the network.

A thorough discussion on how to determine which switch to select based on traffic flow analysis and how many core switches are required to maintain performance is beyond the scope of this course. For a good introduction to network design, read this book that is available from Cisco-press.com: *Top-Down Network Design*, by Priscilla Oppenheimer (2004).

1.1.3 What is a Converged Network?

Refer to
Figure
in online course

Small and medium-sized businesses are embracing the idea of running voice and video services on their data networks. Let us look at how voice and video over IP (*VoIP*) affect a hierarchical network.

Legacy Equipment

Convergence is the process of combining voice and video communications on a data network. Converged networks have existed for a while now, but were only feasible in large enterprise organizations because of the network infrastructure requirements and complex management that was involved to make them work seamlessly. There were high network costs associated with convergence because more expensive switch hardware was required to support the additional bandwidth requirements. Converged networks also required extensive management in relation to Quality of Service (*QoS*), because voice and video data traffic needed to be classified and prioritized on the network. Few individuals had the expertise in voice, video, and data networks to make convergence feasible and functional. In addition, legacy equipment hinders the process. The figure shows a legacy telephone company switch. Most telephone companies today have made the transition to digital-based switches. However, there are many offices that still use analog phones, so they still have existing analog telephone wiring closets. Because analog phones have not yet been replaced, you will also see equipment that has to support both legacy *PBX* telephone systems and IP-based phones. This sort of equipment will slowly be migrated to modern IP-based phone switches.

Click Advanced Technology button in the figure.

Advanced Technology

Converging voice, video, and data networks has become more popular recently in the small to medium-sized business market because of advancements in technology. Convergence is now easier to implement and manage, and less expensive to purchase. The figure shows a high-end VoIP phone and switch combination suitable for a medium-sized business of 250-400 employees. The figure also shows a Cisco Catalyst Express 500 switch and a Cisco 7906G phone suitable for small to medium-sized businesses. This VoIP technology used to be affordable only to enterprises and governments.

Moving to a converged network can be a difficult decision if the business already invested in separate voice, video, and data networks. It is difficult to abandon an investment that still works, but there are several advantages to converging voice, video, and data on a single network infrastructure.

One benefit of a converged network is that there is just one network to manage. With separate voice, video, and data networks, changes to the network have to be coordinated across networks. There are also additional costs resulting from using three sets of network cabling. Using a single network means you just have to manage one wired infrastructure.

Another benefit is lower implementation and management costs. It is less expensive to implement a single network infrastructure than three distinct network infrastructures. Managing a single network is also less expensive. Traditionally, if a business has a separate voice and data network, they have one group of people managing the voice network and another group managing the data network. With a converged network, you have one group managing both the voice and data networks.

Click New Options button in the figure.

New Options

Converged networks give you options that had not existed previously. You can now tie voice and video communications directly into an employee's personal computer system, as shown in the figure. There is no need for an expensive handset phone or videoconferencing equipment. You can accomplish the same function using special software integrated with a personal computer. Softphones, such as the Cisco IP Communicator, offer a lot of flexibility for businesses. The person in the top left of the figure is using a softphone on the computer. When software is used in place of a physical phone, a business can quickly convert to converged networks, because there is no capital expense in purchasing IP phones and the switches needed to power the phones. With the addition of inexpensive webcams, videoconferencing can be added to a softphone. These are just a few examples provided by a broader communications solution portfolio that redefine business processes today.

Refer to
Figure
in online course

Separate Voice, Video and Data Networks

As you see in the figure, a voice network contains isolated phone *lines* running to a PBX switch to allow phone connectivity to the Public Switched Telephone Network (*PSTN*). When a new phone is added, a new line has to be run back to the PBX. The PBX switch is typically located in a *telco* wiring closet, separate from the data and video wiring closets. The wiring closets are usually separated because different support personnel require access to each system. However, using a properly designed hierarchical network, and implementing QoS policies that prioritize the audio data, voice data can be converged onto an existing data network with little to no impact on audio quality.

Click the Video Network button in the figure to see an example of a separate video network.

In this figure, videoconferencing equipment is wired separately from the voice and data networks. Videoconferencing data can consume significant bandwidth on a network. As a result, video networks were maintained separately to allow the videoconferencing equipment to operate at full speed without competing for bandwidth with voice and data streams. Using a properly designed hierarchical network, and implementing QoS policies that prioritize the video data, video can be converged onto an existing data network with little to no impact on video quality.

Click the Data Network button in the figure to see an example of a separate data network.

The data network interconnects the workstations and servers on a network to facilitate resource sharing. Data networks can consume significant data bandwidth, which is why voice, video, and data networks were kept separated for such a long time. Now that properly designed hierarchical networks can accommodate the bandwidth requirements of voice, video, and data communications at the same time, it makes sense to converge them all onto a single hierarchical network.

Refer to
Figure
in online course

Complex Flash: Building a Real-World Hierarchical Network

1.2   Matching Switches to Specific LAN Functions

1.2.1   Considerations for Hierarchical Network Switches

Refer to
Figure
in online course

Traffic Flow Analysis

To select the appropriate switch for a layer in a hierarchical network, you need to have specifications that detail the target traffic flows, user communities, data servers, and data storage servers.

Companies need a network that can meet evolving requirements. A business may start with a few PCs interconnected so that they can share data. As the business adds more employees, devices, such as PCs, printers, and servers, are added to the network. Accompanying the new devices is an increase in network traffic. Some companies are replacing their existing telephone systems with converged VoIP phone systems, which adds additional traffic.

When selecting switch hardware, determine which switches are needed in the core, distribution, and access layers to accommodate the bandwidth requirements of your network. Your plan should take into account future bandwidth requirements. Purchase the appropriate Cisco switch hardware to accommodate both current needs as well as future needs. To help you more accurately choose appropriate switches, perform and record traffic flow analyses on a regular basis.

Traffic Flow Analysis

Traffic flow analysis is the process of measuring the bandwidth usage on a network and analyzing the data for the purpose of performance tuning, capacity planning, and making hardware improvement decisions. Traffic flow analysis is done using traffic flow analysis software. Although there is no precise definition of network traffic flow, for the purposes of traffic flow analysis we can say that network traffic is the amount of data sent through a network for a given period of time. All network data contributes to the traffic, regardless of its purpose or source. Analyzing the various traffic sources and their impact on the network, allows you to more accurately tune and upgrade the network to achieve the best possible performance.

Traffic flow data can be used to help determine just how long you can continue using existing network hardware before it makes sense to upgrade to accommodate additional bandwidth requirements. When you are making your decisions about which hardware to purchase, you should consider port densities and switch forwarding rates to ensure adequate growth capability. Port density and forwarding rates are explained later in this chapter.

There are many ways to monitor traffic flow on a network. You can manually monitor individual switch ports to get the bandwidth utilization over time. When analyzing the traffic flow data, you want to determine future traffic flow requirements based on the capacity at certain times of the day and where most of the data is generated and sent. However, to obtain accurate results, you need to record enough data. Manual recording of traffic data is a tedious process that requires a lot of time and diligence. Fortunately, there are some automated solutions.

Analysis Tools

Many traffic flow analysis tools that automatically record traffic flow data to a database and perform a trend analysis are available. In larger networks, software collection solutions are the only effective method for performing traffic flow analysis. The figure displays sample output from Solarwinds Orion 8.1 NetFlow Analysis, which monitors traffic flow on a network. While the software is collecting data, you can see just how every interface is performing at any given point in time on the network. Using the included charts, you can identify traffic flow problems visually. This is much easier than having to interpret the numbers in a column of traffic flow data.

For a list of some commercial traffic flow collection and analysis tools, visit http://www.cisco.com/warp/public/732/Tech/nmp/netflow/partners/commercial/index.shtml.

For a list of some freeware traffic flow collection and analysis tools, visit http://www.cisco.com/warp/public/732/Tech/nmp/netflow/partners/freeware/index.shtml.

Refer to
Figure
in online course

User Communities Analysis

User community analysis is the process of identifying various groupings of users and their impact on network performance. The way users are grouped affects issues related to port density and traffic flow, which, in turn, influences the selection of network switches. Port density is explained later in this chapter.

In a typical office building, end users are grouped according to their job function, because they require similar access to resources and *applications*. You may find the Human Resource (HR) department located on one floor of an office building, while Finance is located on another floor. Each department has a different number of users and application needs, and requires access to different data resources available through the network. For example, when selecting switches for the wiring closets of the HR and Finance departments, you would choose a switch that had enough ports to meet the department needs and was powerful enough to accommodate the traffic requirements for all the devices on that floor. Additionally, a good network design plan factors in the growth of each department to ensure that there are enough open switch ports that can utilized before the next planned upgrade to the network.

As shown in the figure, the HR department requires 20 workstations for its 20 users. That translates to 20 switch ports needed to connect the workstations to the network. If you were to select an appropriate access layer switch to accommodate the HR department, you would probably choose a

24 port switch, which has enough ports to accommodate the 20 workstations and the uplinks to the distribution layer switches.

Future Growth

But this plan does not account for future growth. Consider what will happen if the HR department grows by five employees. A solid network plan includes the rate of personnel growth over the past five years to be able to anticipate the future growth. With that in mind, you would want to purchase a switch that can accommodate more than 24 ports, such as stackable or modular switches that can scale.

As well as looking at the number of devices on a given switch in a network, you should investigate the network traffic generated by end-user applications. Some user communities use applications that generate a lot of network traffic, while other user communities do not. By measuring the network traffic generated for all applications in use by different user communities, and determining the location of the data source, you can identify the effect of adding more users to that community.

A *workgroup*-sized user community in a small business is supported by a couple of switches and typically connected to the same switch as the server. In medium-sized businesses or enterprises, user communities are supported by many switches. The resources that medium-sized business or enterprise user communities need could be located in geographically separate areas. Consequently, the location of the user communities influences where data stores and server farms are located.

Click the Finance Department button in the figure.

If the Finance users are using a network-intensive application that exchanges data with a specific server on the network, it may make sense to locate the Finance user community close to that server. By locating users close to their servers and data stores, you can reduce the network diameter for their communications, thereby reducing the impact of their traffic across the rest of the network.

One complication of analyzing application usage by user communities is that usage is not always bound by department or physical location. You may have to analyze the impact of the application across many network switches to determine its overall impact.

Refer to
Figure
in online course

Data Stores and Data Servers Analysis

When analyzing traffic on a network, consider where the data stores and servers are located so that you can determine the impact of traffic on the network. Data stores can be servers, storage area networks (SANs), network-attached storage (NAS), tape backup units, or any other device or component where large quantities of data are stored.

When considering the traffic for data stores and servers, consider both *client-server* traffic and server-server traffic.

As you can see in the figure, client-server traffic is the traffic generated when a *client* device accesses data from data stores or servers. Client-server traffic typically traverses multiple switches to reach its destination. Bandwidth aggregation and switch forwarding rates are important factors to consider when attempting to eliminate bottlenecks for this type of traffic.

Click the Server-Server Communication button in the figure.

Server-server traffic is the traffic generated between data storage devices on the network. Some server applications generate very high volumes of traffic between data stores and other servers. To optimize server-server traffic, servers needing frequent access to certain resources should be located in close proximity to each other so that the traffic they generate does not affect the performance of the rest of the network. Servers and data stores are typically located in data centers within a business. A data center is a secured area of the building where servers, data stores, and other network equipment are located. A device can be physically located in the data center but represented in quite a different location in the logical topology. Traffic across data center switches is typically very high due to the server-server and client-server traffic that traverses the switches. As a result, switches selected for data centers should be higher performing switches than the switches you would find in the wiring closets at the access layer.

By examining the data paths for various applications used by different user communities, you can identify potential bottlenecks where performance of the application can be affected by inadequate bandwidth. To improve the performance, you could aggregate links to accommodate the bandwidth, or replace the slower switches with faster switches capable of handling the traffic load.

Refer to Figure in online course

Topology Diagrams

A topology diagram is a graphical representation of a network infrastructure. A topology diagram shows how all switches are interconnected, detailed down to which switch port interconnects the devices. A topology diagram graphically displays any redundant paths or aggregated ports between switches that provide for resiliency and performance. It shows where and how many switches are in use on your network, as well as identifies their configuration. Topology diagrams can also contain information about device densities and user communities. Having a topology diagram allows you to visually identify potential bottlenecks in network traffic so that you can focus your traffic analysis data collection on areas where improvements can have the most significant impact on performance.

A network topology can be very difficult to piece together after the fact if you were not part of the design process. Network *cables* in the wiring closets disappear into the floors and ceilings, making it difficult to trace their destinations. And because devices are spread throughout the building, it is difficult to know how all of the pieces are connected together. With patience, you can determine just how everything is interconnected and then document the network infrastructure in a topology diagram.

The figure displays a simple network topology diagram. Notice how many switches are present in the network, as well as how each switch is interconnected. The topology diagram identifies each switch port used for inter-switch communications and redundant paths between access layer switches and distribution layer switches. The topology diagram also displays where different user communities are located on the network and the location of the servers and data stores.

1.2.2 Switch Features

Refer to Figure in online course

Switch Form Factors

What are the key features of switches that are used in hierarchical networks? When you look up the specifications for a switch, what do all of the acronyms and word phrases mean? What does "PoE" mean and what is "forwarding rate"? In this topic, you will learn about these features.

When you are selecting a switch, you need to decide between fixed configuration or modular configuration, and stackable or non-stackable. Another consideration is the thickness of the switch expressed in number of rack units. For example, the Fixed Configuration Switches shown in the figure are all 1 rack unit (1U). These options are sometimes referred to as switch form factors.

Fixed Configuration Switches

Fixed configuration switches are just as you might expect, fixed in their configuration. What that means is that you cannot add features or options to the switch beyond those that originally came with the switch. The particular model you purchase determines the features and options available. For example, if you purchase a 24-port *gigabit* fixed switch, you cannot add additional ports when you need them. There are typically different configuration choices that vary in how many and what types of ports are included.

Modular Switches

Modular switches offer more flexibility in their configuration. Modular switches typically come with different sized chassis that allow for the installation of different numbers of modular *line cards*. The line cards actually contain the ports. The line card fits into the switch chassis like expansion cards fit into a PC. The larger the chassis, the more modules it can support. As you can see in the figure, there can be many different chassis sizes to choose from. If you bought a modular switch with a 24-port line card, you could easily add an additional 24 port line card, to bring the total number of ports up to 48.

Stackable Switches

Stackable switches can be interconnected using a special *backplane* cable that provides high-bandwidth throughput between the switches. Cisco introduced StackWise technology in one of its switch product lines. StackWise allows you to interconnect up to nine switches using fully redundant backplane connections. As you can see in the figure, switches are stacked one atop of the other, and cables connect the switches in daisy chain fashion. The stacked switches effectively operate as a single larger switch. Stackable switches are desirable where fault tolerance and bandwidth availability are critical and a modular switch is too costly to implement. Using cross-connected connections, the network can recover quickly if a single switch fails. Stackable switches use a special port for interconnections and do not use line ports for inter-switch connections. The speeds are also typically faster than using line ports for connection switches.

Refer to
Figure
in online course

Performance

When selecting a switch for the access, distribution, or core layer, consider the ability of the switch to support the port density, forwarding rates, and bandwidth aggregation requirements of your network.

Port Density

Port density is the number of ports available on a single switch. Fixed configuration switches typically support up to 48 ports on a single device, with options for up to four additional ports for small form-factor pluggable (SFP) devices, as shown in the figure. High port densities allow for better use of space and power when both are in limited supply. If you have two switches that each contain 24 ports, you would be able to support up to 46 devices, because you lose at least one port per switch to connect each switch to the rest of the network. In addition, two power outlets are required. On the other hand, if you have a single 48-port switch, 47 devices can be supported, with only one port used to connect the switch to the rest of the network, and only one power outlet needed to accommodate the single switch.

Modular switches can support very high port densities through the addition of multiple switch port line cards, as shown in the figure. For example, the Catalyst 6500 switch can support in excess of 1,000 switch ports on a single device.

Large *enterprise networks* that support many thousands of network devices require high density, modular switches to make the best use of space and power. Without using a high-density modular switch, the network would need many fixed configuration switches to accommodate the number of devices that need network access. This approach can consume many power outlets and a lot of closet space.

You must also address the issue of uplink bottlenecks. A series of fixed configuration switches may consume many additional ports for bandwidth aggregation between switches for the purpose of achieving target performance. With a single modular switch, bandwidth aggregation is less of an issue because the backplane of the chassis can provide the necessary bandwidth to accommodate the devices connected to the switch port line cards.

Forwarding Rates

Click Forwarding Rates button in the figure to see an example of forwarding rates on switches with different port densities.

Forwarding rates define the processing capabilities of a switch by rating how much data the switch can process per second. Switch product lines are classified by forwarding rates. Entry-layer switches have lower forwarding rates than enterprise-layer switches. Forwarding rates are important to consider when selecting a switch. If the switch forwarding rate is too low, it cannot accommodate full wire-speed communication across all of its switch ports. Wire speed is the data rate that each port on the switch is capable of attaining, either 100 Mb/s *Fast Ethernet* or 1000 Mb/s Gigabit Ethernet. For example, a 48-port gigabit switch operating at full wire speed generates 48 Gb/s of traffic. If the switch only supports a forwarding rate of 32 Gb/s, it cannot run at full wire speed across all ports simultaneously. Fortunately, access layer switches typically do not need to operate at full wire speed because they are physically limited by their uplinks to the distribution layer. This allows you to use less expensive, lower performing switches at the access layer, and use the more expensive, higher performing switches at the distribution and core layers, where the forwarding rate makes a bigger difference.

Link Aggregation

Click the Link Aggregation button in the figure.

As part of bandwidth aggregation, you should determine if there are enough ports on a switch to aggregate to support the required bandwidth. For example, consider a Gigabit Ethernet port, which carries up to 1 Gb/s of traffic. If you have a 24-port switch, with all ports capable of running at gigabit speeds, you could generate up to 24 Gb/s of network traffic. If the switch is connected to the rest of the network by a single network cable, it can only forward 1 Gb/s of the data to the rest of the network. Due to the contention for bandwidth, the data would forward more slowly. That results in 1/24th wire speed available to each of the 24 devices connected to the switch. Wire speed describes the theoretical maximum data transmission rate of a connection. For example, the wire speed of an Ethernet connection is dependent on the physical and electrical properties of the cable, combined with the lowest layer of the connection protocols.

Link aggregation helps to reduce these bottlenecks of traffic by allowing up to eight switch ports to be bound together for data communications, providing up to 8 Gb/s of data throughput when Gigabit Ethernet ports are used. With the addition of multiple 10 Gigabit Ethernet (10GbE) uplinks on some enterprise-layer switches, very high throughput rates can be achieved. Cisco uses the term EtherChannel when describing aggregated switch ports.

As you can see in the figure, four separate ports on switches C1 and D1 are used to create a 4-port EtherChannel. EtherChannel technology allows a group of physical Ethernet links to create one logical Ethernet link for the purpose of providing fault tolerance and high-speed links between switches, routers, and servers. In this example, there is four times the throughput when compared to the single port connection between switches C1 and D2.

Refer to
Figure
in online course

PoE and Layer 3 Functionality

Two other characteristics you want to consider when selecting a switch are Power over Ethernet (*PoE*) and Layer 3 functionality.

Power over Ethernet

Power over Ethernet (PoE) allows the switch to deliver power to a device over the existing Ethernet cabling. As you can see in the figure, this feature can be used by IP phones and some wireless access points. PoE allows you more flexibility when installing wireless access points and IP phones because you can install them anywhere you can run an Ethernet cable. You do not need to consider how to run ordinary power to the device. You should only select a switch that supports PoE if you are actually going to take advantage of the feature, because it adds considerable cost to the switch.

Click the switch icon to see PoE ports.

Click the phone icon to see the phone ports.

Click the wireless access point icon to see its ports.

Layer 3 Functions

Click the Layer 3 Functions button in the figure to see some Layer 3 functions that can be provided by switches in a hierarchical network.

Typically, switches operate at Layer 2 of the *OSI reference model* where they deal primarily with the MAC addresses of devices connected to switch ports. Layer 3 switches offer advanced functionality. Layer 3 switches are also known as *multilayer switches*.

1.2.3 Switch Features in a Hierarchical Network

Refer to
Figure
in online course

Access Layer Switch Features

Now that you know which factors to consider when choosing a switch, let us examine which features are required at each layer in a hierarchical network. You will then be able to match the switch specification with its ability to function as an access, distribution, or core layer switch.

Access layer switches facilitate the connection of end node devices to the network. For this reason, they need to support features such as port security, VLANs, Fast Ethernet/Gigabit Ethernet, PoE, and link aggregation.

Port security allows the switch to decide how many or what specific devices are allowed to connect to the switch. All Cisco switches support port layer security. Port security is applied at the access layer. Consequently, it is an important first line of defense for a network. You will learn about port security in Chapter 2.

VLANs are an important component of a converged network. Voice traffic is typically given a separate VLAN. In this way, voice traffic can be supported with more bandwidth, more redundant connections, and improved security. Access layer switches allow you to set the VLANs for the end node devices on your network.

Port speed is also a characteristic you need to consider for your access layer switches. Depending on the performance requirements for your network, you must choose between Fast Ethernet and Gigabit Ethernet switch ports. Fast Ethernet allows up to 100 Mb/s of traffic per switch port. Fast Ethernet is adequate for IP *telephony* and data traffic on most business networks, however, performance is slower than Gigabit Ethernet ports. Gigabit Ethernet allows up to 1000 Mb/s of traffic per switch port. Most modern devices, such as workstations, notebooks, and IP phones, support Gigabit Ethernet. This allows for much more efficient data transfers, enabling users to be more productive. Gigabit Ethernet does have a drawback-switches supporting Gigabit Ethernet are more expensive.

Another feature requirement for some access layer switches is PoE. PoE dramatically increases the overall price of the switch across all Cisco Catalyst switch product lines, so it should only be considered when voice convergence is required or wireless access points are being implemented, and power is difficult or expensive to run to the desired location.

Link aggregation is another feature that is common to most access layer switches. Link aggregation allows the switch to use multiple links simultaneously. Access layer switches take advantage of link aggregation when aggregating bandwidth up to distribution layer switches.

Because the uplink connection between the access layer switch and the distribution layer switch is typically the bottleneck in communication, the internal forwarding rate of access layer switches does not need to be as high as the link between the distribution and access layer switches. Characteristics such as the internal forwarding rate are less of a concern for access layer switches because they only handle traffic from the end devices and forward it to the distribution layer switches.

In a converged network supporting voice, video and data network traffic, access layer switches need to support QoS to maintain the prioritization of traffic. Cisco IP phones are types of equipment that are found at the access layer. When a Cisco IP phone is plugged into an access layer switch port configured to support voice traffic, that switch port tells the IP phone how to send its voice traffic. QoS needs to be enabled on access layer switches so that voice traffic the IP phone has priority over, for example, data traffic.

Refer to
Figure
in online course

Distribution Layer Switch Features

Distribution layer switches have a very important role on the network. They collect the data from all the access layer switches and forward it to the core layer switches. As you will learn later in this course, traffic that is generated at Layer 2 on a switched network needs to be managed, or segmented into VLANs, so it does not needlessly consume bandwidth throughout the network. Distribution layer switches provides the inter-VLAN routing functions so that one VLAN can communicate with another on the network. This routing typically takes place at the distribution layer because distribution layer switches have higher processing capabilities than the access layer switches. Distribution layer switches alleviate the core switches from needing to perform that task since the core is busy handling the forwarding of very high volumes of traffic. Because inter-VLAN routing is performed at the distribution layer, the switches at this layer need to support Layer 3 functions.

Security Policies

Another reason why Layer 3 functionality is required for distribution layer switches is because of the advanced security policies that can be applied to network traffic. Access lists are used to control how traffic flows through the network. An Access Control List (*ACL*) allows the switch to prevent certain types of traffic and permit others. ACLs also allow you to control which network devices can communicate on the network. Using ACLs is processing-intensive because the switch needs to inspect every packet and see if it matches one of the ACL rules defined on the switch. This inspection is performed at the distribution layer, because the switches at this layer typically have the processing capability to handle the additional load, and it also simplifies the use of ACLs. Instead of using ACLs for every access layer switch in the network, they are defined on the fewer distribution layer switches, making management of the ACLs much easier.

Quality of Service

The distribution layer switches also need to support QoS to maintain the prioritization of traffic coming from the access layer switches that have implemented QoS. Priority policies ensure that audio and video communications are guaranteed adequate bandwidth to maintain an acceptable quality of service. To maintain the priority of the voice data throughout the network, all of the switches that forward voice data must support QoS; if not all of the network devices support QoS, the benefits of QoS will be reduced. This results in poor performance and quality for audio and video communications.

The distribution layer switches are under high demand on the network because of the functions that they provide. It is important that distribution switches support redundancy for adequate availability. Loss of a distribution layer switch could have significant impact on the rest of the network because all access layer traffic passes through the distribution layer switches. Distribution layer switches are typically implemented in pairs to ensure availability. It is also recommended that distribution layer switches support multiple, *hot swappable* power supplies. Having more than one power supply allows the switch to continue operating even if one of the power supplies failed during operation. Having hot swappable power supplies allows you to change a failed power supply while the switch is still running. This allows you to repair the failed component without impacting the functionality of the network.

Finally, distribution layer switches need to support link aggregation. Typically, access layer switches use multiple links to connect to a distribution layer switch to ensure adequate bandwidth to accommodate the traffic generated on the access layer, and provide fault tolerance in case a link is lost. Because distribution layer switches accept incoming traffic from multiple access layer switches, they need to be able to forward all of that traffic as fast as possible to the core layer switches. As a result, distribution layer switches also need high-bandwidth aggregated links back to the core layer switches. Newer distribution layer switches support aggregated 10 Gigabit Ethernet (10GbE) uplinks to the core layer switches.

Refer to
Figure
in online course

Core Layer Switch Features

The core layer of a hierarchical topology is the high-speed backbone of the network and requires switches that can handle very high forwarding rates. The required forwarding rate is largely dependent on the number of devices participating in the network. You determine your necessary forwarding rate by conducting and examining various traffic flow reports and user communities analyses. Based on your results, you can identify an appropriate switch to support the network. Take care to evaluate your needs for the present and near future. If you choose an inadequate switch to run in the core of the network, you face potential bottleneck issues in the core, slowing down all communications on the network.

Link Aggregation

The core layer also needs to support link aggregation to ensure adequate bandwidth coming into the core from the distribution layer switches. Core layer switches should have support for aggregated 10GbE connections, which is currently the fastest available Ethernet connectivity option. This allows corresponding distribution layer switches to deliver traffic as efficiently as possible to the core.

Redundancy

The availability of the core layer is also critical, so you should build in as much redundancy as you can. Layer 3 redundancy typically has a faster convergence than Layer 2 redundancy in the event of hardware failure. Convergence in this context refers to the time it takes for the network to adapt to a change, not to be confused with a converged network that supports data, audio, and video communications. With that in mind, you want to ensure that your core layer switches support Layer 3 functions. A complete discussion on the implications of Layer 3 redundancy is beyond the scope of this course. It remains an open question about the need for Layer 2 redundancy in this context. Layer 2 redundancy is examined in Chapter 5 when we discuss the spanning tree protocol (*STP*). Also, look for core layer switches that support additional hardware redundancy features like redundant power supplies that can be swapped while the switch continues to operate. Because of the high workload carried by core layer switches, they tend to operate hotter than access or distribution layer switches, so they should have more sophisticated cooling options. Many true, core layer-capable switches have the ability to swap cooling fans without having to turn the switch off.

For example, it would be disruptive to shut down a core layer switch to change a power supply or a fan in the middle of the day when the network usage is at its highest. To perform a hardware replacement, you could expect to have at least a 5 minute network outage, and that is if you are very fast at performing the maintenance. In a more realistic situation, the switch could be down for 30 minutes or more, which most likely is not acceptable. With hot-swappable hardware, there is no downtime during switch maintenance.

QoS is an important part of the services provided by core layer switches. For example, service providers (who provide IP, data storage, e-mail and other services) and enterprise Wide Area Networks (*WANs*), are adding more voice and video traffic to an already growing amount of data traffic. At the core and network edge, mission-critical and time-sensitive traffic such as voice should receive higher QoS guarantees than less time-sensitive traffic such as file transfers or e-mail. Since high-speed WAN access is often prohibitively expensive, adding bandwidth at the core layer is not an option. Because QoS provides a software based solution to prioritize traffic, core layer switches can provide a cost effect way of supporting optimal and differentiated use of existing bandwidth.

1.2.4 Switches for Small and Medium Sized Business (SMB)

Refer to
Figure
in online course

The features of Cisco Catalyst Switches

Now that you know which switch features are used at which layer in a hierarchical network, you will learn about the Cisco switches that are applicable for each layer in the hierarchical network model. Today, you cannot simply select a Cisco switch by considering the size of a business. A small business with 12 employees might be integrated into the network of a large multinational enterprise and require all of the advanced LAN services available at the corporate head office. The following classification of Cisco switches within the hierarchical network model represents a starting point for your deliberations on which switch is best for a given application. The classification presented reflects how you might see the range of Cisco switches if you were a multinational enterprise. For example, the port densities of the Cisco 6500 switch only makes sense as an access layer switch where there are many hundreds of users in one area, such as the floor of a stock exchange. If you think of the needs of a medium-sized business, a switch that is shown as an access layer switch, the Cisco 3560 for example, could be used as a distribution layer switch if it met the criteria determined by the network designer for that application.

Cisco has seven switch product lines. Each product line offers different characteristics and features, allowing you to find the right switch to meet the functional requirements of your network. The Cisco switch product lines are:

- Catalyst Express 500
- Catalyst 2960
- Catalyst 3560
- Catalyst 3750
- Catalyst 4500
- Catalyst 4900
- Catalyst 6500

Catalyst Express 500

The Catalyst Express 500 is Cisco's entry-layer switch. It offers the following:

- Forwarding rates from 8.8 Gb/s to 24 Gb/s

- Layer 2 port security

- Web-based management

- Converged data/IP communications support

This switch series is appropriate for access layer implementations where high port density is not required. The Cisco Catalyst Express 500 series switches are scaled for small business environments ranging from 20 to 250 employees. The Catalyst Express 500 series switches are available in different fixed configurations:

- Fast Ethernet and Gigabit Ethernet connectivity

- Up to 24 10/100 ports with optional PoE or 12 10/100/1000 ports

Catalyst Express 500 series switches do not allow management through the Cisco *IOS* CLI. They are managed using a built-in web management interface, the Cisco Network Assistant or the new Cisco Configuration Manager developed specifically for the Catalyst Express 500 series switches. The Catalyst Express does not support *console* access.

To learn more about the Cisco Express 500 series of switches, go to http://www.cisco.com/en/US/products/ps6545/index.html.

Catalyst 2960

The Catalyst 2960 series switches enable entry-layer enterprise, medium-sized, and branch office networks to provide enhanced LAN services. The Catalyst 2960 series switches are appropriate for access layer implementations where access to power and space is limited. The CCNA Exploration 3 LAN Switching and Wireless labs are based on the features of the Cisco 2960 switch.

The Catalyst 2960 series switches offers the following:

- Forwarding rates from 16 Gb/s to 32 Gb/s

- Multilayered switching

- QoS features to support IP communications

- Access control lists (ACLs)

- Fast Ethernet and Gigabit Ethernet connectivity

- Up to 48 10/100 ports or 10/100/1000 ports with additional dual purpose gigabit uplinks

The Catalyst 2960 series of switches do not support PoE.

The Catalyst 2960 series supports the Cisco IOS CLI, integrated web management interface, and Cisco Network Assistant. This switch series supports console and auxiliary access to the switch.

To learn more about the Catalyst 2960 series of switches, visit http://www.cisco.com/en/US/products/ps6406/index.html.

Catalyst 3560

The Cisco Catalyst 3560 series is a line of enterprise-class switches that include support for PoE, QoS, and advanced security features such as ACLs. These switches are ideal access layer switches for small enterprise LAN access or branch-office converged network environments.

The Cisco Catalyst 3560 Series supports forwarding rates of 32 Gb/s to 128 Gb/s (Catalyst 3560-E switch series).

The Catalyst 3560 series switches are available in different fixed configurations:

- Fast Ethernet and Gigabit Ethernet connectivity

- Up to 48 10/100/1000 ports, plus four small form-factor pluggable (SFP) ports

- Optional 10 Gigabit Ethernet connectivity in the Catalyst 3560-E models

- Optional Integrated PoE (Cisco pre-*standard* and *IEEE* 802.3af); up to 24 ports with 15.4 watts or 48 ports with 7.3 watts

To learn more about the Catalyst 3560 series of switches, visit http://www.cisco.com/en/US/products/ hw/switches/ps5528/index.html.

Catalyst 3750

The Cisco Catalyst 3750 series of switches are ideal for access layer switches in midsize organizations and enterprise branch offices. This series offers forwarding rates from 32 Gb/s to 128 Gb/s (Catalyst 3750-E switch series). The Catalyst 3750 series supports Cisco StackWise technology. StackWise technology allows you to interconnect up to nine physical Catalyst 3750 switches into one logical switch using a high-performance (32 Gb/s), redundant, backplane connection.

The Catalyst 3750 series switches are available in different stackable fixed configurations:

- Fast Ethernet and Gigabit Ethernet connectivity

- Up to 48 10/100/1000 ports, plus four SFP ports

- Optional 10 Gigabit Ethernet connectivity in the Catalyst 3750-E models

- Optional Integrated PoE (Cisco pre-standard and IEEE 802.3af); up to 24 ports with 15.4 watts or 48 ports with 7.3 watts

To learn more about the Catalyst 3750 series of switches, visit http://www.cisco.com/en/US/products/ hw/switches/ps5023/index.html.

Catalyst 4500

The Catalyst 4500 is the first midrange modular switching platform offering multilayer switching for enterprises, small- to medium-sized businesses, and service providers.

With forwarding rates up to 136 Gb/s, the Catalyst 4500 series is capable of managing traffic at the distribution layer. The modular capability of the Catalyst 4500 series allows for very high port densities through the addition of switch port line cards to its modular chassis. The Catalyst 4500 series offers multilayer QoS and sophisticated routing functions.

The Catalyst 4500 series switches are available in different modular configurations:

- Modular 3, 6, 7, and 10 slot chassis offering different layers of scalability

- High port density: up to 384 Fast Ethernet or Gigabit Ethernet ports available in copper or fiber with 10 Gigabit uplinks

- PoE (Cisco pre-standard and IEEE 802.3af)

- Dual, hot-swappable internal AC or DC power supplies

- Advanced hardware-assisted IP routing capabilities

To learn more about the Catalyst 4500 series of switches, visit http://www.cisco.com/en/US/products/ hw/switches/ps4324/index.html.

Refer to
Figure
in online course

Catalyst 4900

The Catalyst 4900 series switches are designed and optimized for server switching by allowing very high forwarding rates. The Cisco Catalyst 4900 is not a typical access layer switch. It is a specialty access layer switch designed for data center deployments where many servers may exist in close proximity. This switch series supports dual, redundant power supplies and fans that can be swapped out while the switch is still running. This allows the switches to achieve higher availability, which is critical in data center deployments.

The Catalyst 4900 series switches support advanced QoS features, making them ideal candidates for the back-end IP telephony hardware. Catalyst 4900 series switches do not support the Stack-Wise feature of the Catalyst 3750 series nor do they support PoE.

The Catalyst 4900 series switches are available in different fixed configurations:

- Up to 48 10/100/1000 ports with four SFP ports or 48 10/100/1000 ports with two 10GbE ports

- Dual, hot-swappable internal AC or DC power supplies

- Hot-swappable fan trays

To learn more about the Catalyst 4900 series of switches, visit http://www.cisco.com/en/US/products/ps6021/index.html.

Catalyst 6500

The Catalyst 6500 series modular switch is optimized for secure, converged voice, video, and data networks. The Catalyst 6500 is capable of managing traffic at the distribution and core layers. The Catalyst 6500 series is the highest performing Cisco switch, supporting forwarding rates up to 720 Gb/s. The Catalyst 6500 is ideal for very large network environments found in enterprises, medium-sized businesses, and service providers.

The Catalyst 6500 series switches are available in different modular configurations:

- Modular 3, 4, 6, 9, and 13 slot chassis

- LAN/WAN service modules

- PoE up to 420 IEEE 802.3af Class 3 (15.4W) PoE devices

- Up to 1152 10/100 ports, 577 10/100/1000 ports, 410 SFP Gigabit Ethernet ports, or 64 10 Gigabit Ethernet ports

- Dual, hot-swappable internal AC or DC power supplies

- Advanced hardware-assisted IP routing capabilities

To learn more about the Catalyst 6500 series of switches, visit http://www.cisco.com/en/US/products/hw/switches/ps708/index.html.

The following tool can help identify the correct switch for an implementation: http://www.cisco.com/en/US/products/hw/switches/products_promotion0900aecd8050364f.html.

The following guide provides a detailed comparison of current switch offerings from Cisco: http://www.cisco.com/en/US/prod/switches/ps5718/ps708/networking_solutions_products_genericcontent0900aecd805f0955.pdf.

Refer to **Packet
Tracer Activity**
for this chapter

Packet Tracer is integrated throughout this course. You must know how to navigate the Packet Tracer environment to complete this course. Use the tutorials if you need a review of Packet Tracer fundamentals. The tutorials are located in the Packet Tracer Help menu.

This activity focuses on building a hierarchical topology, from the core to the distribution and access layers.

Activity Instructions (PDF)

1.3 Chapter Labs

1.3.1 Review of Concepts from Exploration 1

Refer to Lab Activity for this chapter

In this lab, you will design and configure a small routed network and verify connectivity across multiple network devices. This requires creating and assigning two subnetwork blocks, connecting *hosts* and network devices, and configuring host computers and one Cisco router for basic network connectivity. Switch1 has a default configuration and does not require additional configuration. You will use common commands to test and document the network. The zero *subnet* is used.

Refer to Packet Tracer Activity for this chapter

In this activity, you will design and configure a small routed network and verify connectivity across multiple network devices. This requires creating and assigning two subnetwork blocks, connecting hosts and network devices, and configuring host computers and one Cisco router for basic network connectivity. Switch1 has a default configuration and does not require additional configuration. You will use common commands to test and document the network. The zero subnet is used.

Detailed instructions are provided within the activity as well as in the PDF link below.

Activity Instructions (PDF)

1.3.2 Review of Concepts from Exploration 1 - Challenge

Refer to Lab Activity for this chapter

In this lab, you will design and configure a small routed network and verify connectivity across multiple network devices. This requires creating and assigning two subnetwork blocks, connecting hosts and network devices, and configuring host computers and one Cisco router for basic network connectivity. Switch1 has a default configuration and does not require additional configuration. You will use common commands to test and document the network. The zero subnet is used.

Refer to Packet Tracer Activity for this chapter

In this activity, you will design and configure a small routed network and verify connectivity across multiple network devices. This requires creating and assigning two subnetwork blocks, connecting hosts and network devices, and configuring host computers and one Cisco router for basic network connectivity. Switch1 has a default configuration and does not require additional configuration. You will use common commands to test and document the network. The zero subnet is used.

Detailed instructions are provided within the activity as well as in the PDF link below.

Activity Instructions (PDF)

1.3.3 Troubleshooting a Small Network

Refer to Lab Activity for this chapter

In this lab, you are given a completed configuration for a small routed network. The configuration contains design and configuration errors that conflict with stated requirements and prevent end-to-end communication. You will examine the given design and identify and correct any design errors. You will then cable the network, configure the hosts, and load configurations onto the router. Finally, you will troubleshoot the connectivity problems to determine where the errors are occurring and correct them using the appropriate commands. When all errors have been corrected, each host should be able to communicate with all other configured network elements and with the other host.

Refer to **Packet Tracer Activity** for this chapter

The configuration contains design and configuration errors that conflict with stated requirements and prevent end-to-end communication. You will troubleshoot the connectivity problems to determine where the errors are occurring and correct them using the appropriate commands. When all errors have been corrected, each host should be able to communicate with all other configured network elements and with the other host.

Detailed instructions are provided within the activity as well as in the PDF link below.

Activity Instructions (PDF)

Refer to
Figure
in online course

Chapter Summary

In this chapter, we discussed the hierarchical design model. Implementing this model improves the performance, scalability, availability, manageability, and maintainability of the network. Hierarchical network topologies facilitate network convergence by enhancing the performance necessary for voice and video data to be combined onto the existing data network.

Refer to
Figure
in online course

Traffic flow, user communities, data stores and server location, and topology diagram analysis are used to help identify network bottlenecks. The bottlenecks can then be addressed to improve the performance of the network and accurately determine appropriate hardware requirements to satisfy the desired performance of the network.

Refer to **Packet Tracer Activity** for this chapter

We surveyed the different switch features, such as form factor, performance, PoE, and Layer 3 support and how they relate to the different layers of the hierarchical network design. An array of Cisco Catalyst switch product lines is available to support any application or business size.

This activity reviews the skills you acquired in the CCNA Exploration: Network Fundamentals course. The skills include subnetting, building a network, applying an addressing scheme, and testing connectivity. You should review those skills before proceeding. In addition, this activity reviews the basics of using the Packet Tracer program. Packet Tracer is integrated throughout this course. You must know how to navigate the Packet Tracer environment to complete this course. Use the tutorials if you need a review of Packet Tracer fundamentals. The tutorials are located in the Packet Tracer Help menu.

Detailed instructions are provided within the activity as well as in the PDF link below.

Activity Instructions (PDF)

Go to
the online course
to take the quiz.

Chapter Quiz

Take the chapter quiz to test your knowledge.

Your Chapter Notes

CHAPTER 2

Basic Switch Concepts and Configuration

Chapter Introduction

Refer to **Figure** in online course

In this chapter, you will build upon the skills learned in CCNA Exploration 4.0: Network Fundamentals, reviewing and reinforcing these skills with in-depth practice activities. You will learn about some key malicious threats to switches and learn to enable a switch with a secure initial configuration.

2.1 Introduction to Ethernet/802.3 LANs

2.1.1 Key Elements of Ethernet/802.3 Networks

Refer to **Figure** in online course

In this topic, you will learn about key components of the Ethernet standard that play a significant role in the design and implementation of switched networks. You will explore how Ethernet communications function and how switches play a role in the communication process.

CSMA/CD

Ethernet signals are transmitted to every host connected to the LAN using a special set of rules to determine which station can access the network. The set of rules that Ethernet uses is based on the IEEE carrier sense multiple access/collision detect (*CSMA/CD*) technology. You may recall from CCNA Exploration: Networking Fundamentals that CSMA/CD is only used with half-duplex communication typically found in hubs. Full-duplex switches do not use CSMA/CD.

Carrier Sense

In the CSMA/CD *access method*, all network devices that have *messages* to send must listen before transmitting.

If a device detects a signal from another device, it waits for a specified amount of time before attempting to transmit.

When there is no traffic detected, a device transmits its message. While this transmission is occurring, the device continues to listen for traffic or *collisions* on the LAN. After the message is sent, the device returns to its default listening mode.

Multi-access

If the distance between devices is such that the latency of the signals of one device means that signals are not detected by a second device, the second device may also start to transmit. The media now has two devices transmitting signals at the same time. The messages propagate across the media until they encounter each other. At that point, the signals mix and the messages are destroyed, a collision has occurred. Although the messages are corrupted, the jumble of remaining signals continues to propagate across the media.

Collision Detection

When a device is in listening mode, it can detect when a collision occurs on the shared media, because all devices can detect an increase in the *amplitude* of the signal above the normal level.

When a collision occurs, the other devices in listening mode, as well as all the transmitting devices, detect the increase in the signal amplitude. Every device that is transmitting continues to transmit to ensure that all devices on the network detect the collision.

Jam Signal and Random *Backoff*

When a collision is detected, the transmitting devices send out a jamming signal. The jamming signal notifies the other devices of a collision, so that they invoke a backoff *algorithm*. This backoff algorithm causes all devices to stop transmitting for a random amount of time, which allows the collision signals to subside.

After the *delay* has expired on a device, the device goes back into the "listening before transmit" mode. A random backoff period ensures that the devices that were involved in the collision do not try to send traffic again at the same time, which would cause the whole process to repeat. However, during the backoff period, a third device may transmit before either of the two involved in the collision have a chance to re-transmit.

Click the Play button to see the animation.

Refer to
Figure
in online course

Ethernet Communications

Reference the selected Ethernet Communications area in the figure.

Communications in a switched LAN network occur in three ways: *unicast*, broadcast, and *multicast*:

Unicast: Communication in which a frame is sent from one host and addressed to one specific destination. In unicast transmission, there is just one sender and one receiver. Unicast transmission is the predominant form of transmission on LANs and within the Internet. Examples of protocols that use unicast transmissions include HTTP, *SMTP*, FTP, and *Telnet*.

Broadcast: Communication in which a frame is sent from one address to all other addresses. In this case, there is just one sender, but the information is sent to all connected receivers. Broadcast transmission is essential when sending the same message to all devices on the LAN. An example of a broadcast transmission is the address resolution query that the address resolution protocol (*ARP*) sends to all computers on a LAN.

Multicast: Communication in which a frame is sent to a specific group of devices or clients. Multicast transmission clients must be members of a logical *multicast group* to receive the information. An example of multicast transmission is the video and voice transmissions associated with a network-based, collaborative business meeting.

Ethernet Frame

Click the Ethernet Frame button in the figure.

The first course in our series, CCNA Exploration: Networking Fundamentals, described the structure of the Ethernet frame in detail. To briefly review, the Ethernet frame structure adds *headers* and *trailers* around the Layer 3 *PDU* to encapsulate the message being sent. Both the Ethernet header and trailer have several sections (or fields) of information that are used by the Ethernet protocol. The figure shows the structure of the current Ethernet frame standard, the revised IEEE 802.3 (Ethernet).

Roll over each field name to see its description.

Preamble and Start Frame Delimiter Fields

The Preamble (7 *bytes*) and Start Frame Delimiter (SFD) (1 byte) fields are used for *synchronization* between the sending and receiving devices. These first 8 bytes of the frame are used to get the attention of the receiving nodes. Essentially, the first few bytes tell the receivers to get ready to receive a new frame.

Destination MAC Address Field

The Destination MAC Address field (6 bytes) is the identifier for the intended recipient. This address is used by Layer 2 to assist a device in determining if a frame is addressed to it. The address in the frame is compared to the MAC address in the device. If there is a match, the device accepts the frame.

Source MAC Address Field

The Source MAC Address field (6 bytes) identifies the frame's originating *NIC* or interface. Switches use this address to add to their lookup tables.

Length/Type Field

The Length/Type field (2 bytes) defines the exact length of the frame's data field. This field is used later as part of the Frame Check Sequence (*FCS*) to ensure that the message was received properly. Only a frame length or a frame type can be entered here. If the purpose of the field is to designate a type, the Type field describes which protocol is implemented. When a node receives a frame and the Length/Type field designates a type, the node determines which higher layer protocol is present. If the two-*octet* value is equal to or greater than 0x0600 *hexadecimal* or 1536 decimal, the contents of the Data Field are decoded according to the protocol indicated; if the two-byte value is less than 0x0600 then the value represents the length of the data in the frame.

Data and Pad Fields

The Data and Pad fields (46 to 1500 bytes) contain the encapsulated data from a higher layer, which is a generic Layer 3 PDU, or more commonly, an *IPv4* packet. All frames must be at least 64 bytes long (minimum length aides the detection of collisions). If a small packet is encapsulated, the Pad field is used to increase the size of the frame to the minimum size.

Frame Check Sequence Field

The FCS field (4 bytes) detects errors in a frame. It uses a cyclic redundancy check (*CRC*). The sending device includes the results of a CRC in the FCS field of the frame. The receiving device receives the frame and generates a CRC to look for errors. If the calculations match, no error has occurred. If the calculations do not match, the frame is dropped.

MAC Address

Click the MAC Address button in the figure.

In CCNA Exploration: Networking Fundamentals, you learned about the MAC address. An Ethernet MAC address is a two-part 48-*bit binary* value expressed as 12 hexadecimal digits. The address formats might be similar to 00-05-9A-3C-78-00, 00:05:9A:3C:78:00, or 0005.9A3C.7800.

All devices connected to an Ethernet LAN have MAC-addressed interfaces. The NIC uses the MAC address to determine if a message should be passed to the upper layers for processing. The MAC address is permanently encoded into a ROM chip on a NIC. This type of MAC address is referred to as a burned in address (BIA). Some vendors allow local modification of the MAC address. The MAC address is made up of the organizational unique identifier (*OUI*) and the vendor assignment number.

Roll over each field name to see its description.

Organizational Unique Identifier

The OUI is the first part of a MAC address. It is 24 bits long and identifies the manufacturer of the NIC card. The IEEE regulates the assignment of OUI numbers. Within the OUI, there are 2 bits that have meaning only when used in the destination address, as follows:

Broadcast or multicast bit: Indicates to the receiving interface that the frame is destined for all or a group of end stations on the LAN segment.

Locally administered address bit: If the vendor-assigned MAC address can be modified locally, this bit should be set.

Vendor Assignment Number

The vendor-assigned part of the MAC address is 24 bits long and uniquely identifies the Ethernet hardware. It can be a BIA or modified by software indicated by the local bit.

Refer to
Figure
in online course

Duplex Settings

There are two types of duplex settings used for communications on an Ethernet network: *half duplex* and *full duplex*. The figure shows the two duplex settings available on modern network equipment.

Half Duplex: Half-duplex communication relies on unidirectional data flow where sending and receiving data are not performed at the same time. This is similar to how walkie-talkies or two-way radios function in that only one person can talk at any one time. If someone talks while someone else is already speaking, a collision occurs. As a result, half-duplex communication implements CSMA/CD to help reduce the potential for collisions and detect them when they do happen. Half-duplex communications have performance issues due to the constant waiting, because data can only flow in one direction at a time. Half-duplex connections are typically seen in older hardware, such as hubs. Nodes that are attached to hubs that share their connection to a switch port must operate in half-duplex mode because the end computers must be able to detect collisions. Nodes can operate in a half-duplex mode if the NIC card cannot be configured for full duplex operations. In this case the port on the switch defaults to a half-duplex mode as well. Because of these limitations, full-duplex communication has replaced half duplex in more current hardware.

Full Duplex: In full-duplex communication, data flow is bidirectional, so data can be sent and received at the same time. The bidirectional support enhances performance by reducing the wait time between transmissions. Most Ethernet, Fast Ethernet, and Gigabit Ethernet NICs sold today offer full-duplex capability. In full-duplex mode, the collision detect *circuit* is disabled. Frames sent by the two connected end nodes cannot collide because the end nodes use two separate circuits in the network cable. Each full-duplex connection uses only one port. Full-duplex connections require a switch that supports full duplex or a direct connection between two nodes that each support full duplex. Nodes that are directly attached to a dedicated switch port with NICs that support full duplex should be connected to switch ports that are configured to operate in full-duplex mode.

Standard, shared hub-based Ethernet configuration efficiency is typically rated at 50 to 60 percent of the 10-Mb/s bandwidth. Full-duplex Fast Ethernet, compared to 10-Mb/s bandwidth, offers 100 percent efficiency in both directions (100-Mb/s transmit and 100-Mb/s receive).

Refer to
Figure
in online course

Switch Port Settings

A port on a switch needs to be configured with duplex settings that match the media type. Later in this chapter, you will configure duplex settings. The Cisco Catalyst switches have three settings:

- The `auto` option sets autonegotiation of duplex mode. With autonegotiation enabled, the two ports communicate to decide the best mode of operation.

- The `full` option sets full-duplex mode.

- The **half** option sets half-duplex mode.

For Fast Ethernet and 10/100/1000 ports, the default is auto. For *100BASE-FX* ports, the default is full. The 10/100/1000 ports operate in either half- or full-duplex mode when they are set to 10 or 100 Mb/s, but when set to 1,000 Mb/s, they operate only in full-duplex mode.

Note: Autonegotiation can produce unpredictable results. By default, when autonegotiation fails, the Catalyst switch sets the corresponding switch port to half-duplex mode. This type of failure happens when an attached device does not support autonegotiation. If the device is manually configured to operate in half-duplex mode, it matches the default mode of the switch. However, autonegotiation errors can happen if the device is manually configured to operate in full-duplex mode. Having half-duplex on one end and full-duplex on the other causes late collision errors at the half-duplex end. To avoid this situation, manually set the duplex parameters of the switch to match the attached device. If the switch port is in full-duplex mode and the attached device is in half-duplex mode, check for FCS errors on the switch full-duplex port.

auto-MDIX

Connections between specific devices, such as switch-to-switch or switch-to-router, once required the use of certain cable types (cross-over, straight-through). Instead, you can now use the **mdix auto** interface configuration command in the CLI to enable the automatic medium-dependent interface crossover (auto-MDIX) feature.

When the auto-MDIX feature is enabled, the switch detects the required cable type for copper Ethernet connections and configures the interfaces accordingly. Therefore, you can use either a crossover or a straight-through cable for connections to a copper 10/100/1000 port on the switch, regardless of the type of device on the other end of the connection.

The auto-MDIX feature is enabled by default on switches running Cisco IOS Release 12.2(18)SE or later. For releases between Cisco IOS Release 12.1(14)EA1 and 12.2(18)SE, the auto-MDIX feature is disabled by default.

Refer to
Figure
in online course

MAC Addressing and Switch MAC Address Tables

Switches use MAC addresses to direct network communications through their switch fabric to the appropriate port toward the destination node. The switch fabric is the integrated circuits and the accompanying machine programming that allows the data paths through the switch to be controlled. For a switch to know which port to use to transmit a unicast frame, it must first learn which nodes exist on each of its ports.

A switch determines how to handle incoming data frames by using its MAC address table. A switch builds its MAC address table by recording the MAC addresses of the nodes connected to each of its ports. Once a MAC address for a specific node on a specific port is recorded in the address table, the switch then knows to send traffic destined for that specific node out the port mapped to that node for subsequent transmissions.

When an incoming data frame is received by a switch and the destination MAC address is not in the table, the switch forwards the frame out all ports, except for the port on which it was received. When the destination node responds, the switch records the node's MAC address in the address table from the frame's source address field. In networks with multiple interconnected switches, the MAC address tables record multiple MAC addresses for the ports connecting the switches which reflect the node's beyond. Typically, switch ports used to interconnect two switches have multiple MAC addresses recorded in the MAC address table.

To see how this works, **click the steps in the figure.**

The following describes this process:

Step 1. The switch receives a broadcast frame from PC 1 on Port 1.

Step 2. The switch enters the source MAC address and the switch port that received the frame into the address table.

Step 3. Because the destination address is a broadcast, the switch *floods* the frame to all ports, except the port on which it received the frame.

Step 4. The destination device replies to the broadcast with a unicast frame addressed to PC 1.

Step 5. The switch enters the source MAC address of PC 2 and the port number of the switch port that received the frame into the address table. The destination address of the frame and its associated port is found in the MAC address table.

Step 6. The switch can now forward frames between source and destination devices without flooding, because it has entries in the address table that identify the associated ports.

2.1.2 Design Considerations for Ethernet/802.3 Networks

Refer to
Figure
in online course

In this topic, you will learn about the Ethernet design guidelines needed for interpreting hierarchical network designs for small and medium-sized businesses. This topic focuses on broadcast and *collision domains* and how they affect LAN designs.

Bandwidth and Throughput

A major disadvantage of Ethernet 802.3 networks is collisions. Collisions occur when two hosts transmit frames simultaneously. When a collision occurs, the transmitted frames are corrupted or destroyed. The sending hosts stop sending further transmissions for a random period, based on the Ethernet 802.3 rules of CSMA/CD.

Because Ethernet has no way of controlling which node will be transmitting at any time, we know that collisions will occur when more than one node attempts to gain access to the network. Ethernet's resolution for collisions does not occur instantaneously. Also, a node involved in a collision cannot start transmitting until the matter is resolved. As more devices are added to the shared media the likelihood of collisions increases. Because of this, it is important to understand that when stating the bandwidth of the Ethernet network is 10 Mb/s, full bandwidth for transmission is available only after any collisions have been resolved. The net throughput of the port (the average data that is effectively transmitted) will be considerably reduced as a function of how many other nodes want to use the network. A hub offers no mechanisms to either eliminate or reduce these collisions and the available bandwidth that any one node has to transmit is correspondingly reduced. As a result, the number of nodes sharing the Ethernet network will have effect on the throughput or productivity of the network.

Collision Domains

When expanding an Ethernet LAN to accommodate more users with more bandwidth requirements, the potential for collisions increases. To reduce the number of nodes on a given network segment, you can create separate physical network segments, called collision domains.

The network area where frames originate and collide is called the collision domain. All shared media environments, such as those created by using hubs, are collision domains. When a host is connected to a switch port, the switch creates a dedicated connection. This connection is considered an individual collision domain, because traffic is kept separate from all other traffic, thereby eliminating the potential for a collision. The figure shows unique collision domains in a switched environment. For example, if a 12-port switch has a device connected to each port, 12 collision domains are created.

As you now know, a switch builds a MAC address table by learning the MAC addresses of the hosts that are connected to each switch port. When two connected hosts want to communicate with each other, the switch uses the switching table to establish a connection between the ports. The circuit is maintained until the *session* is terminated. In the figure, Host A and Host B want to communicate with each other. The switch creates the connection that is referred to as a microsegment. The microsegment behaves as if the network has only two hosts, one host sending and one receiving, providing maximum utilization of the available bandwidth.

Switches reduce collisions and improve bandwidth use on network segments because they provide dedicated bandwidth to each network segment.

Refer to
Figure
in online course

Broadcast Domains

Although switches *filter* most frames based on MAC addresses, they do not filter broadcast frames. For other switches on the LAN to get broadcasted frames, broadcast frames must be forwarded by switches. A collection of interconnected switches forms a single broadcast domain. Only a Layer 3 *entity*, such as a router, or a virtual LAN (VLAN), can stop a Layer 3 broadcast domain. Routers and VLANs are used to segment both collision and broadcast domains. The use of VLANs to segment broadcast domains will be discussed in the next chapter.

When a device wants to send out a Layer 2 broadcast, the destination MAC address in the frame is set to all ones. By setting the destination to this value, all the devices accept and process the broadcasted frame.

The broadcast domain at Layer 2 is referred to as the MAC broadcast domain. The MAC broadcast domain consists of all devices on the LAN that receive frame broadcasts by a host to all other machines on the LAN. This is shown in the first half of the animation.

When a switch receives a broadcast frame, it forwards the frame to each of its ports, except the incoming port where the switch received the broadcast frame. Each attached device recognizes the broadcast frame and processes it. This leads to reduced network efficiency, because bandwidth is used to propagate the broadcast traffic.

When two switches are connected, the broadcast domain is increased. In this example, a broadcast frame is forwarded to all connected ports on switch S1. Switch S1 is connected to switch S2. The frame is propagated to all devices connected to switch S2. This is shown in the second half of the animation.

Refer to
Figure
in online course

Network Latency

Latency is the time a frame or a packet takes to travel from the source station to the final destination. Users of network-based applications experience latency when they have to wait many minutes to access data stored in a data center or when a website takes many minutes to load in a *browser*. Latency has at least three sources.

First, there is the time it takes the source NIC to place voltage pulses on the wire, and the time it takes the destination NIC to interpret these pulses. This is sometimes called NIC delay, typically around 1 microsecond for a *10BASE-T* NIC.

Second, there is the actual *propagation delay* as the signal takes time to travel through the cable. Typically, this is about 0.556 microseconds per 100 m for Cat 5 UTP. Longer cable and slower nominal velocity of propagation (*NVP*) result in more propagation delay.

Third, latency is added based on network devices that are in the path between two devices. These are either Layer 1, Layer 2, or Layer 3 devices. These three contributors to latency can be discerned from the animation as the frame traverses the network.

Latency does not depend solely on distance and number of devices. For example, if three properly configured switches separate two computers, the computers may experience less latency than if two properly configured routers separated them. This is because routers conduct more complex and time-intensive functions. For example, a router must analyze Layer 3 data, while switches just analyze the Layer 2 data. Since Layer 2 data is present earlier in the frame structure than the Layer 3 data, switches can process the frame more quickly. Switches also support the high transmission rates of voice, video, and data networks by employing application-specific integrated circuits (ASIC) to provide hardware support for many networking tasks. Additional switch features such as port-based memory *buffering*, port level QoS, and *congestion* management, also help to reduce network latency.

Switch-based latency may also be due to oversubscribed switch fabric. Many entry-level switches do not have enough internal throughput to manage full bandwidth capabilities on all ports simultaneously. The switch needs to be able to manage the amount of peak data expected on the network. As the switching technology improves, the latency through the switch is no longer the issue. The predominant cause of network latency in a switched LAN is more a function of the media being transmitted, *routing protocols* used, and types of applications running on the network.

Refer to **Figure** in online course

Network Congestion

The primary reason for segmenting a LAN into smaller parts is to isolate traffic and to achieve better use of bandwidth per user. Without segmentation, a LAN quickly becomes clogged with traffic and collisions. The figure shows a network that is subject to congestion by multiple node devices on a hub-based network.

These are the most common causes of network congestion:

- Increasingly powerful computer and network technologies. Today, CPUs, buses, and peripherals are much faster and more powerful than those used in early LANs, therefore they can send more data at higher rates through the network, and they can process more data at higher rates.

- Increasing volume of network traffic. Network traffic is now more common because remote resources are necessary to carry out basic work. Additionally, broadcast messages, such as address resolution queries sent out by ARP, can adversely affect end-station and network performance.

- High-bandwidth applications. Software applications are becoming richer in their functionality and are requiring more and more bandwidth. Desktop publishing, engineering design, video on demand (*VoD*), electronic learning (e-learning), and streaming video all require considerable processing power and speed.

Refer to **Figure** in online course

LAN Segmentation

LANs are segmented into a number of smaller collision and broadcast domains using routers and switches. Previously, bridges were used, but this type of network equipment is rarely seen in a modern switched LAN. The figure shows the routers and switches segmenting a LAN.

In the figure the network is segmented into four collision domains using the switch.

Roll over the Collision Domain to see the size of each collision domain.

However, the broadcast domain, in the figure spans the entire network.

Roll over the Broadcast Domain to see the size of broadcast domain.

Bridges and Switches

Although bridges and switches share many attributes, several distinctions differentiate these technologies. Bridges are generally used to segment a LAN into a couple of smaller segments. Switches are generally used to segment a large LAN into many smaller segments. Bridges have only a few ports for LAN connectivity, whereas switches have many.

Routers

Even though the *LAN switch* reduces the size of collision domains, all hosts connected to the switch, and in the same VLAN, are still in the same broadcast domain. Because routers do not forward broadcast traffic by default, they can be used to create broadcast domains. Creating additional, smaller broadcast domains with a router reduces broadcast traffic and provides more available bandwidth for unicast communications. Each router interface connects to a separate network, containing broadcast traffic within the LAN segment in which it originated.

Click the Controlled Collision and Broadcast Domain button to see the effect of introducing routers and more switches into the network.

Roll over the two text areas to identify the different broadcast and collision domains.

2.1.3 LAN Design Considerations

Refer to
Figure
in online course

Controlling Network Latency

When designing a network to reduce latency, you need to consider the latency caused by each device on the network. Switches can introduce latency on a network when oversubscribed on a busy network. For example, if a core level switch has to support 48 ports, each one capable of running at 1000 Mb/s full duplex, the switch should support around 96 Gb/s internal throughput if it is to maintain full wirespeed across all ports simultaneously. In this example, the throughput requirements stated are typical of core-level switches, not of access-level switches.

The use of higher layer devices can also increase latency on a network. When a Layer 3 device, such as a router, needs to examine the Layer 3 addressing information contained within the frame, it must read further into the frame than a Layer 2 device, which creates a longer processing time. Limiting the use of higher layer devices can help reduce network latency. However, appropriate use of Layer 3 devices helps prevent contention from broadcast traffic in a large broadcast domain or the high collision rate in a large collision domain.

Removing Bottlenecks

Bottlenecks on a network are places where high network congestion results in slow performance.

Click on the Removing Network Bottlenecks button in the figure.

In this figure which shows six computers connected to a switch, a single server is also connected to the same switch. Each workstation and the server are all connected using a 1000 Mb/s NIC. What happens when all six computers try to access the server at the same time? Does each workstation get 1000 Mb/s dedicated access to the server? No, all the computers have to share the 1000 Mb/s connection that the server has to the switch. Cumulatively, the computers are capable of 6000 Mb/s to the switch. If each connection was used at full capacity, each computer would be able to use only 167 Mb/s, one-sixth of the 1000 Mb/s bandwidth. To reduce the bottleneck to the server, additional network cards can be installed, which increases the total bandwidth the server is capable of receiving. The figure shows five NIC cards in the server and approximately five times the bandwidth. The same logic applies to network topologies. When switches with multiple nodes are interconnected by a single 1000 Mb/s connection, a bottleneck is created at this single interconnect.

Higher capacity links (for example, upgrading from 100 Mb/s to 1000 Mb/s connections) and using multiple links leveraging link aggregation technologies (for example, combining two links as if they were one to double a connection's capacity) can help to reduce the bottlenecks created by inter-switch links and router links. Although configuring link aggregation is outside the scope of this course, it is important to consider a device's capabilities when assessing a network's needs. How many ports and of what speed is the device capable of? What is the internal throughput of the device? Can it handle the anticipated traffic loads considering its placement in the network?

Refer to
Figure
in online course

Refer to
Figure
in online course

2.2 Forwarding Frames using a Switch

2.2.1 Switch Forwarding Methods

Switch Packet Forwarding Methods

In this topic, you will learn how switches forward Ethernet frames on a network. Switches can operate in different modes that can have both positive and negative effects.

In the past, switches used one of the following forwarding methods for switching data between network ports: store-and-forward or cut-through switching. Referencing the Switch Forwarding Methods button shows these two methods. However, store-and-forward is the sole forwarding method used on current models of Cisco Catalyst switches.

Store-and-Forward Switching

In store-and-forward switching, when the switch receives the frame, it stores the data in buffers until the complete frame has been received. During the storage process, the switch analyzes the frame for information about its destination. In this process, the switch also performs an error check using the Cyclic Redundancy Check (CRC) trailer portion of the Ethernet frame.

CRC uses a mathematical formula, based on the number of bits (1s) in the frame, to determine whether the received frame has an error. After confirming the integrity of the frame, the frame is forwarded out the appropriate port toward its destination. When an error is detected in a frame, the switch discards the frame. Discarding frames with errors reduces the amount of bandwidth consumed by corrupt data. Store-and-forward switching is required for Quality of Service (QoS) analysis on converged networks where frame classification for traffic prioritization is necessary. For example, voice over IP data streams need to have priority over web-browsing traffic.

Click on the Store-and-Forward Switching button and play the animation for a demonstration of the store-and-forward process.

Cut-through Switching

In cut-through switching, the switch acts upon the data as soon as it is received, even if the transmission is not complete. The switch buffers just enough of the frame to read the destination MAC address so that it can determine to which port to forward the data. The destination MAC address is located in the first 6 bytes of the frame following the preamble. The switch looks up the destination MAC address in its switching table, determines the outgoing interface port, and forwards the frame onto its destination through the designated switch port. The switch does not perform any error checking on the frame. Because the switch does not have to wait for the entire frame to be completely buffered, and because the switch does not perform any error checking, cut-through switching is faster than store-and-forward switching. However, because the switch does not perform any error checking, it forwards corrupt frames throughout the network. The corrupt frames consume bandwidth while they are being forwarded. The destination NIC eventually discards the corrupt frames.

Click on the Cut-Through Switching button and play the animation for a demonstration of the cut-through switching process.

There are two variants of cut-through switching:

- Fast-forward switching: Fast-forward switching offers the lowest level of latency. Fast-forward switching immediately forwards a packet after reading the destination address. Because fast-forward switching starts forwarding before the entire packet has been received, there may be times when packets are relayed with errors. This occurs infrequently, and the destination network *adapter* discards the faulty packet upon receipt. In fast-forward mode, latency is measured from the first bit received to the first bit transmitted. Fast-forward switching is the typical cut-through method of switching.

- Fragment-free switching: In fragment-free switching, the switch stores the first 64 bytes of the frame before forwarding. Fragment-free switching can be viewed as a compromise between store-and-forward switching and cut-through switching. The reason fragment-free switching stores only the first 64 bytes of the frame is that most network errors and collisions occur during the first 64 bytes. Fragment-free switching tries to enhance cut-through switching by performing a small error check on the first 64 bytes of the frame to ensure that a collision has not occurred before forwarding the frame. Fragment-free switching is a compromise between the high latency and high integrity of store-and-forward switching, and the low latency and reduced integrity of cut-through switching.

Some switches are configured to perform cut-through switching on a per-port basis until a user-defined error threshold is reached and then they automatically change to store-and-forward. When the error rate falls below the threshold, the port automatically changes back to cut-through switching.

2.2.2 Symmetric and Asymmetric Switching

Refer to
Figure
in online course

Symmetric and Asymmetric Switching

In this topic, you will learn the differences between symmetric and asymmetric switching in a network. LAN switching may be classified as symmetric or asymmetric based on the way in which bandwidth is allocated to the switch ports.

Symmetric switching provides switched connections between ports with the same bandwidth, such as all 100 Mb/s ports or all 1000 Mb/s ports. An asymmetric LAN switch provides switched connections between ports of unlike bandwidth, such as a combination of 10 Mb/s, 100 Mb/s, and 1000 Mb/s ports. The figure shows the differences between symmetric and asymmetric switching.

Asymmetric

Asymmetric switching enables more bandwidth to be dedicated to a server switch port to prevent a bottleneck. This allows smoother traffic flows where multiple clients are communicating with a server at the same time. Memory buffering is required on an asymmetric switch. For the switch to match the different data rates on different ports, entire frames are kept in the memory buffer and are moved to the port one after the other as required.

Symmetric

On a symmetric switch all ports are of the same bandwidth. Symmetric switching is optimized for a reasonably distributed traffic load, such as in a peer-to-peer desktop environment.

A network manager must evaluate the needed amount of bandwidth for connections between devices to accommodate the data flow of network-based applications. Most current switches are asymmetric switches because this type of switch offers the greatest flexibility.

2.2.3 Memory Buffering

Refer to
Figure
in online course

Port Based and Shared Memory Buffering

As you learned in a previous topic, a switch analyzes some or all of a packet before it forwards it to the destination host based on the forwarding method. The switch stores the packet for the brief time in a memory buffer. In this topic, you will learn how two types of memory buffers are used during switch forwarding.

An Ethernet switch may use a buffering technique to store frames before forwarding them. Buffering may also be used when the **destination port** is busy due to congestion and the switch stores the frame until it can be transmitted. The use of memory to store the data is called memory buffering. Memory buffering is built into the hardware of the switch and, other than increasing the amount of memory available, is not configurable.

There are two methods of memory buffering: port-based and shared memory.

Port-based Memory Buffering

In port-based memory buffering, frames are stored in *queues* that are linked to specific incoming and outgoing ports. A frame is transmitted to the outgoing port only when all the frames ahead of it in the queue have been successfully transmitted. It is possible for a single frame to delay the transmission of all the frames in memory because of a busy destination port. This delay occurs even if the other frames could be transmitted to open destination ports.

Shared Memory Buffering

Shared memory buffering deposits all frames into a common memory buffer that all the ports on the switch share. The amount of buffer memory required by a port is dynamically allocated. The frames in the buffer are linked dynamically to the destination port. This allows the packet to be received on one port and then transmitted on another port, without moving it to a different queue.

The switch keeps a map of frame to port links showing where a packet needs to be transmitted. The map link is cleared after the frame has been successfully transmitted. The number of frames stored in the buffer is restricted by the size of the entire memory buffer and not limited to a single port buffer. This permits larger frames to be transmitted with fewer dropped frames. This is important to asymmetric switching, where frames are being exchanged between different rate ports.

2.2.4 Layer 2 and Layer 3 Switching

Refer to
Figure
in online course

Layer 2 and Layer 3 Switching

In this topic, you will review the concept of Layer 2 switching and learn about Layer 3 switching.

A Layer 2 LAN switch performs switching and filtering based only on the OSI *Data Link layer* (Layer 2) MAC address. A Layer 2 switch is completely transparent to network protocols and user applications. Recall that a Layer 2 switch builds a MAC address table that it uses to make forwarding decisions.

A Layer 3 switch, such as the Catalyst 3560, functions similarly to a Layer 2 switch, such as the Catalyst 2960, but instead of using only the Layer 2 MAC address information for forwarding decisions, a Layer 3 switch can also use *IP address* information. Instead of only learning which MAC addresses are associated with each of its ports, a Layer 3 switch can also learn which IP addresses are associated with its interfaces. This allows the Layer 3 switch to direct traffic throughout the network based on IP address information.

Layer 3 switches are also capable of performing Layer 3 routing functions, reducing the need for dedicated routers on a LAN. Because Layer 3 switches have specialized switching hardware, they can typically route data as quickly as they can switch.

Layer 3 Switch and Router Comparison

Refer to **Figure** in online course

In the previous topic, you learned that Layer 3 switches examine Layer 3 information in an Ethernet packet to make forwarding decisions. Layer 3 switches can route packets between different LAN segments similarly to dedicated routers. However, Layer 3 switches do not completely replace the need for routers on a network.

Routers perform additional Layer 3 services that Layer 3 switches are not capable of performing. Routers are also capable of performing packet forwarding tasks not found on Layer 3 switches, such as establishing remote access connections to remote networks and devices. Dedicated routers are more flexible in their support of WAN interface cards (WIC), making them the preferred, and sometimes only, choice for connecting to a WAN. Layer 3 switches can provide basic routing functions in a LAN and reduce the need for dedicated routers.

Refer to **Figure** in online course

2.3 Switch Management Configuration

2.3.1 Navigating Command-Line Interface Modes

Refer to **Figure** in online course

The Command Line Interface Modes

In this topic, you will review what you learned in CCNA Exploration: Network Fundamentals about how to navigate the various command line interface (*CLI*) modes.

As a security feature, *Cisco IOS software* separated the *EXEC* sessions into these access levels:

- *User EXEC:* Allows a person to access only a limited number of basic monitoring commands. User EXEC mode is the default mode you enter after logging in to a Cisco switch from the CLI. User EXEC mode is identified by the > prompt.

- *Privileged EXEC:* Allows a person to access all device commands, such as those used for configuration and management, and can be password-protected to allow only authorized users to access the device. Privileged EXEC mode is identified by the # prompt.

To change from user EXEC mode to privileged EXEC mode, enter the `enable` command. To change from privileged EXEC mode to user EXEC mode, enter the `disable` command. On a real network, the switch prompts for the password. Enter the correct password. By default, the password is not configured. The figure shows the Cisco IOS commands used to navigate from user EXEC mode to privileged EXEC mode and back again.

Click the user EXEC and privileged EXEC mode button in the figure.

Navigating Configuration Modes

Once you have entered privileged EXEC mode on the Cisco switch, you can access other configuration modes. Cisco IOS software uses a hierarchy of commands in its command-mode structure. Each command mode supports specific Cisco IOS commands related to a type of operation on the device.

There are many configuration modes. For now, you will explore how to navigate two common configuration modes: global configuration mode and interface configuration mode.

Click the Navigating Configuration Modes button in the figure.

Global Configuration Mode

The example starts with the switch in privileged EXEC mode. To configure global switch parameters such as the switch hostname or the switch IP address used for switch management purposes, use global configuration mode. To access global configuration mode, enter the `configure terminal` command in privileged EXEC mode. The prompt changes to `(config)#`.

Interface Configuration Mode

Configuring interface-specific parameters is a common task. To access interface configuration mode from global configuration mode, enter the `interface` *<interface name>* command. The prompt changes to `(config-if)#`. To exit interface configuration mode, use the `exit` command. The prompt switches back to `(config)#`, letting you know that you are in global configuration mode. To exit global configuration mode, enter the `exit` command again. The prompt switches to #, signifying privileged EXEC mode.

Refer to
Figure
in online course

GUI-based Alternatives to the CLI

There are a number of graphical management alternatives for managing a Cisco switch. Using a *GUI* offers simplified switch management and configuration without in-depth knowledge of the Cisco CLI.

Click the Cisco Network Assistant button in the figure.

Cisco Network Assistant

Cisco Network Assistant is a PC-based GUI *network management* application optimized for small and medium-sized LANs. You can configure and manage groups of switches or standalone switches. The figure shows the management interface for Network Assistant. Cisco Network Assistant is available at no cost and can be downloaded from Cisco (CCO username/password required):

http://www.cisco.com/en/US/prod/collateral/netmgtsw/ps6504/ps5931/
product_data_sheet0900aecd8068820a.html

Click the *CiscoView* Application button in the figure.

CiscoView Application

The CiscoView device-management application displays a physical view of the switch that you can use to set configuration parameters and to view switch status and performance information. The CiscoView application, purchased separately, can be a standalone application or part of a Simple Network Management Protocol (*SNMP*) platform. The figure shows the management interface for the CiscoView Device Manager. Learn more about CiscoView Device Manager at:

http://www.cisco.com/en/US/products/sw/cscowork/ps4565/prod_bulletin0900aecd802948b0.html

Click the Cisco Device Manager button in the figure.

Cisco Device Manager

Cisco Device Manager is web-based software that is stored in the switch memory. You can use Device Manager to configure and manage switches. You can access Device Manager from anywhere in your network through a web browser. The figure shows the management interface.

Click the SNMP Network Management button in the figure.

SNMP Network Management

You can manage switches from a SNMP-compatible management station, such as HP OpenView. The switch is able to provide comprehensive management information and provide four Remote Monitoring (*RMON*) groups. SNMP network management is more common in large enterprise networks.

2.3.2 Using the Help Facility

Refer to
Figure
in online course

Context Sensitive Help

The Cisco IOS CLI offers two types of help:

- *Word help:* If you do not remember an entire command but do remember the first few characters, enter the character sequence followed by a question mark (**?**). Do not include a space before the question mark.

A list of commands that start with the characters that you entered is displayed. For example, entering **sh?** returns a list of all commands that begin with the sh character sequence.

- *Command syntax help:* If you are unfamiliar with which commands are available in your current context within the Cisco IOS CLI, or if you do not know the parameters required or available to complete a given command, enter the **?** command.

When only **?** is entered, a list of all available commands in the current context is displayed. If the **?** command is entered after a specific command, the command arguments are displayed. If <cr> is displayed, no other arguments are needed to make the command function. Make sure to include a space before the question mark to prevent the Cisco IOS CLI from performing word help rather than command syntax help. For example, enter **show ?** to get a list of the command options supported by the **show** command.

The figure shows the Cisco help functions.

Using the example of setting the device clock, let's see how CLI help works. If the device clock needs to be set but the **clock** command syntax is not known, the context-sensitive help provides a means to check the syntax.

Context-sensitive help supplies the whole command even if you enter just the first part of the command, such as **cl?**.

If you enter the command **clock** followed by the Enter key, an error message indicates that the command is incomplete. To view the required parameters for the **clock** command, enter **?**, preceded by a space. In the **clock ?** example, the help output shows that the keyword **set** is required after **clock**.

If you now enter the command **clock set**, another error message appears indicating that the command is still incomplete. Now add a space and enter the **?** command to display a list of command arguments that are available at that point for the given command.

The additional arguments needed to set the clock on the device are displayed: the current time using hours, minutes, and seconds. For an excellent resource on how to use the Cisco IOS CLI, visit:

http://www.cisco.com/univercd/cc/td/doc/product/software/ios124/124cg/hcf_c/ch10/index.htm.

Refer to
Figure
in online course

Console Error Messages

Console error messages help identify problems when an incorrect command has been entered. The figure provides example error messages, what they mean, and how to get help when they are displayed.

2.3.3 Accessing the Command History

Refer to
Figure
in online course

The Command History Buffer

When you are configuring many interfaces on a switch, you can save time retyping commands by using the Cisco IOS command history buffer. In this topic, you will learn how to configure the command history buffer to support your configuration efforts.

The Cisco CLI provides a history or record of commands that have been entered. This feature, called command history, is particularly useful in helping recall long or complex commands or entries.

With the command history feature, you can complete the following tasks:

- Display the contents of the command buffer.

- Set the command history buffer size.

- Recall previously entered commands stored in the history buffer. There is a buffer for each configuration mode.

By default, command history is enabled, and the system records the last 10 command lines in its history buffer. You can use the **show history** command to view recently entered EXEC commands.

Refer to
Figure
in online course

Configure the Command History Buffer

In Cisco network products that support the Cisco IOS software, command history is enabled by default, and the last 10 command lines are recorded in the history buffer.

The command history can be disabled for the current terminal session only by using the **terminal no history** command in user or privileged EXEC mode. When command history is disabled, the device no longer retains any previously entered command lines.

To revert the terminal history size back to its default value of 10 lines, enter the **terminal no history size** command in privileged EXEC mode. The figure provides an explanation and example of these Cisco IOS commands.

2.3.4 The Switch Boot Sequence

Refer to
Figure
in online course

Describe the Boot Sequence

In this topic, you will learn the sequence of Cisco IOS commands that a switch executes from the off state to displaying the login prompt. After a Cisco switch is turned on, it goes through the following boot sequence:

The switch loads the boot loader software. The boot loader is a small program stored in ROM and is run when the switch is first turned on.

The boot loader:

- Performs low-level CPU initialization. It initializes the CPU registers, which control where physical memory is mapped, the quantity of memory, and its speed.

- Performs power-on self-test (*POST*) for the CPU subsystem. It tests the CPU *DRAM* and the portion of the flash device that makes up the flash file system.

- Initializes the flash file system on the system board.

- Loads a default operating system software image into memory and boots the switch. The boot loader finds the Cisco IOS image on the switch by first looking in a directory that has the same name as the image file (excluding the .bin extension). If it does not find it there, the boot loader software searches each subdirectory before continuing the search in the original directory.

The operating system then initializes the interfaces using the Cisco IOS commands found in the operating system configuration file, config.text, stored in the switch flash memory.

Recovering from a System Crash

The boot loader also provides access into the switch if the operating system cannot be used. The boot loader has a command-line facility that provides access to the files stored on *Flash memory* before the operating system is loaded. From the boot loader command line you can enter commands to format the flash file system, reinstall the operating system software image, or recover from a lost or forgotten password.

2.3.5 Prepare to Configure the Switch

Refer to
Figure
in online course

Prepare to Configure the Switch

The initial startup of a Catalyst switch requires the completion of the following steps:

Step 1. Before starting the switch, verify the following:

All network cable connections are secure.

Your PC or terminal is connected to the console port.

Your terminal emulator application, such as HyperTerminal, is running and configured correctly.

The figure illustrates how to connect a PC to a switch using the console port.

Click the Configure Hyperterminal button in the figure.

The figure shows the correct configuration of HyperTerminal, which can be used to view the console of a Cisco device.

Step 2. Attach the power cable plug to the switch power supply socket. The switch will start. Some Catalyst switches, including the Cisco Catalyst 2960 series, do not have power buttons.

Step 3. Observe the boot sequence as follows:

When the switch is on, the POST begins. During POST, the *LEDs* blink while a series of tests determine that the switch is functioning properly. When the POST has completed, the SYST LED rapidly blinks green. If the switch fails POST, the SYST LED turns amber. When a switch fails the POST test, it is necessary to repair the switch.

Observe the Cisco IOS software output text on the console.

Click the View Boot Process on Console button in the figure.

The figure shows the boot process on the console of a Cisco switch.

During the initial startup of the switch, if POST failures are detected, they are reported to the console and the switch does not start. If POST completes successfully, and the switch has not been configured before, you are prompted to configure the switch.

2.3.6 Basic Switch Configuration

Refer to
Figure
in online course

Management Interface Considerations

An access layer switch is much like a PC in that you need to configure an IP address, a *subnet mask*, and a default gateway. To manage a switch remotely using *TCP/IP*, you need to assign the switch an IP address. In the figure, you want to manage S1 from PC1, a computer used for managing the network. To do this, you need to assign switch S1 an IP address. This IP address is assigned to a virtual interface called a virtual LAN (VLAN), and then it is necessary to ensure the VLAN is assigned to a specific port or ports on the switch.

The default configuration on the switch is to have the management of the switch controlled through VLAN 1. However, a best practice for basic switch configuration is to change the management VLAN to a VLAN other than VLAN 1. The implications and reasoning behind this action are explained in the next chapter. The figure illustrates the use of VLAN 99 as the management VLAN; however, it is important to consider that an interface other than VLAN 99 can be considered for the management interface.

Note: You will learn more about VLANs in the next chapter. Here the focus is on providing management access to the switch using an alternative VLAN. Some of the commands introduced here are explained more thoroughly in the next chapter.

For now, VLAN 99 is created and assigned an IP address. Then the appropriate port on switch S1 is assigned to VLAN 99. The figure also shows this configuration information.

Click the Configure Management Interface button in the figure.

Configure Management Interface

To configure an IP address and subnet mask on the management VLAN of the switch, you must be in VLAN interface configuration mode. Use the command `interface vlan 99` and enter the ip address configuration command. You must use the `no shutdown` interface configuration command to make this Layer 3 interface operational. When you see "interface VLAN x", that refers to the Layer 3 interface associated with VLAN x. Only the management VLAN has an interface VLAN associated with it.

Note that a Layer 2 switch, such as the Cisco Catalyst 2960, only permits a single VLAN interface to be active at a time. This means that the Layer 3 interface, interface VLAN 99, is active, but the Layer 3 interface, interface VLAN 1, is not active.

Click the Configure Default Gateway button in the figure.

Configure Default Gateway

You need to configure the switch so that it can forward IP packets to distant networks. The default gateway is the mechanism for doing this. The switch forwards IP packets with destination IP addresses outside the local network to the default gateway. In the figure, router R1 is the next-hop router. Its IP address is 172.17.99.1.

To configure a default gateway for the switch, use the `ip default-gateway` command. Enter the IP address of the next-hop router interface that is directly connected to the switch where a default gateway is being configured. Make sure you save the configuration running on a switch or router. Use the `copy running-config startup-config` command to back up your configuration.

Click the Verify Configuration button in the figure.

Verify Configuration

The top screen shot in the figure is an abbreviated screen output showing that VLAN 99 has been configured with an IP address and subnet mask, and Fast Ethernet port F0/18 has been assigned the VLAN 99 management interface.

Show the IP Interfaces

Use the `show ip interface brief` to verify port operation and status. You will practice using the `switchport access vlan 99` command in a hands on lab and a Packet Tracer activity.

The `mdix auto` Command

You used to be required to use certain cable types (cross-over, straight-through) when connecting between specific devices, switch-to-switch or switch-to-router. Instead, you can now use the `mdix auto` interface configuration command in the CLI to enable the automatic medium-dependent interface crossover (auto-MDIX) feature.

When the auto-MDIX feature is enabled, the switch detects the required cable type for copper Ethernet connections and configures the interfaces accordingly. Therefore, you can use either a crossover or a straight-through cable for connections to a copper 10/100/1000 port on the switch, regardless of the type of device on the other end of the connection.

The auto-MDIX feature was introduced in Cisco IOS Release 12.2(25)FX.

Refer to **Figure** in online course

Configure Duplex and Speed

You can use the **duplex** interface configuration command to specify the duplex mode of operation for switch ports. You can manually set the duplex mode and speed of switch ports to avoid inter-vendor issues with autonegotiation. Although there can be issues when you configure switch port duplex settings to **auto**, in this example, S1 and S2 switches have the same duplex settings and speeds. The figure describes the steps to configure the port F0/1 on the S1 switch.

Refer to **Figure** in online course

Configure a Web Interface

Modern Cisco switches have a number of web-based configuration tools that require that the switch is configured as an HTTP server. These applications include the Cisco web browser user interface, Cisco Router and Security Device Manager (SDM), and IP Phone and Cisco IOS Telephony Service applications.

To control who can access the HTTP services on the switch, you can optionally configure *authentication*. Authentication methods can be complex. You may have so many people using the HTTP services that you require a separate server specifically to handle user authentication. *AAA* and *TACACS* authentication modes are examples that use this type of remote authentication method. AAA and TACACS are authentication protocols that can be used in networks to validate user credentials. You may need to have a less complex authentication method. The **enable** method requires users to use the server's enable password. The local authentication method requires the user to use the login username, password, and privilege level access combination specified in the local system configuration (by the **username** global configuration command).

For more information on TACACS, visit: http://www.cisco.com/en/US/tech/tk583/tk642/ tsd_technology_support_sub-protocol_home.html.

For more information on AAA, visit: http://www.cisco.com/en/US/products/ps6638/ products_data_sheet09186a00804fe332.html.

Refer to **Figure** in online course

Managing the MAC Address Table

Switches use MAC address tables to determine how to forward traffic between ports. These MAC tables include dynamic and static addresses. The figure shows a sample MAC address table from the output of the **show mac-address-table** command that includes static and dynamic MAC addresses.

Note: The MAC address table was previously referred to as content addressable memory (*CAM*) or as the CAM table.

Dynamic addresses are source MAC addresses that the switch learns and then ages when they are not in use. You can change the aging time setting for MAC addresses. The default time is 300 seconds. Setting too short an aging time can cause addresses to be prematurely removed from the table. Then, when the switch receives a packet for an unknown destination, it floods the packet to all ports in the same LAN (or VLAN) as the receiving port. This unnecessary flooding can impact performance. Setting too long an aging time can cause the address table to be filled with unused addresses, which prevents new addresses from being learned. This can also cause flooding.

The switch provides dynamic addressing by learning the source MAC address of each frame that it receives on each port, and then adding the source MAC address and its associated port number to the MAC address table. As computers are added or removed from the network, the switch updates the MAC address table, adding new entries and aging out those that are currently not in use.

A *network administrator* can specifically assign static MAC addresses to certain ports. Static addresses are not aged out, and the switch always knows which port to send out traffic destined for that specific MAC address. As a result, there is no need to relearn or refresh which port the MAC address is connected to. One reason to implement static MAC addresses is to provide the network administrator complete control over access to the network. Only those devices that are known to the network administrator can connect to the network.

To create a static mapping in the MAC address table, use the `mac-address-table static` <*MAC address*> `vlan` {`1-4096`, `ALL`} `interface` *interface-id* command.

To remove a static mapping in the MAC address table, use the `no mac-address-table static` <*MAC address*> `vlan` {`1-4096`, `ALL`} `interface` *interface-id* command.

The maximum size of the MAC address table varies with different switches. For example, the Catalyst 2960 series switch can store up to 8,192 MAC addresses. There are other protocols that may limit the absolute number of MAC address available to a switch.

2.3.7 Verifying Switch Configuration

Refer to
Figure
in online course

Using the Show Commands

Now that you have performed the initial switch configuration, you should confirm that the switch has been configured correctly. In this topic, you will learn how to verify the switch configuration using various `show` commands.

Click the Show Commands button in the figure.

When you need to verify the configuration of your Cisco switch, the `show` command is very useful. The `show` command is executed from privileged EXEC mode. The figure presents some of the key options for the `show` command that verify nearly all configurable switch features. There are many additional `show` commands that you will learn throughout this course.

Click the Show Running-config button in the figure.

One of the more valuable `show` commands is the `show running-config` command. This command displays the configuration currently running on the switch. Use this command to verify that you have correctly configured the switch. The figure shows an abbreviated output from the `show running-config` command. The three periods indicate missing content. The figure has highlighted screen output of the S1 switch showing:

- Fast Ethernet 0/18 interface configured with the management VLAN 99

- VLAN 99 configured with an IP address of 172.17.99.11 255.255.0.0

- Default gateway set to 172.17.50.1

- HTTP server configured

Click the Show Interfaces button in the figure.

Another commonly used command is the `show interfaces` command, which displays status and statistics information on the network interfaces of the switch. The `show interfaces` command is used frequently while configuring and monitoring network devices. Recall that you can type partial commands at the command prompt and, as long as no other command option is the same, the Cisco IOS software interprets the command correctly. For example, you can use `show int` for this command. The figure shows the output from a `show interfaces FastEthernet 0/1` command.

The first highlighted line in the figure indicates that the Fast Ethernet 0/1 interface is up and running. The next highlighted line shows that the duplex is auto-duplex and the speed is auto-speed.

2.3.8 Basic Switch Management

Refer to
Figure
in online course

Back up and Restore Switch Configurations

A typical job for an apprentice network technician is to load a switch with a configuration. In this topic, you will learn how to load and store a configuration on the switch flash memory and to a *TFTP* server.

Click the Backup Configurations button in the figure.

Backing Up the Configuration

You have already learned how to back up the running configuration of a switch to the startup configuration file. You have used the `copy running-config startup-config` privileged EXEC command to back up the configurations you have made so far. As you may already know, the running configuration is saved in DRAM and the startup configuration is stored in the NVRAM section of Flash memory. When you issue the `copy running-config startup-config` command, the Cisco IOS software copies the running configuration to NVRAM so that when the switch boots, the startup-config with your new configuration is loaded.

You do not always want to save configuration changes you make to the running configuration of a switch. For example, you might want to change the configuration for a short time period rather than permanently.

If you want to maintain multiple different startup-config files on the device, you can copy the configuration to different filenames, using the `copy startup-config flash:`*filename* command. Storing multiple startup-config versions allows you to roll back to a point in time if your configuration has problems. The figure shows three examples of backing up the configuration to Flash memory. The first is the formal and complete syntax. The second is the syntax commonly used. Use the first syntax when you are unfamiliar with the network device you are working with, and use the second syntax when you know that the destination is the flash NVRAM installed on the switch. The third is the syntax used to save a copy of the startup-config file in flash.

Click the Restoring Configurations button in the figure.

Restoring the Configuration

Restoring a configuration is a simple process. You just need to copy the saved configuration over the current configuration. For example, if you had a saved configuration called config.bak1, you could restore it over your existing startup-config by entering this Cisco IOS command `copy flash:config.bak1 startup-config`. Once the configuration has been restored to the startup-config, you restart the switch so that it reloads the new startup configuration by using the `reload` command in privileged EXEC mode.

The `reload` command halts the system. If the system is set to restart on error, it reboots itself. Use the `reload` command after configuration information is entered into a file and saved to the startup configuration.

Note: You cannot reload from a virtual terminal if the switch is not set up for automatic booting. This restriction prevents the system from dropping to the *ROM* monitor (ROMMON) and thereby taking the system out of the remote user's control.

After issuing the `reload` command, the system prompts you to answer whether or not to save the configuration. Normally you would indicate "yes", but in this particular case you need to answer "no". If you answered "yes", the file you just restored would be overwritten. In every case you need to consider whether or not the current running configuration is the one you want to be active after reload.

For more details on the **reload** command, review the Cisco IOS Configuration Fundamentals Command Reference, Release 12.4 found at this website: http://www.cisco.com/en/US/docs/ios/fundamentals/command/reference/cf_book.html.

Note: There is also the option of entering the **copy startup-config running-config** command. Unfortunately, this command does not entirely overwrite the running configuration; it only adds existing commands from the startup configuration to the running configuration. This can cause unintended results, so be careful when you do this.

Refer to
Figure
in online course

Back up Configuration Files to a TFTP Server

Once you have configured your switch with all the options you want to set, it is a good idea to back up the configuration on the network where it can then be archived along with the rest of your network data being backed up nightly. Having the configuration stored safely off the switch protects it in the event there is some major catastrophic problem with your switch.

Some switch configurations take many hours to get working correctly. If you lost the configuration because of switch hardware failure, a new switch needs to be configured. If there is a backup configuration for the failed switch, it can be loaded quickly onto the new switch. If there is no backup configuration, you must configure the new switch from scratch.

You can use TFTP to back up your configuration files over the network. Cisco IOS software comes with a built-in TFTP client that allows you to connect to a TFTP server on your network.

Note: There are free TFTP server software packages available on the Internet that you can use if you do not already have a TFTP server running. One commonly used TFTP server is from www.solarwinds.com.

Backing up the Configuration

To upload a configuration file from a switch to a TFTP server for storage, follow these steps:

Step 1. Verify that the TFTP server is running on your network.

Step 2. Log in to the switch through the console port or a Telnet session. Enable the switch and then ping the TFTP server.

Step 3. Upload the switch configuration to the TFTP server. Specify the IP address or hostname of the TFTP server and the destination filename. The Cisco IOS command is: **#copy system:running-config tftp:**[[[//location]/directory]/filename] or **#copy nvram:startup-config tftp:**[[[//location]/directory]/filename].

The figure shows an example of backing up the configuration to a TFTP server.

Restoring the Configuration

Once the configuration is stored successfully on the TFTP server, it can be copied back to the switch using the following steps:

Step 1. Copy the configuration file to the appropriate TFTP directory on the TFTP server if it is not already there.

Step 2. Verify that the TFTP server is running on your network.

Step 3. Log in to the switch through the console port or a Telnet session. Enable the switch and then ping the TFTP server.

Step 4. Download the configuration file from the TFTP server to configure the switch. Specify the IP address or hostname of the TFTP server and the name of the file to download. The Cisco IOS command is: `#copy tftp:[[[//location]/directory]/filename] system:running-config` or `#copy tftp:[[[//location]/directory]/filename] nvram:startup-config`.

If the configuration file is downloaded into the running-config, the commands are executed as the file is parsed line by line. If the configuration file is downloaded into the startup-config, the switch must be reloaded for the changes to take effect.

Clearing Configuration Information

Refer to **Figure** in online course

You can clear the configuration information from the startup configuration. You might do this to prepare a used switch to be shipped to a customer or a different department and you want to ensure that the switch gets reconfigured. When you erase the startup configuration file when the switch reboots, it enters the setup program so that you can reconfigure the switch with new settings.

To clear the contents of your startup configuration, use the `erase nvram:` or the `erase startup-config` privileged EXEC command. The figure shows an example of erasing the configuration files stored in NVRAM.

Caution: You cannot restore the startup configuration file after it has been erased, so make sure that you have a backup of the configuration in case you need to restore it at a later point.

Deleting a Stored Configuration File

You may have been working on a complex configuration task and stored many backup copies of your files in Flash. To delete a file from Flash memory, use the `delete flash:filename` privileged EXEC command. Depending on the setting of the file prompt global configuration command, you might be prompted for confirmation before you delete a file. By default, the switch prompts for confirmation when deleting a file.

Caution: You cannot restore the startup configuration file after it has been deleted, so make sure that you have a backup of the configuration in case you need to restore it at a later point.

After the configuration has been erased or deleted, you can reload the switch to initiate a new configuration for the switch.

Refer to **Packet Tracer Activity** for this chapter

Basic switch management is the foundation for configuring switches. This activity focuses on navigating command-line interface modes, using help functions, accessing the command history, configuring boot sequence parameters, setting speed and duplex settings, as well as managing the MAC address table and switch configuration file. Skills learned in this activity are necessary for configuring basic switch security in later chapters. Detailed instructions are provided within the activity as well as in the PDF link below.

Activity Instructions (PDF)

2.4 Configuring Switch Security

2.4.1 Configure Password Options

Refer to **Figure** in online course

Configure Console Access

In this topic, you will learn how to configure passwords for the console access, virtual terminal, and EXEC mode. You will also learn how to encrypt and recover passwords on a switch.

Data is very valuable and must be zealously guarded and protected. The U.S. Federal Bureau of Investigation (FBI) estimates that businesses lose $67.2 billion annually because of computer-related crime. Personal customer data in particular sells for very high prices. The following are some current prices for stolen data:

- Automatic teller machine (ATM) or debit card with personal identification number (PIN): $500

- Driver's license number: $150

- Social Security number: $100

- Credit card number with expiration date: $15 to $20

Securing your switches starts with protecting them from unauthorized access.

You can perform all configuration options directly from the console. To access the console, you need to have local physical access to the device. If you do not secure the console port properly, a malicious user could compromise the switch configuration.

Secure the Console

To secure the console port from unauthorized access, set a password on the console port using the **password** *<password>* line configuration mode command. Use the **line console 0** command to switch from global configuration mode to line configuration mode for console 0, which is the console port on Cisco switches. The prompt changes to (config-line)#, indicating that the switch is now in line configuration mode. From line configuration mode, you can set the password for the console by entering the **password** *<password>* command. To ensure that a user on the console port is required to enter the password, use the **login** command. Even when a password is defined, it is not required to be entered until the **login** command has been issued.

The figure shows the commands used to configure and require the password for console access. Recall that you can use the **show running-config** command to verify your configuration. Before you complete the switch configuration, remember to save the running configuration file to the startup configuration.

Remove Console Password

If you need to remove the password and requirement to enter the password at login, use the following steps:

Step 1. Switch from privileged EXEC mode to global configuration mode. Enter the **configure terminal** command.

Step 2. Switch from global configuration mode to line configuration mode for console 0. The command prompt (config-line)# indicates that you are in line configuration mode. Enter the command **line console 0**.

Step 3. Remove the password from the console line using the **no password** command.

Step 4. Remove the requirement to enter the password at login to the console line using the **no login** command.

Step 5. Exit line configuration mode and return to privileged EXEC mode using the **end** command.

Refer to
Figure
in online course

Secure the vty Ports

The vty ports on a Cisco switch allow you to access the device remotely. You can perform all configuration options using the vty terminal ports. You do not need physical access to the switch to access the vty ports, so it is very important to secure the vty ports. Any user with network access to the switch can establish a vty remote terminal connection. If the vty ports are not properly secured, a malicious user could compromise the switch configuration.

To secure the vty ports from unauthorized access, you can set a vty password that is required before access is granted.

To set the password on the vty ports, you must be in line configuration mode.

There can be many vty ports available on a Cisco switch. Multiple ports permit more than one administrator to connect to and manage the switch. To secure all vty lines, make sure that a password is set and login is enforced on all lines. Leaving some lines unsecured compromises security and allows unauthorized users access to the switch.

Use the `line vty 0 4` command to switch from global configuration mode to line configuration mode for vty lines 0 through 4.

Note: If the switch has more vty lines available, adjust the range to secure them all. For example, a Cisco 2960 has lines 0 through 15 available.

The figure shows the commands used to configure and require the password for vty access. You can use the `show running-config` command to verify your configuration and the `copy running-config startup config` command to save your work.

Remove the vty Password

If you need to remove the password and requirement to enter the password at login, use the following steps:

Step 1. Switch from privileged EXEC mode to global configuration mode. Enter the `configure terminal` command.

Step 2. Switch from global configuration mode to line configuration mode for vty terminals 0 through 4. The command prompt (`config-line`)# indicates that you are in line configuration mode. Enter the command `line vty 0 4`.

Step 3. Remove the password from the vty lines using the `no password` command.

Caution: If no password is defined and login is still enabled, there is no access to the vty lines.

Step 4. Remove the requirement to enter the password at login to the vty lines using the `no login` command.

Step 5. Exit line configuration mode and return to privileged EXEC mode using the `end` command.

Refer to
Figure
in online course

Configure EXEC Mode Passwords

Privileged EXEC mode allows any user enabling that mode on a Cisco switch to configure any option available on the switch. You can also view all the currently configured settings on the switch, including some of the unencrypted passwords! For these reasons, it is important to secure access to privileged EXEC mode.

The `enable password` global configuration command allows you to specify a password to restrict access to privileged EXEC mode. However, one problem with the `enable password` command is that it stores the password in readable text in the startup-config and running-config. If someone were to gain access to a stored startup-config file, or temporary access to a Telnet or console session that is logged in to privileged EXEC mode, they could see the password. As a result, Cisco introduced a new password option to control access to privileged EXEC mode that stores the password in an encrypted format.

You can assign an encrypted form of the enable password, called the enable secret password, by entering the `enable secret` command with the desired password at the global configuration mode prompt. If the enable secret password is configured, it is used instead of the enable password, not in addition to it. There is also a safeguard built into the Cisco IOS software that notifies you when setting the enable secret password to the same password that is used for the enable password. If identical passwords are entered, the IOS will accept the password but will warn you they are the same and instruct you to re-enter a new password.

The figure shows the commands used to configure privileged EXEC mode passwords. You can use the `show running-config` command to verify your configuration and the `copy running-config startup config` command to save your work.

Remove EXEC Mode Password

If you need to remove the password requirement to access privileged EXEC mode, you can use the `no enable password` and the `no enable secret` commands from global configuration mode.

Refer to Figure in online course

Configure Encrypted Passwords

When configuring passwords in Cisco IOS CLI, by default all passwords, except for the enable secret password, are stored in clear text format within the startup-config and running-config. The figure shows an abbreviated screen output from the `show running-config` command on the S1 switch. The clear text passwords are highlighted in orange. It is universally accepted that passwords should be encrypted and not stored in clear text format. The Cisco IOS command `service password-encryption` enables service password *encryption*.

When the `service password-encryption` command is entered from global configuration mode, all system passwords are stored in an encrypted form. As soon as the command is entered, all the currently set passwords are converted to encrypted passwords. At the bottom of the figure, the encrypted passwords are highlighted in orange.

If you want to remove the requirement to store all system passwords in an encrypted format, enter the `no service password-encryption` command from global configuration mode. Removing password encryption does not convert currently encrypted passwords back into readable text. However, all newly set passwords are stored in clear text format.

Note: The encryption standard used by the `service password-encryption` command is referred to as type 7. This encryption standard is very weak and there are easily accessible tools on the Internet for decrypting passwords encrypted with this standard. Type 5 is more secure but must be invoked manually for each password configured.

Refer to Figure in online course

Enable Password Recovery

After you set passwords to control access to the Cisco IOS CLI, you need to make sure you remember them. In case you have lost or forgotten access passwords, Cisco has a password recovery mechanism that allows administrators to gain access to their Cisco devices. The password recovery process requires physical access to the device. The figure shows a screen capture of the console display indicating that password recovery has been enabled. You will see this display after Step 3 below.

Note that you may not be able to actually recover the passwords on the Cisco device, especially if password encryption has been enabled, but you are able to reset them to a new value.

For more information on the password procedure, visit: http://www.cisco.com/en/US/products/sw/iosswrel/ps1831/products_tech_note09186a00801746e6.shtml.

To recover the password on a Cisco 2960 switch, use the following steps:

Step 1. Connect a terminal or PC with terminal-emulation software to the switch console port.

Step 2. Set the line speed on the emulation software to 9600 baud.

Step 3. Power off the switch. Reconnect the power cord to the switch and within 15 seconds, press the Mode button while the System LED is still flashing green. Continue pressing the Mode button until the System LED turns briefly amber and then solid green. Then release the Mode button.

Step 4. Initialize the Flash file system using the `flash_init` command.

Step 5. Load any helper files using the `load_helper` command.

Step 6. Display the contents of Flash memory using the `dir flash` command:

The switch file system appears:

```
Directory of flash:
   13 drwx 192 Mar 01 1993 22:30:48 c2960-lanbase-mz.122-25.FX
   11 -rwx 5825 Mar 01 1993 22:31:59 config.text
   18 -rwx 720 Mar 01 1993 02:21:30 vlan.dat
16128000 bytes total (10003456 bytes free)
```

Step 7. Rename the configuration file to config.text.old, which contains the password definition, using the `rename flash:config.text flash:config.text.old` command.

Step 8. Boot the system with the `boot` command.

Step 9. You are prompted to start the setup program. Enter **N** at the prompt, and then when the system prompts whether to continue with the configuration dialog, enter **N**.

Step 10. At the switch prompt, enter privileged EXEC mode using the `enable` command.

Step 11. Rename the configuration file to its original name using the `rename flash:config.text.old flash:config.text` command.

Step 12. Copy the configuration file into memory using the `copy flash:config.text system:running-config` command. After this command has been entered, the follow is displayed on the console:

```
Source filename [config.text]?
Destination filename [running-config]?
```

Press Return in response to the confirmation prompts. The configuration file is now reloaded, and you can change the password.

Step 13. Enter global configuration mode using the `configure terminal` command.

Step 14. Change the password using the `enable secret` *password* command.

Step 15. Return to privileged EXEC mode using the `exit` command.

Step 16. Write the running configuration to the startup configuration file using the `copy running-config startup-config` command.

Step 17. Reload the switch using the `reload` command.

Note: The password recovery procedure can be different depending on the Cisco switch series, so you should refer to the product documentation before you attempt a password recovery.

2.4.2 Login Banners

Refer to
Figure
in online course

Configure a Login Banner

The Cisco IOS command set includes a feature that allows you to configure messages that anyone logging onto the switch sees. These messages are called login banners and message of the day (MOTD) banners. In this topic, you will learn how to configure them.

You can define a customized banner to be displayed before the username and password login prompts by using the `banner login` command in global configuration mode. Enclose the banner text in quotations or using a delimiter different from any character appearing in the MOTD string.

The figure shows the S1 switch being configured with a login banner **Authorized Personnel Only!**

To remove the MOTD banner, enter the **no** format of this command in global configuration mode, for example, S1(config)#`no banner login`.

Refer to **Figure** in online course

Configure a MOTD Banner

The MOTD banner displays on all connected terminals at login and is useful for sending messages that affect all network users (such as impending system shutdowns). The MOTD banner displays before the login banner if it is configured.

Define the MOTD banner by using the `banner motd` command in global configuration mode. Enclose the banner text in quotations.

The figure shows the S1 switch being configured with a MOTD banner to display **Device maintenance will be occurring on Friday!**

To remove the login banner, enter the **no** format of this command in global configuration mode, for example S1(config)#`no banner motd`.

2.4.3 Configure Telnet and SSH

Refer to **Figure** in online course

Telnet and SSH

Older switches may not support secure communication with Secure Shell (SSH). This topic will help you choose between the Telnet and SSH methods of communicating with a switch.

There are two choices for remotely accessing a vty on a Cisco switch.

Telnet is the original method that was supported on early Cisco switch models. Telnet is a popular protocol used for terminal access because most current operating systems come with a Telnet client built in. However, Telnet is an insecure way of accessing a network device, because it sends all communications across the network in clear text. Using network monitoring software, an attacker can read every keystroke that is sent between the Telnet client and the Telnet service running on the Cisco switch. Because of the security concerns of the Telnet protocol, SSH has become the preferred protocol for remotely accessing virtual terminal lines on a Cisco device.

SSH gives the same type of access as Telnet with the added benefit of security. Communication between the SSH client and SSH server is encrypted. SSH has gone through a few versions, with Cisco devices currently supporting both SSHv1 and SSHv2. It is recommended that you implement SSHv2 when possible, because it uses a more enhanced security encryption algorithm than SSHv1.

The figure presents the differences between the two protocols.

Refer to **Figure** in online course

Configuring Telnet

Telnet is the default vty-supported protocol on a Cisco switch. When a management IP address is assigned to the Cisco switch, you can connect to it using a Telnet client. Initially, the vty lines are unsecured allowing access by any user attempting to connect to them.

In the previous topic, you learned how to secure access to the switch over the vty lines by requiring password authentication. This makes running the Telnet service a little more secure.

Because Telnet is the default transport for the vty lines, you do not need to specify it after the initial configuration of the switch has been performed. However, if you have switched the transport protocol on the vty lines to permit only SSH, you need to enable the Telnet protocol to permit Telnet access manually.

If you need to re-enable the Telnet protocol on a Cisco 2960 switch, use the following command from line configuration mode: `(config-line)#transport input telnet` or `(config-line)#transport input all`.

By permitting all transport protocols, you still permit SSH access to the switch as well as Telnet access.

Refer to
Figure
in online course

Configuring SSH

SSH is a cryptographic security feature that is subject to export restrictions. To use this feature, a cryptographic image must be installed on your switch.

The SSH feature has an SSH server and an SSH integrated client, which are applications that run on the switch. You can use any SSH client running on a PC or the Cisco SSH client running on the switch to connect to a switch running the SSH server.

The switch supports SSHv1 or SSHv2 for the server component. The switch supports only SSHv1 for the client component.

SSH supports the Data Encryption Standard (*DES*) algorithm, the Triple DES (3DES) algorithm, and password-based user authentication. DES offers 56-bit encryption, and 3DES offers 168-bit encryption. Encryption takes time, but DES takes less time to encrypt text than 3DES. Typically, encryption standards are specified by the client, so if you have to configure SSH, ask which one to use. (The discussion of data encryption methods is beyond the scope of this course.)

To implement SSH, you need to generate RSA keys. RSA involves a public key, kept on a public RSA server, and a private key, kept only by the sender and receiver. The public key can be known to everyone and is used for encrypting messages. Messages encrypted with the public key can only be decrypted using the private key. This is known as asymmetric encryption and will be discussed in greater detail in the Exploration: Accessing the WAN course.

You need to generate the encrypted RSA keys using the `crypto key generate rsa` command.

This procedure is required if you are configuring the switch as an SSH server. Beginning in privileged EXEC mode, follow these steps to configure a hostname and an IP domain name and to generate an RSA key pair.

Step 1. Enter global configuration mode using the `configure terminal` command.

Step 2. Configure a hostname for your switch using the `hostname` *hostname* command.

Step 3. Configure a host domain for your switch using the `ip domain-name` *domain_name* command.

Step 4. Enable the SSH server for local and remote authentication on the switch and generate an RSA key pair using the `crypto key generate rsa` command.

When you generate RSA keys, you are prompted to enter a modulus length. Cisco recommends using a modulus size of 1024 bits. A longer modulus length might be more secure, but it takes longer to generate and to use.

Step 5. Return to privileged EXEC mode using the `end` command.

Step 6. Show the status of the SSH server on the switch using the `show ip ssh` or `show ssh` command.

To delete the RSA key pair, use the `crypto key zeroize rsa` global configuration command. After the RSA key pair is deleted, the SSH server is automatically disabled.

Configuring the SSH Server

Beginning in privileged EXEC mode, follow these steps to configure the SSH server.

Step 1. Enter global configuration mode using the `configure terminal` command.

Step 2. (Optional) Configure the switch to run SSHv1 or SSHv2 using the `ip ssh version` [1 ¦ 2] command.

If you do not enter this command or do not specify a keyword, the SSH server selects the latest SSH version supported by the SSH client. For example, if the SSH client supports SSHv1 and SSHv2, the SSH server selects SSHv2.

Step 3. Configure the SSH control parameters:

- Specify the *time-out* value in seconds; the default is 120 seconds. The range is 0 to 120 seconds. For a SSH connect to be established, a number of phases must be completed, such as connection, protocol negotiation, and parameter negation. The time-out value applies to the amount of time the switch allows for a connection to be established.

By default, up to five simultaneous, encrypted SSH connections for multiple CLI-based sessions over the network are available (session 0 to session 4). After the execution shell starts, the CLI-based session time-out value returns to the default of 10 minutes.

- Specify the number of times that a client can re-authenticate to the server. The default is 3; the range is 0 to 5. For example, a user can allow the SSH session to sit for more than 10 minutes three times before the SSH session is terminated.

Repeat this step when configuring both parameters. To configure both parameters use the `ip ssh` {`timeout` *seconds* ¦ `authentication-retries` *number*} command.

Step 4. Return to privileged EXEC mode using the end command.

Step 5. Display the status of the SSH server connections on the switch using the `show ip ssh` or the `show ssh` command.

Step 6. (Optional) Save your entries in the configuration file using the `copy running-config startup-config` command.

If you want to prevent non-SSH connections, add the `transport input ssh` command in line configuration mode to limit the switch to SSH connections only. Straight (non-SSH) Telnet connections are refused.

For a detailed discussion on SSH, visit: http://www.cisco.com/en/US/tech/tk583/tk617/tsd_technology_support_protocol_home.html.

For an overview of RSA technology, visit http://en.wikipedia.org/wiki/Public-key_cryptography.

For a detailed discussion on RSA technology, visit: http://www.rsa.com/rsalabs/node.asp?id=2152.

Refer to **Figure** in online course

2.4.4 Common Security Attacks

Security Attacks

Unfortunately, basic switch security does not stop malicious attacks from occurring. In this topic, you will learn about a few common security attacks and how dangerous they are. This topic provides introductory level information about security attacks. The details of how some of these common attacks work are beyond the scope of the course. If you find network security of interest, you should explore the course CCNA Exploration: Accessing the WAN.

MAC Address Flooding

MAC address flooding is a common attack. Recall that the MAC address table in a switch contains the MAC addresses available on a given physical port of a switch and the associated VLAN parameters for each. When a Layer 2 switch receives a frame, the switch looks in the MAC address table for the destination MAC address. All Catalyst switch models use a MAC address table for Layer 2 switching. As frames arrive on switch ports, the source MAC addresses are learned and recorded in the MAC address table. If an entry exists for the MAC address, the switch forwards the frame to the MAC address port designated in the MAC address table. If the MAC address does not exist, the switch acts like a hub and forwards the frame out every other port on the switch. MAC address table overflow attacks are sometimes referred to as MAC flooding attacks. To understand the mechanism of a MAC address table overflow attack, recall the basic operation of a switch.

Click the Step 1 button in the figure to see how MAC address table overflow attack begins.

In the figure, host A sends traffic to host B. The switch receives the frames and looks up the destination MAC address in its MAC address table. If the switch cannot find the destination MAC in the MAC address table, the switch then copies the frame and broadcasts it out every switch port.

Click the Step 2 button in the figure to see the next step.

Host B receives the frame and sends a reply to host A. The switch then learns that the MAC address for host B is located on port 2 and writes that information into the MAC address table.

Host C also receives the frame from host A to host B, but because the destination MAC address of that frame is host B, host C drops that frame.

Click the Step 3 button in the figure to see the next step.

Now, any frame sent by host A (or any other host) to host B is forwarded to port 2 of the switch and not broadcast out every port.

The key to understanding how MAC address table overflow attacks work is to know that MAC address tables are limited in size. MAC flooding makes use of this limitation to bombard the switch with fake source MAC addresses until the switch MAC address table is full. The switch then enters into what is known as a fail-open mode, starts acting as a *hub*, and broadcasts packets to all the machines on the network. As a result, the attacker can see all of the frames sent from a victim host to another host without a MAC address table entry.

Click the Step 4 button in the figure to see how an attacker uses legitimate tools maliciously.

The figure shows how an attacker can use the normal operating characteristics of the switch to stop the switch from operating.

MAC flooding can be performed using a network attack tool. The network intruder uses the attack tool to flood the switch with a large number of invalid source MAC addresses until the MAC address table fills up. When the MAC address table is full, the switch floods all ports with incoming traffic because it cannot find the port number for a particular MAC address in the MAC address table. The switch, in essence, acts like a hub.

Some network attack tools can generate 155,000 MAC entries on a switch per minute. Depending on the switch, the maximum MAC address table size varies. In the figure, the attack tool is running on the host with MAC address C in the bottom right of the screen. This tool floods a switch with packets containing randomly generated source and destination MAC and IP addresses. Over a short period of time, the MAC address table in the switch fills up until it cannot accept new entries. When the MAC address table fills up with invalid source MAC addresses, the switch begins to forward all frames that it receives to every port.

Refer to
Figure
in online course

Click the Step 5 button in the figure to see the next step.

As long as the network attack tool is left running, the MAC address table on the switch remains full. When this happens, the switch begins to broadcast all received frames out every port so that frames sent from host A to host B are also broadcast out of port 3 on the switch.

Spoofing Attacks

Click the Spoofing button in the figure.

One way an attacker can gain access to network traffic is to spoof responses that would be sent by a valid DHCP server. The DHCP spoofing device replies to client DHCP requests. The legitimate server may also reply, but if the *spoofing* device is on the same segment as the client, its reply to the client may arrive first. The intruder DHCP reply offers an IP address and supporting information that designates the intruder as the default gateway or Domain Name System (*DNS*) server. In the case of a gateway, the clients then forward packets to the attacking device, which in turn, sends them to the desired destination. This is referred to as a man-in-the-middle attack, and it may go entirely undetected as the intruder intercepts the data flow through the network.

You should be aware of another type of DHCP attack called a DHCP starvation attack. The attacker PC continually requests IP addresses from a real DHCP server by changing their source MAC addresses. If successful, this kind of DHCP attack causes all of the leases on the real DHCP server to be allocated, thus preventing the real users (DHCP clients) from obtaining an IP address.

To prevent DHCP attacks, use the DHCP snooping and port security features on the Cisco Catalyst switches.

Cisco Catalyst DHCP Snooping and Port Security Features

DHCP snooping is a Cisco Catalyst feature that determines which switch ports can respond to DHCP requests. Ports are identified as trusted and untrusted. Trusted ports can source all DHCP messages; untrusted ports can source requests only. Trusted ports host a DHCP server or can be an uplink toward the DHCP server. If a rogue device on an untrusted port attempts to send a DHCP response packet into the network, the port is shut down. This feature can be coupled with DHCP options in which switch information, such as the port ID of the DHCP request, can be inserted into the DHCP request packet.

Click the DHCP Snooping button.

Untrusted ports are those not explicitly configured as trusted. A DHCP binding table is built for untrusted ports. Each entry contains a client MAC address, IP address, lease time, binding type, VLAN number, and port ID recorded as clients make DHCP requests. The table is then used to filter subsequent DHCP traffic. From a DHCP snooping perspective, untrusted access ports should not send any DHCP server responses.

These steps illustrate how to configure DHCP snooping on a Cisco IOS switch:

Step 1. Enable DHCP snooping using the `ip dhcp snooping` global configuration command.

Step 2. Enable DHCP snooping for specific VLANs using the `ip dhcp snooping vlan number` [*number*] command.

Step 3. Define ports as trusted or untrusted at the interface level by defining the trusted ports using the `ip dhcp snooping trust` command.

Step 4. (Optional) Limit the rate at which an attacker can continually send bogus DHCP requests through untrusted ports to the DHCP server using the `ip dhcp snooping limit rate` *rate* command.

Refer to
Figure
in online course

CDP Attacks

The Cisco Discovery Protocol (*CDP*) is a proprietary protocol that all Cisco devices can be configured to use. CDP discovers other Cisco devices that are directly connected, which allows the devices to auto-configure their connection in some cases, simplifying configuration and connectivity. CDP messages are not encrypted.

By default, most Cisco routers and switches have CDP enabled. CDP information is sent in periodic broadcasts that are updated locally in each device's CDP database. Because CDP is a Layer 2 protocol, it is not propagated by routers.

CDP contains information about the device, such as the IP address, software version, platform, capabilities, and the native VLAN. When this information is available to an attacker, they can use it to find exploits to attack your network, typically in the form of a Denial of Service (DoS) attack.

The figure is a portion of an Ethereal packet trace showing the inside of a CDP packet. The Cisco IOS software version discovered via CDP, in particular, would allow the attacker to research and determine whether there were any security vulnerabilities specific to that particular version of code. Also, because CDP is unauthenticated, an attacker could craft bogus CDP packets and have them received by the attacker's directly connected Cisco device.

To address this vulnerability, it is recommended that you disable the use of CDP on devices that do not need to use it.

Refer to **Figure** in online course

Telnet Attacks

The Telnet protocol can be used by an attacker to gain remote access to a Cisco network switch. In an earlier topic, you configured a login password for the vty lines and set the lines to require password authentication to gain access. This provides an essential and basic level of security to help protect the switch from unauthorized access. However, it is not a secure method of securing access to the vty lines. There are tools available that allow an attacker to launch a brute force password cracking attack against the vty lines on the switch.

Brute Force Password Attack

The first phase of a brute force password attack starts with the attacker using a list of common passwords and a program designed to try to establish a Telnet session using each word on the dictionary list. Luckily, you are smart enough not to use a dictionary word, so you are safe for now. In the second phase of a brute force attack, the attacker uses a program that creates sequential character combinations in an attempt to "guess" the password. Given enough time, a brute force password attack can crack almost all passwords used.

The simplest thing that you can do to limit the vulnerability to brute force password attacks is to change your passwords frequently and use strong passwords randomly mixing upper and lowercase letters with numerals. More advanced configurations allow you to limit who can communicate with the vty lines by using access lists, but that is beyond the scope of this course.

DoS Attack

Another type of Telnet attack is the DoS attack. In a DoS attack, the attacker exploits a flaw in the Telnet server software running on the switch that renders the Telnet service unavailable. This sort of attack is mostly a nuisance because it prevents an administrator from performing switch management functions.

Vulnerabilities in the Telnet service that permit DoS attacks to occur are usually addressed in security patches that are included in newer Cisco IOS revisions. If you are experiencing a DoS attack against the Telnet service, or any other service on a Cisco device, check to see if there is a newer Cisco IOS revision available.

Refer to
Figure
in online course

2.4.5 Security Tools

After you have configured switch security, you need to verify that you have not left any weakness for an attacker to exploit. Network security is a complex and changing topic. In this section, you are introduced to how network security tools are one component used to protect a network from malicious attacks.

Network security tools help you test your network for various weaknesses. They are tools that allow you to play the roles of a hacker and a network security analyst. Using these tools, you can launch an attack and audit the results to determine how to adjust your security policies to prevent a given attack.

The features used by network security tools are constantly evolving. For example, network security tools once focused only on the services listening on the network and examined these services for flaws. Today, viruses and worms are able to propagate because of flaws in mail clients and web browsers. Modern network security tools not only detect the remote flaws of the hosts on the network, but also determine if there are application level flaws, such as missing patches on client computers. Network security extends beyond network devices, all the way to the desktop of users. Security auditing and penetration testing are two basic functions that network security tools perform.

Network Security Audit

Network security tools allow you to perform a security audit of your network. A security audit reveals what sort of information an attacker can gather simply by monitoring network traffic. Network security auditing tools allow you to flood the MAC table with bogus MAC addresses. Then you can audit the switch ports as the switch starts flooding traffic out all ports as the legitimate MAC address mappings are aged out and replaced with more bogus MAC address mappings. In this way, you can determine which ports are compromised and have not been correctly configured to prevent this type of attack.

Timing is an important factor in performing the audit successfully. Different switches support varying numbers of MAC addresses in their MAC table. It can be tricky to determine the ideal amount of spoofed MAC addresses to throw out on the network. You also have to contend with the age-out period of the MAC table. If the spoofed MAC addresses start to age out while you are performing your network audit, valid MAC addresses start to populate the MAC table, limiting the data that you can monitor with a network auditing tool.

Network Penetration Testing

Network security tools can also be used for penetration testing against your network. This allows you to identify weaknesses within the configuration of your networking devices. There are numerous attacks that you can perform, and most tool suites come with extensive documentation detailing the syntax needed to execute the desired attack. Because these types of tests can have adverse effects on the network, they are carried out under very controlled conditions, following documented procedures detailed in a comprehensive network security policy. Of course, if you have a small classroom-based network, you can arrange to work with your instructor to try your own network penetration tests.

Refer to
Figure
in online course

In the next topic, you will learn how to implement port security on your Cisco switches so that you can ensure these network security tests do not reveal any flaws in your security configuration.

Network Security Tools Features

A secure network really is a process not a product. You cannot just enable a switch with a secure configuration and declare the job done. To say you have a secure network, you need to have a comprehensive network security plan defining how to regularly verify that your network can withstand the latest malicious network attacks. The changing landscape of security risks means that you need auditing and penetration tools that can be updated to look for the latest security risks. Common features of a modern network security tool include:

- Service identification: Tools are used to target hosts using the Internet Assigned Numbers Authority (*IANA*) port numbers. These tools should also be able to discover an FTP server running on a non-standard port or a web server running on port 8080. The tool should also be able to test all the services running on a host.

- Support of SSL services: Testing services that use SSL level security, including HTTPS, SMTPS, IMAPS, and security certificate.

- Non-destructive and destructive testing: Performing non-destructive security audits on a routine basis that do not compromise or only moderately compromise network performance. The tools should also let you perform destructive audits that significantly degrade network performance. Destructive auditing allows you to see how well your network withstands attacks from intruders.

- Database of vulnerabilities: Vulnerabilities change all the time.

Network security tools need to be designed so they can plug in a module of code and then run a test for that vulnerability. In this way, a large database of vulnerabilities can be maintained and uploaded to the tool to ensure that the most recent vulnerabilities are being tested.

You can use network security tools to:

- Capture chat messages
- Capture files from *NFS* traffic
- Capture HTTP requests in Common Log Format
- Capture mail messages in Berkeley mbox format
- Capture passwords
- Display captured URLs in browser in real time
- Flood a switched LAN with random MAC addresses
- Forge replies to DNS address / pointer queries
- Intercept packets on a switched LAN

Refer to
Figure
in online course

2.4.6 Configuring Port Security

Using Port Security to Mitigate Attacks

In this topic, you will learn about the issues to consider when configuring port security on a switch. Key port security Cisco IOS commands are summarized. You will also learn about configuring static and dynamic port security.

Click the Port Security button in the figure.

Port Security

A switch that does not provide port security allows an attacker to attach a system to an unused, enabled port and to perform information gathering or attacks. A switch can be configured to act like a hub, which means that every system connected to the switch can potentially view all network traffic passing through the switch to all systems connected to the switch. Thus, an attacker could collect traffic that contains usernames, passwords, or configuration information about the systems on the network.

All switch ports or interfaces should be secured before the switch is deployed. Port security limits the number of valid MAC addresses allowed on a port. When you assign secure MAC addresses to a secure port, the port does not forward packets with *source addresses* outside the group of defined addresses.

If you limit the number of secure MAC addresses to one and assign a single secure MAC address to that port, the workstation attached to that port is assured the full bandwidth of the port, and only that workstation with that particular secure MAC address can successfully connect to that switch port.

If a port is configured as a secure port and the maximum number of secure MAC addresses is reached, a security violation occurs when the MAC address of a workstation attempting to access the port is different from any of the identified secure MAC addresses. The figure summarizes these points.

Click the Secure MAC Address Types button in the figure.

Secure MAC Address Types

There are a number of ways to configure port security. The following describes the ways you can configure port security on a Cisco switch:

- *Static secure MAC addresses:* MAC addresses are manually configured by using the `switchport port-security mac-address` *mac-address* interface configuration command. MAC addresses configured in this way are stored in the address table and are added to the running configuration on the switch.

- *Dynamic secure MAC addresses:* MAC addresses are dynamically learned and stored only in the address table. MAC addresses configured in this way are removed when the switch restarts.

- *Sticky secure MAC addresses:* You can configure a port to dynamically learn MAC addresses and then save these MAC addresses to the running configuration.

Sticky MAC Addresses

Sticky secure MAC addresses have these characteristics:

- When you enable sticky learning on an interface by using the `switchport port-security mac-address sticky` interface configuration command, the interface converts all the dynamic secure MAC addresses, including those that were dynamically learned before sticky learning was enabled, to sticky secure MAC addresses and adds all sticky secure MAC addresses to the running configuration.

- If you disable sticky learning by using the `no switchport port-security mac-address sticky` interface configuration command, the sticky secure MAC addresses remain part of the address table but are removed from the running configuration.

- When you configure sticky secure MAC addresses by using the `switchport port-security mac-address sticky` *mac-address* interface configuration command, these addresses are added to the address table and the running configuration. If port security is disabled, the sticky secure MAC addresses remain in the running configuration.

■ If you save the sticky secure MAC addresses in the configuration file, when the switch restarts or the interface shuts down, the interface does not need to relearn these addresses. If you do not save the sticky secure addresses, they are lost.

■ If you disable sticky learning and enter the `switchport port-security mac-address sticky` *mac-address* interface configuration command, an error message appears, and the sticky secure MAC address is not added to the running configuration.

Click the Security Violation Modes button in the figure.

Security Violation Modes

It is a security violation when either of these situations occurs:

■ The maximum number of secure MAC addresses have been added to the address table, and a station whose MAC address is not in the address table attempts to access the interface.

■ An address learned or configured on one secure interface is seen on another secure interface in the same VLAN.

You can configure the interface for one of three violation modes, based on the action to be taken if a violation occurs. The figure presents which kinds of data traffic are forwarded when one of the following security violation modes are configured on a port:

■ *protect:* When the number of secure MAC addresses reaches the limit allowed on the port, packets with unknown source addresses are dropped until you remove a sufficient number of secure MAC addresses or increase the number of maximum allowable addresses. You are not notified that a security violation has occurred.

■ *restrict:* When the number of secure MAC addresses reaches the limit allowed on the port, packets with unknown source addresses are dropped until you remove a sufficient number of secure MAC addresses or increase the number of maximum allowable addresses. In this mode, you are notified that a security violation has occurred. Specifically, an SNMP trap is sent, a syslog message is logged, and the violation counter increments.

Refer to
Figure
in online course

■ *shutdown:* In this mode, a port security violation causes the interface to immediately become error-disabled and turns off the port LED. It also sends an SNMP trap, logs a syslog message, and increments the violation counter. When a secure port is in the error-disabled state, you can bring it out of this state by entering the `shutdown` and `no shutdown` interface configuration commands. This is the default mode.

Configure Port Security

Click the Default Configuration button in the figure.

The ports on a Cisco switch are preconfigured with defaults. The figure summarizes the default port security configuration.

Click the Configure Dynamic Port Security button in the figure.

The figure shows the Cisco IOS CLI commands needed to configure port security on the Fast Ethernet F0/18 port on S1 switch. Notice that the example does not specify a violation mode. In this example, the violation mode is set to `shutdown`.

Click the Configure Sticky Port Security button in the figure.

Refer to
Figure
in online course

The figure shows how to enable sticky port security on Fast Ethernet port 0/18 of switch S1. As stated earlier, you can configure the maximum number of secure MAC addresses. In this example, you can see the Cisco IOS command syntax used to set the maximum number of MAC addresses to 50. The violation mode is set to `shutdown` by default.

There are other port security settings that you may find useful. For a complete listing of port security configuration options, visit: http://www.cisco.com/en/US/docs/switches/lan/catalyst2960/software/release/12.2_44_se/configuration/guide/swtrafc.html

Verify Port Security

After you have configured port security for your switch, you want to verify that it has been configured correctly. You need to check each interface to verify that you have set the port security correctly. You also have to check to make sure that you have configured static MAC addresses correctly.

Verify Port Security Settings

To display port security settings for the switch or for the specified interface, use the `show port-security` [`interface` *interface-id*] command.

The output displays the following:

- Maximum allowed number of secure MAC addresses for each interface
- Number of secure MAC addresses on the interface
- Number of security violations that have occurred
- Violation mode

Verify Secure MAC Addresses

Refer to
Figure
in online course

Click the Verify Secure MAC Addresses button in the figure.

To display all secure MAC addresses configured on all switch interfaces or on a specified interface with aging information for each, use the `show port-security` [`interface` *interface-id*] address command.

2.4.7 Securing Unused Ports

Disable Unused Ports

In this topic, you will learn how to use a simple Cisco IOS command to secure unused switch ports. A simple method many administrators use to help secure their network from unauthorized access is to disable all unused ports on a network switch. For example, imagine that a Cisco 2960 switch has 24 ports. If there are three Fast Ethernet connections in use, good security practice demands that you disable the 21 unused ports. The figure shows partial output for this configuration.

Refer to **Packet
Tracer Activity**
for this chapter

It is simple to disable multiple ports on a switch. Navigate to each unused port and issue this Cisco IOS `shutdown` command. An alternate way to shutdown multiple ports is to use the `interface range` command. If a port needs to be activated, you can manually enter the `no shutdown` command on that interface.

The process of enabling and disabling ports can become a tedious task, but the value in terms of enhancing security on your network is well worth the effort.

Refer to
Lab Activity
for this chapter

In this activity, you will configure basic switch commands and then configure and test port security. Detailed instructions are provided within the activity as well as in the PDF link below.

Activity Instructions (PDF)

2.5 Chapter Labs

Refer to **Packet Tracer Activity** for this chapter

2.5.1 Basic Switch Configuration

In this lab, you will examine and configure a standalone LAN switch. Although a switch performs basic functions in its default out-of-the-box condition, there are a number of parameters that a network administrator should modify to ensure a secure and optimized LAN. This lab introduces you to the basics of switch configuration.

In this activity, you will examine and configure a standalone LAN switch. Although a switch performs basic functions in its default out-of-the-box condition, there are a number of parameters that a network administrator should modify to ensure a secure and optimized LAN. This activity introduces you to the basics of switch configuration.

Detailed instructions are provided within the activity as well as in the PDF link below.

Activity Instructions (PDF)

Refer to **Lab Activity** for this chapter

2.5.2 Managing Switch Operating System and Configuration Files

Refer to **Lab Activity** for this chapter

In this lab, you will create and save a basic switch configuration to a TFTP server. You will use a TFTP server to load a configuration to the switch and to upgrade the Cisco IOS software. You will also use password recovery procedures to access a switch for which the password is unknown.

2.5.3 Managing Switch Operating System and Configuration Files - Challenge

Cable a network that is similar to the one in the topology diagram. Then, create a console connection to the switch. If necessary, refer to Lab 1.3.1. The output shown in this lab is from a 2960 switch. If you use other switches, the switch outputs and interface descriptions may appear different.

Chapter Summary

Refer to
Figure
in online course

In this chapter, we discussed IEEE 802.3 Ethernet communication using unicast, broadcast, and multicast traffic. Early implementations of Ethernet networks needed to use CSMA/CD to help prevent and detect collisions between frames on the network. Duplex settings and LAN segmentation improve performance and reduce the need for CSMA/CD.

LAN design is a process with the intended end result a determination of how a LAN is to be implemented. LAN design considerations include collision domains, broadcast domains, network latency, and LAN segmentation.

We discussed how switch forwarding methods influence LAN performance and latency. Memory buffering plays a role in switch forwarding, symmetric and asymmetric switching, and multilayer switching.

An introduction to navigating the Cisco IOS CLI on a Cisco Catalyst 2960 switch was presented. Built-in help functions are used to identify commands and command options. The Cisco IOS CLI maintains a command history that allows you to more quickly configure repetitive switch functions.

We discussed the initial switch configuration and how to verify the switch configuration. Backing up a switch configuration and restoring a switch configuration are key skills for anyone administering a switch.

We learned how to secure access to the switch: implementing passwords to protect console and virtual terminal lines, implementing passwords to limit access to privileged EXEC mode, configuring system-wide password encryption, and enabling SSH. There are a number of security risks common to Cisco Catalyst switches, many of which are mitigated by using port security.

Refer to
Figure
in online course

Refer to **Packet
Tracer Activity**
for this chapter

In this Packet Tracer Skills Integration Challenge activity, you will configure basic switch management, including general maintenance commands, passwords, and port security. This activity provides you an opportunity to review previously acquired skills. Detailed instructions are provided within the activity as well as in the PDF link below.

Activity Instructions (PDF)

Chapter Quiz

Go to
the online course
to take the quiz.

Take the chapter quiz to test your knowledge.

Your Chapter Notes

Chapter Introduction

Network performance can be a factor in an organization's productivity and its reputation for delivering as promised. One of the contributing technologies to excellent network performance is the separation of large broadcast domains into smaller ones with VLANs. Smaller broadcast domains limit the number of devices participating in broadcasts and allow devices to be separated into functional groupings, such as database services for an accounting department and high-speed data transfer for an engineering department. In this chapter, you will learn how to configure, manage, and troubleshoot VLANs and *trunks*.

3.1 Introducing VLANs

3.1.1 Introducing VLANs

Before VLANs

To appreciate why VLANs are being widely used today, consider a small community college with student dorms and the faculty offices all in one building. The figure shows the student computers in one LAN and the faculty computers in another LAN. This works fine because each department is physically together, so it is easy to provide them with their network resources.

Click the Many Buildings button in the figure.

A year later, the college has grown and now has three buildings. In the figure, the original network is the same, but student and faculty computers are spread out across three buildings. The student dorms remain on the fifth floor and the faculty offices remain on the third floor. However, now the IT department wants to ensure that student computers all share the same security features and bandwidth controls. How can the network accommodate the shared needs of the geographically separated departments? Do you create a large LAN and wire each department together? How easy would it be to make changes to that network? It would be great to group the people with the resources they use regardless of their geographic location, and it would make it easier to manage their specific security and bandwidth needs.

VLAN Overview

The solution for the community college is to use a networking technology called a virtual LAN (VLAN). A VLAN allows a network administrator to create groups of logically networked devices that act as if they are on their own independent network, even if they share a common infrastructure with other VLANs. When you configure a VLAN, you can name it to describe the primary role of the users for that VLAN. As another example, all of the student computers in a school can be configured in the "Student" VLAN. Using VLANs, you can logically segment switched networks based on functions, departments, or project teams. You can also use a VLAN to geographically structure your network to support the growing reliance of companies on home-based workers. In the figure, one VLAN is created for students and another for faculty. These VLANs allow the network administrator to implement access and security policies to particular groups of users. For example, the faculty, but not the students, can be allowed access to e-learning management servers for developing online course materials.

Click the Details button in the figure.

VLAN Details

A VLAN is a logically separate IP subnetwork. VLANs allow multiple IP networks and subnets to exist on the same switched network. The figure shows a network with three computers. For computers to communicate on the same VLAN, each must have an IP address and a subnet mask that is consistent for that VLAN. The switch has to be configured with the VLAN and each port in the VLAN must be assigned to the VLAN. A switch port with a singular VLAN configured on it is called an access port. Remember, just because two computers are physically connected to the same switch does not mean that they can communicate. Devices on two separate networks and subnets must communicate via a router (Layer 3), whether or not VLANs are used. You do not need VLANs to have multiple networks and subnets on a switched network, but there are definite advantages to using VLANs.

Refer to
Figure
in online course

Benefits of a VLAN

User productivity and network adaptability are key drivers for business growth and success. Implementing VLAN technology enables a network to more flexibly support business goals. The primary benefits of using VLANs are as follows:

- *Security -* Groups that have sensitive data are separated from the rest of the network, decreasing the chances of confidential information breaches. Faculty computers are on VLAN 10 and completely separated from student and guest data traffic.

- *Cost reduction -* Cost savings result from less need for expensive network upgrades and more efficient use of existing bandwidth and uplinks.

- *Higher performance -* Dividing flat Layer 2 networks into multiple logical workgroups (broadcast domains) reduces unnecessary traffic on the network and boosts performance.

- *Broadcast storm* mitigation - Dividing a network into VLANs reduces the number of devices that may participate in a broadcast storm. As discussed in the "Configure a Switch" chapter, LAN segmentation prevents a broadcast storm from propagating to the whole network. In the figure you can see that although there are six computers on this network, there are only three broadcast domains: Faculty, Student, and Guest.

- *Improved IT staff efficiency -* VLANs make it easier to manage the network because users with similar network requirements share the same VLAN. When you provision a new switch, all the policies and procedures already configured for the particular VLAN are implemented when the ports are assigned. It is also easy for the IT staff to identify the function of a VLAN by giving it an appropriate name. In the figure, for easy identification VLAN 20 has been named "Student", VLAN 10 could be named "Faculty", and VLAN 30 "Guest."

- *Simpler project or application management -* VLANs aggregate users and network devices to support business or geographic requirements. Having separate functions makes managing a project or working with a specialized application easier, for example, an e-learning development platform for faculty. It is also easier to determine the scope of the effects of upgrading network services.

Refer to
Figure
in online course

VLAN ID Ranges

Access VLANs are divided into either a normal range or an extended range.

Normal Range VLANs

- Used in small- and medium-sized business and enterprise networks.

- Identified by a VLAN ID between 1 and 1005.

- IDs 1002 through 1005 are reserved for *Token Ring* and *FDDI* VLANs.

- IDs 1 and 1002 to 1005 are automatically created and cannot be removed. You will learn more about VLAN 1 later in this chapter.

- Configurations are stored within a VLAN database file, called vlan.dat. The vlan.dat file is located in the flash memory of the switch.

- The VLAN trunking protocol (*VTP*), which helps manage VLAN configurations between switches, can only learn normal range VLANs and stores them in the VLAN database file.

Extended Range VLANs

- Enable service providers to extend their infrastructure to a greater number of customers. Some global enterprises could be large enough to need extended range VLAN IDs.

- Are identified by a VLAN ID between 1006 and 4094.

- Support fewer VLAN features than normal range VLANs.

- Are saved in the running configuration file.

- VTP does not learn extended range VLANs.

255 VLANs Configurable

One Cisco Catalyst 2960 switch can support up to 255 normal range and extended range VLANs, although the number configured affects the performance of the switch hardware. Because an enterprise network may need a switch with a lot of ports, Cisco has developed enterprise-level switches that can be joined or stacked together to create a single switching unit consisting of nine separate switches. Each separate switch can have 48 ports, which totals 432 ports on a single switching unit. In this case, the 255 VLAN limit per single switch could be a constraint for some enterprise customers.

3.1.2 Types of VLANs

Refer to **Figure** in online course

Today there is essentially one way of implementing VLANs - port-based VLANs. A port-based VLAN is associated with a port called an access VLAN.

However in the network there are a number of terms for VLANs. Some terms define the type of network traffic they carry and others define a specific function a VLAN performs. The following describes common VLAN terminology:

Roll over the Data VLAN button in the figure.

Data VLAN

A data VLAN is a VLAN that is configured to carry only user-generated traffic. A VLAN could carry voice-based traffic or traffic used to manage the switch, but this traffic would not be part of a data VLAN. It is common practice to separate voice and management traffic from data traffic. The importance of separating user data from switch management control data and voice traffic is highlighted by the use of a special term used to identify VLANs that only carry user data - a "data VLAN". A data VLAN is sometimes referred to as a user VLAN.

Roll over the Default VLAN button in the figure.

Default VLAN

All switch ports become a member of the default VLAN after the initial boot up of the switch. Having all the switch ports participate in the default VLAN makes them all part of the same broadcast domain. This allows any device connected to any switch port to communicate with other devices on other switch ports. The default VLAN for Cisco switches is VLAN 1. VLAN 1 has all the features of any VLAN, except that you cannot rename it and you can not delete it. By default, Layer 2 control traffic, such as CDP and spanning tree protocol traffic, are associated with VLAN 1. In the figure, VLAN 1 traffic is forwarded over the VLAN trunks connecting the S1, S2, and S3 switches. It is a security best practice to change the default VLAN to a VLAN other than VLAN 1; this entails configuring all the ports on the switch to be associated with a default VLAN other than VLAN 1. VLAN trunks support the transmission of traffic from more than one VLAN. Although VLAN trunks are mentioned throughout this section, they are explained in the next section on VLAN trunking.

Note: Some network administrators use the term "default VLAN" to mean a VLAN other than VLAN 1 defined by the network administrator as the VLAN that all ports are assigned to when they are not in use. In this case, the only role that VLAN 1 plays is that of handling Layer 2 control traffic for the network.

Roll over the Native VLAN button in the figure.

Native VLAN

A native VLAN is assigned to an 802.1Q trunk port. An 802.1Q trunk port supports traffic coming from many VLANs (tagged traffic) as well as traffic that does not come from a VLAN (untagged traffic). The 802.1Q trunk port places untagged traffic on the native VLAN. In the figure, the native VLAN is VLAN 99. Untagged traffic is generated by a computer attached to a switch port that is configured with the native VLAN. Native VLANs are set out in the IEEE 802.1Q specification to maintain backward compatibility with untagged traffic common to legacy LAN scenarios. For our purposes, a native VLAN serves as a common identifier on opposing ends of a trunk link. It is a best practice to use a VLAN other than VLAN 1 as the native VLAN.

Roll over the Management VLAN button in the figure.

Management VLAN

A management VLAN is any VLAN you configure to access the management capabilities of a switch. VLAN 1 would serve as the management VLAN if you did not proactively define a unique VLAN to serve as the management VLAN. You assign the management VLAN an IP address and subnet mask. A switch can be managed via HTTP, Telnet, SSH, or SNMP. Since the out-of-the-box configuration of a Cisco switch has VLAN 1 as the default VLAN, you see that VLAN 1 would be a bad choice as the management VLAN; you wouldn't want an arbitrary user connecting to a switch to default to the management VLAN. Recall that you configured the management VLAN as VLAN 99 in the Basic Switch Concepts and Configuration chapter.

On the next page we will explore the one remaining VLAN type: voice VLANs.

Refer to
Figure
in online course

Voice VLANs

It is easy to appreciate why a separate VLAN is needed to support Voice over IP (VoIP). Imagine you are receiving an emergency call and suddenly the quality of the transmission degrades so much you cannot understand what the caller is saying. VoIP traffic requires:

■ Assured bandwidth to ensure voice quality

- Transmission priority over other types of network traffic

- Ability to be routed around congested areas on the network

- Delay of less than 150 milliseconds (ms) across the network

To meet these requirements, the entire network has to be designed to support VoIP. The details of how to configure a network to support VoIP are beyond the scope of the course, but it is useful to summarize how a voice VLAN works between a switch, a Cisco IP phone, and a computer.

In the figure, VLAN 150 is designed to carry voice traffic. The student computer PC5 is attached to the Cisco IP phone, and the phone is attached to switch S3. PC5 is in VLAN 20, which is used for student data. The F0/18 port on S3 is configured to be in voice mode so that it will tell the phone to tag voice frames with VLAN 150. Data frames coming through the Cisco IP phone from PC5 are left untagged. Data destined for PC5 coming from port F0/18 is tagged with VLAN 20 on the way to the phone, which strips the VLAN tag before the data is forwarded to PC5. Tagging refers to the addition of bytes to a field in the data frame which is used by the switch to identify which VLAN the data frame should be sent to. You will learn later about how data frames are tagged.

Click The Details button in the figure.

A Cisco Phone is a Switch

The Cisco IP Phone contains an integrated three-port 10/100 switch as shown in the Figure. The ports provide dedicated connections to these devices:

- Port 1 connects to the switch or other voice-over-IP (VoIP) device.

- Port 2 is an internal 10/100 interface that carries the IP phone traffic.

- Port 3 (access port) connects to a PC or other device.

The figure shows one way to connect an IP Phone.

The voice VLAN feature enables switch ports to carry IP voice traffic from an IP phone. When the switch is connected to an IP Phone, the switch sends messages that instruct the attached IP phone to send voice traffic tagged with the voice VLAN ID 150. The traffic from the PC attached to the IP Phone passes through the IP phone untagged. When the switch port has been configured with a voice VLAN, the link between the switch and the IP phone acts as a trunk to carry both the tagged voice traffic and untagged data traffic.

Note: Communication between the switch and IP phone is facilitated by the CDP protocol. This protocol is discussed in greater detail in the CCNA Exploration: Routing Protocols and Concepts course.

Click the Sample Configuration button in the figure.

Sample Configuration

The figure shows sample output. A discussion of the Cisco IOS commands are beyond the scope of this course, but you can see that the highlighted areas in the sample output show the F0/18 interface configured with a VLAN configured for data (VLAN 20) and a VLAN configured for voice (VLAN 150).

Refer to
Figure
in online course

Network Traffic Types

In CCNA Exploration: Network Fundamentals, you learned about the different kinds of traffic a LAN handles. Because a VLAN has all the characteristics of a LAN, a VLAN must accommodate the same network traffic as a LAN.

Network Management and Control Traffic

Many different types of network management and control traffic can be present on the network, such as Cisco Discovery Protocol (CDP) updates, Simple Network Management Protocol (SNMP) traffic, and Remote Monitoring (RMON) traffic.

Roll over the Network Management button in the figure.

IP Telephony

The types of IP telephony traffic are *signaling* traffic and voice traffic. Signaling traffic is, responsible for call setup, progress, and teardown, and traverses the network end to end. The other type of telephony traffic consists of data packets of the actual voice conversation. As you just learned, in a network configured with VLANs, it is strongly recommended to assign a VLAN other than VLAN 1 as the management VLAN. Data traffic should be associated with a data VLAN (other than VLAN 1), and voice traffic is associated with a voice VLAN.

Roll over the IP Telephony button in the figure.

IP Multicast

IP multicast traffic is sent from a particular source address to a multicast group that is identified by a single IP and MAC destination-group address pair. Examples of applications that generate this type of traffic are Cisco IP/TV broadcasts. Multicast traffic can produce a large amount of data streaming across the network. When the network must support multicast traffic, VLANs should be configured to ensure multicast traffic only goes to those user devices that use the service provided, such as remote video or audio applications. Routers must be configured to ensure that multicast traffic is forwarded to the network areas where it is requested.

Roll over the IP Multicast button in the figure.

Normal Data

Normal data traffic is related to file creation and storage, print services, e-mail database access, and other shared network applications that are common to business uses. VLANs are a natural solution for this type of traffic because you can segment users by their functions or geographic area to more easily manage their specific needs.

Roll over the Normal Data button in the figure.

Scavenger Class

The Scavenger class is intended to provide less-than best-effort services to certain applications. Applications assigned to this class have little or no contribution to the organizational objectives of the enterprise and are typically entertainment oriented in nature. These include peer-to-peer media-sharing applications (KaZaa, Morpheus, Groekster, Napster, iMesh, and so on), gaming applications (Doom, Quake, Unreal Tournament, and so on), and any entertainment video applications.

3.1.3 Switch Port Membership Modes

Switch Ports

Refer to
Figure
in online course

Switch ports are Layer 2-only interfaces associated with a physical port. Switch ports are used for managing the physical interface and associated Layer 2 protocols. They do not handle routing or bridging. Switch ports belong to one or more VLANs.

VLAN Switch Port Modes

When you configure a VLAN, you must assign it a number ID, and you can optionally give it a name. The purpose of VLAN implementations is to judiciously associate ports with particular VLANs. You configure the port to forward a frame to a specific VLAN. As mentioned previously, you can configure a VLAN in voice mode to support voice and data traffic coming from a Cisco IP phone. You can configure a port to belong to a VLAN by assigning a membership mode that specifies the kind of traffic the port carries and the VLANs to which it can belong. A port can be configured to support these VLAN types:

- *Static VLAN -* Ports on a switch are manually assigned to a VLAN. Static VLANs are configured using the Cisco CLI. This can also be accomplished with GUI management applications, such as the Cisco Network Assistant. However, a convenient feature of the CLI is that if you assign an interface to a VLAN that does not exist, the new VLAN is created for you. To see a sample static-VLAN configuration, **click the Static Mode Example button** in the figure. When you are done, **click the Port Modes button** in the figure. This configuration will not be examined in detail now. You will see this configuration later in the chapter.

- *Dynamic VLAN -* This mode is not widely used in production networks and is not explored in this course. However, it is useful to know what a dynamic VLAN is. A dynamic port VLAN membership is configured using a special server called a VLAN Membership Policy Server (VMPS). With the VMPS, you assign switch ports to VLANs dynamically, based on the source MAC address of the device connected to the port. The benefit comes when you move a host from a port on one switch in the network to a port on another switch in the network, the switch dynamically assigns the new port to the proper VLAN for that host.

- *Voice VLAN -* A port is configured to be in voice mode so that it can support an IP phone attached to it. Before you configure a voice VLAN on the port, you need to first configure a VLAN for voice and a VLAN for data. In the figure, VLAN 150 is the voice VLAN, and VLAN 20 is the data VLAN. It is assumed that the network has been configured to ensure that voice traffic can be transmitted with a priority status over the network. When a phone is first plugged into a switch port that is in voice mode, the switch port sends messages to the phone providing the phone with the appropriate voice VLAN ID and configuration. The IP phone tags the voice frames with the voice VLAN ID and forwards all voice traffic through the voice VLAN.

To examine parts of a voice mode configuration, **click the Voice Mode Example button** in the figure:

- The configuration command `mls qos trust cos` ensures that voice traffic is identified as priority traffic. Remember that the entire network must be set up to prioritize voice traffic. You cannot just configure the port with this command.

- The `switchport voice vlan 150` command identifies VLAN 150 as the voice VLAN. You can see this verified in the bottom screen capture: `Voice VLAN: 150 (VLAN0150)`.

- The `switchport access vlan 20` command configures VLAN 20 as the access mode (data) VLAN. You can see this verified in the bottom screen capture: `Access Mode VLAN: 20 (VLAN0020)`.

For more details about configuring a voice VLAN, visit this Cisco.com site: http://www.cisco.com/en/US/docs/switches/lan/catalyst2975/software/release/12.2_46_ex/configuration/guide/swvoip.html.

3.1.4 Controlling Broadcast Domains with VLANs

Refer to **Figure** in online course

Network Without VLANS

In normal operation, when a switch receives a broadcast frame on one of its ports, it forwards the frame out all other ports on the switch. In the figure, the entire network is configured in the same subnet, 172.17.40.0/24. As a result, when the faculty computer, PC1, sends out a broadcast frame, switch S2 sends that broadcast frame out all of its ports. Eventually the entire network receives it; the network is one broadcast domain.

Click the Network broadcasts with VLAN segmentation button in the figure.

Network with VLANs

In the figure, the network has been segmented into two VLANs: Faculty as VLAN 10 and Student as VLAN 20. When the broadcast frame is sent from the faculty computer, PC1, to switch S2, the switch forwards that broadcast frame only to those switch ports configured to support VLAN 10.

In the figure, the ports that make up the connection between switches S2 and S1 (ports F0/1) and between S1 and S3 (ports F0/3) have been configured to support all the VLANs in the network. This connection is called a trunk. You will learn more about trunks later in this chapter.

When S1 receives the broadcast frame on port F0/1, S1 forwards that broadcast frame out the only port configured to support VLAN 10, port F0/3. When S3 receives the broadcast frame on port F0/3, it forwards that broadcast frame out the only port configured to support VLAN 10, port F0/11. The broadcast frame arrives at the only other computer in the network configured on VLAN 10, faculty computer PC4.

When VLANs are implemented on a switch, the transmission of unicast, multicast, and broadcast traffic from a host on a particular VLAN are constrained to the devices that are on the VLAN.

Refer to
Figure
in online course

Controlling Broadcast Domains with Switches and Routers

Breaking up a big broadcast domain into several smaller ones reduces broadcast traffic and improves network performance. Breaking up domains into VLANs also allows for better information confidentiality within an organization. Breaking up broadcast domains can be performed either with VLANs (on switches) or with routers. A router is needed any time devices on different Layer 3 networks need to communicate, regardless whether VLANs are used.

Click the Intra-VLAN Communication button and click the Play button to start the animation.

Intra-VLAN Communication

In the figure, PC1, wants to communicate with another device, PC4. PC1 and PC4 are both in VLAN 10. Communicating with a device in the same VLAN is called intra-VLAN communication. The following describes how this process is accomplished:

Step 1. PC1 in VLAN 10 sends its ARP request frame (broadcast) to switch S2. Switches S2 and S1 send the ARP request frame out all ports on VLAN 10. Switch S3 sends the ARP request out port F0/11 to PC4 on VLAN 10.

Step 2. The switches in the network forward the ARP reply frame (unicast) to PC1. PC1 receives the reply which contains the MAC address of PC4.

Step 3. PC1 now has the destination MAC address of PC4 and uses this to create a unicast frame with PC4's MAC address as the destination. Switches S2, S1 and S3 deliver the frame to PC4.

Click the Inter-VLAN Communication button and click the Play button to start the animation.

Inter-VLAN Communication

In the figure, PC1 in VLAN 10 wants to communicate with PC5 in VLAN 20. Communicating with a device in another VLAN is called inter-VLAN communication.

Note: There are two connections from switch S1 to the router: one to carry transmissions on VLAN 10, and the other to carry transmissions on VLAN 20 to the router interface.

The following describes how this process is accomplished:

Step 1. PC1 in VLAN 10 wants to communicate with PC5 in VLAN 20. PC1 sends an ARP request frame for the MAC address of the default gateway R1.

Step 2. The router R1 replies with an ARP reply frame from its interface configured on VLAN 10.

All switches forward the ARP reply frame and PC1 receives it. The ARP reply contains the MAC address of the default gateway.

Step 3. PC1 then creates an Ethernet frame with the MAC address of the Default Gateway. The frame is sent from switch S2 to S1.

Step 4. The router R1 sends an ARP request frame on VLAN 20 to determine the MAC address of PC5. Switches, S1, S2, S3, broadcast the ARP request frame out ports configured for VLAN 20. PC5 on VLAN 20 receives the ARP request frame from router R1.

Step 5. PC5 on VLAN 20 sends an ARP reply frame to switch S3. Switches S3 and S1 forward the ARP reply frame to router R1 with the destination MAC address of interface F0/2 on router R1.

Step 6. Router R1 sends the frame received from PC1 though S1 and S3 to PC5 (on VLAN 20).

Refer to
Figure
in online course

Controlling Broadcast Domains with VLANs and Layer 3 Forwarding

In the last chapter, you learned about some of the differences between Layer 2 and Layer 3 switches. The figure shows the Catalyst 3750G-24PS switch, one of many Cisco switches that supports Layer 3 routing. The icon that represents a Layer 3 switch is shown. A discussion of Layer 3 switching is beyond the scope of this course, but a brief description of the switch virtual interface (SVI) technology that allows a Layer 3 switch to route transmissions between VLANs is helpful.

SVI

SVI is a logical interface configured for a specific VLAN. You need to configure an SVI for a VLAN if you want to route between VLANs or to provide IP host connectivity to the switch. By default, an SVI is created for the default VLAN (VLAN 1) to permit remote switch administration.

Click the Layer 3 Forwarding Example button in the figure to see an animation that presents a simplified representation of how a Layer 3 switch controls broadcast domains.

Layer 3 Forwarding

A Layer 3 switch has the ability to route transmissions between VLANs. The procedure is the same as described for the inter-VLAN communication using a separate router, except that the SVIs act as the router interfaces for routing the data between VLANs. The animation describes this process.

In the animation, PC1 wants to communicate with PC5. The following steps outline the communication through the Layer 3 switch S1:

Step 1. PC1 sends an ARP request broadcast on VLAN10. S2 forwards the ARP request out all ports configured for VLAN 10.

Step 2. Switch S1 forwards the ARP request out all ports configured for VLAN 10, including the SVI for VLAN 10. Switch S3 forwards the ARP request out all ports configured for VLAN 10.

Step 3. The SVI for VLAN 10 in switch S1 knows the location of VLAN 20. The SVI for VLAN 10 in switch S1 sends an ARP reply back to PC1 with this information.

Step 4. PC1 sends data, destined for PC5, as a unicast frame through switch S2 to the SVI for VLAN 10 in switch S1.

Step 5. The SVI for VLAN 20 sends an ARP request broadcast out all switch ports configured for VLAN 20. Switch S3 sends that ARP request broadcast out all switch ports configured for VLAN 20.

Step 6. PC5 on VLAN 20 sends an ARP reply. Switch S3 sends that ARP reply to S1. Switch S1 forwards the ARP reply to the SVI for VLAN 20.

Step 7. The SVI for VLAN 20 forwards the data, sent from PC1, in a unicast frame to PC5 using the destination address it learned from the ARP reply in step 6.

Refer to **Packet Tracer Activity** for this chapter

This activity opens in simulation mode and with completion at 100%. The purpose of the activity is to observe how broadcast traffic is forwarded by the switches when VLANs are configured and when VLANs are not configured. Detailed instructions are provided within the activity as well as in the PDF link below.

Activity Instructions (PDF)

3.2 VLAN Trunking

3.2.1 VLAN Trunks

Refer to **Figure** in online course

What is a Trunk?

It is hard to describe VLANs without mentioning VLAN trunks. You learned about controlling network broadcasts with VLAN segmentation, and you saw how VLAN trunks transmitted traffic to different parts of the network configured in one VLAN. In the figure, the links between switches S1 and S2, and S1 and S3, are configured to transmit traffic coming from VLAN 10, 20, 30, and 99. This network simply could not function without VLAN trunks. You will find that most networks that you encounter are configured with VLAN trunks. This section brings together the knowledge you already have on VLAN trunking and provides the details you need to be able to configure VLAN trunking in a network.

Definition of a VLAN Trunk

A trunk is a point-to-point link between two network devices that carries more than one VLAN. A VLAN trunk allows you to extend the VLANs across an entire network. Cisco supports IEEE 802.1Q for coordinating trunks on Fast Ethernet and Gigabit Ethernet interfaces. You will learn about 802.1Q later in this section.

A VLAN trunk does not belong to a specific VLAN, rather it is a conduit for VLANs between switches and routers.

Refer to **Figure** in online course

What Problem Does a Trunk Solve?

In the figure, you see the standard topology used in this chapter, except instead of the VLAN trunk that you are used to seeing between switches S1 and S2, there is a separate link for each subnet. There are four separate links connecting switches S1 and S2, leaving three fewer ports to allocate to end-user devices. Each time a new subnetwork is considered, a new link is needed for each switch in the network.

Click the With VLAN Trunks button in the figure.

In the figure, the network topology shows a VLAN trunk connecting switches S1 and S2 with a single physical link. This is the way a network should be configured.

Refer to **Figure** in online course

802.1Q Frame Tagging

Remember that switches are Layer 2 devices. They only use the Ethernet frame header information to forward packets. The frame header does not contain information about which VLAN the frame should belong to. Subsequently, when Ethernet frames are placed on a trunk they need additional information about the VLANs they belong to. This is accomplished by using the 802.1Q encapsulation header. This header adds a tag to the original Ethernet frame specifying the VLAN to which the frame belongs.

Frame tagging has been mentioned a number of times. The first time was in reference to the voice mode configuration on a switch port. There you learned that once configured, a Cisco phone (which includes a small switch) tags voice frames with a VLAN ID. You also learned that VLAN IDs can be in a normal range, 1-1005, and an extended range, 1006-4094. How do VLAN IDs get inserted into a frame?

VLAN Frame Tagging Overview

Before exploring the details of an 802.1Q frame, it is helpful to understand what a switch does when it forwards a frame out a trunk link. When the switch receives a frame on a port configured in access mode with a static VLAN, the switch takes apart the frame and inserts a VLAN tag, re-calculates the FCS and sends the tagged frame out a trunk port.

Note: An animation of the trunking operation is presented later in this section.

VLAN Tag Field Details

The VLAN tag field consists of an EtherType field, a tag control information field,and the FCS field.

EtherType field

Set to the hexadecimal value of 0x8100. This value is called the tag protocol ID (TPID) value. With the EtherType field set to the TPID value, the switch receiving the frame knows to look for information in the tag control information field.

Tag control information field

The tag control information field contains:

- *3 bits of user priority* - Used by the 802.1p standard, which specifies how to provide expedited transmission of Layer 2 frames. A description of the IEEE 802.1p is beyond the scope of this course; however, you learned a little about it earlier in the discussion on voice VLANs.

- *1 bit of Canonical Format Identifier (CFI)* - Enables Token Ring frames to be carried across Ethernet links easily.

- *12 bits of VLAN ID (VID)* - VLAN identification numbers; supports up to 4096 VLAN IDs.

FCS field

After the switch inserts the EtherType and tag control information fields, it recalculates the FCS values and inserts it into the frame.

Refer to
Figure
in online course

Native VLANs and 802.1Q Trunking

Now that you know more about how a switch tags a frame with the correct VLAN, it is time to explore how the native VLAN supports the switch in handling tagged and untagged frames that arrive on an 802.1Q trunk port.

Tagged Frames on the Native VLAN

Some devices that support trunking tag native VLAN traffic as a default behavior. Control traffic sent on the native VLAN should be untagged. If an 802.1Q trunk port receives a tagged frame on the native VLAN, it drops the frame. Consequently, when configuring a switch port on a Cisco switch, you need to identify these devices and configure them so that they do not send tagged frames on the native VLAN. Devices from other vendors that support tagged frames on the native VLAN include IP phones, servers, routers, and non-Cisco switches.

Untagged Frames on the Native VLAN

When a Cisco switch trunk port receives untagged frames it forwards those frames to the native VLAN. As you may recall, the default native VLAN is VLAN 1. When you configure an 802.1Q trunk port, a default Port VLAN ID (PVID) is assigned the value of the native VLAN ID. All untagged traffic coming in or out of the 802.1Q port is forwarded based on the PVID value. For example, if VLAN 99 is configured as the native VLAN, the PVID is 99 and all untagged traffic is forward to VLAN 99. If the native VLAN has not been reconfigured, the PVID value is set to VLAN 1.

Click the Native VLAN Configuration Example button in the figure.

In this example, VLAN 99 will be configured as the native VLAN on port F0/1 on switch S1. This example shows how to reconfigure the native VLAN from its default setting of VLAN 1.

Starting in privileged EXEC mode, the figure describes how to configure the native VLAN on port F0/1 on switch S1 as an IEEE 802.1Q trunk with native VLAN 99.

Click the Native VLAN Verification button in the figure.

Using the `show interfaces` *interface-id* `switchport` command, you can quickly verify that you have correctly reconfigured the native VLAN from VLAN 1 to VLAN 99. The highlighted output in the screen capture indicates that the configuration was successful.

3.2.2 Trunking Operation

Refer to
Figure
in online course

A Trunk in Action

You have learned how a switch handles untagged traffic on a trunk link. You now know that frames traversing a trunk are tagged with the VLAN ID of the access port the frame arrived on. In the figure, PC1 on VLAN 10 and PC3 on VLAN 30 send broadcast frames to switch S2. Switch S2 tags these frames with the appropriate VLAN ID and then forwards the frames over the trunk to switch S1. Switch S1 reads the VLAN ID on the frames and broadcasts them to each port configured to support VLAN 10 and VLAN 30. Switch S3 receives these frames and strips off the VLAN IDs and forwards them as untagged frames to PC4 on VLAN 10 and PC6 on VLAN 30.

Click Play on the animation toolbar in the figure.

3.2.3 Trunking Modes

Refer to
Figure
in online course

You have learned how 802.1Q trunking works on Cisco switch ports. Now it is time to examine the 802.1Q trunk port mode configuration options. First we need to discuss a Cisco legacy trunking protocol called inter-switch link (ISL), because you will see this option in the switch software configuration guides.

IEEE, Not ISL

Although a Cisco switch can be configured to support two types of trunk ports, IEEE 802.1Q and ISL, today only 802.1Q is used. However, legacy networks may still use ISL, and it is useful to learn about each type of trunk port.

- An IEEE 802.1Q trunk port supports simultaneous tagged and untagged traffic. An 802.1Q trunk port is assigned a default PVID, and all untagged traffic travels on the port default PVID. All untagged traffic and tagged traffic with a null VLAN ID are assumed to belong to the port default PVID. A packet with a VLAN ID equal to the outgoing port default PVID is sent untagged. All other traffic is sent with a VLAN tag.

- In an ISL trunk port, all received packets are expected to be encapsulated with an ISL header, and all transmitted packets are sent with an ISL header. Native (non-tagged) frames received from an ISL trunk port are dropped. ISL is no longer a recommended trunk port mode, and it is not supported on a number of Cisco switches.

DTP

Dynamic Trunking Protocol (DTP) is a Cisco proprietary protocol. Switches from other vendors do not support DTP. DTP is automatically enabled on a switch port when certain trunking modes are configured on the switch port.

DTP manages trunk negotiation only if the port on the other switch is configured in a trunk mode that supports DTP. DTP supports both ISL and 802.1Q trunks. This course focuses on the 802.1Q implementation of DTP. A detailed discussion on DTP is beyond the scope of this course; however, you will enable it in the labs and activities associated with the chapter. Switches do not need DTP to do trunking, and some Cisco switches and routers do not support DTP. To learn about DTP support on Cisco switches, visit: http://www.cisco.com/en/US/tech/tk389/tk689/technologies_tech_note09186a008017f86a.shtml.

Trunking Modes

A switch port on a Cisco switch supports a number of trunking modes. The trunking mode defines how the port negotiates using DTP to set up a trunk link with its peer port. The following provides a brief description of the available trunking modes and how DTP is implemented in each.

On (default)

The switch port periodically sends DTP frames, called advertisements, to the remote port. The command used is `switchport mode trunk`. The local switch port advertises to the remote port that it is dynamically changing to a trunking state. The local port then, regardless of what DTP information the remote port sends as a response to the advertisement, changes to a trunking state. The local port is considered to be in an unconditional (always on) trunking state.

Dynamic auto

The switch port periodically sends DTP frames to the remote port. The command used is `switchport mode dynamic auto`. The local switch port advertises to the remote switch port that it is able to trunk but does not request to go to the trunking state. After a DTP negotiation, the local port ends up in trunking state only if the remote port trunk mode has been configured to be on or desirable. If both ports on the switches are set to auto, they do not negotiate to be in a trunking state. They negotiate to be in the access (non-trunk) mode state.

Dynamic desirable

DTP frames are sent periodically to the remote port. The command used is `switchport mode dynamic desirable`. The local switch port advertises to the remote switch port that it is able to trunk and asks the remote switch port to go to the trunking state. If the local port detects that the remote has been configured in on, desirable, or auto mode, the local port ends up in trunking state. If the remote switch port is in the nonegotiate mode, the local switch port remains as a nontrunking port.

Turn off DTP

You can turn off DTP for the trunk so that the local port does not send out DTP frames to the remote port. Use the command `switchport nonegotiate`. The local port is then considered to be in an unconditional trunking state. Use this feature when you need to configure a trunk with a switch from another switch vendor.

A Trunk Mode Example

In the figure, the F0/1 ports on switches S1 and S2 are configured with trunk mode on. The F0/3 ports on switches S1 and S3 are configured to be in auto trunk mode. When the switch configurations are completed and the switches are fully configured, which link will be a trunk?

Click the Which link will be configured as a trunk? button in the figure.

The link between switches S1 and S2 becomes a trunk because the F0/1 ports on switches S1 and S2 are configured to ignore all DTP advertisements and come up and stay in trunk port mode. The F0/3 ports on switches S1 and S3 are set to auto, so they negotiate to be in the default state, the access (non-trunk) mode state. This results in an inactive trunk link. When you configure a trunk port to be in trunk port mode, there is no ambiguity about which state the trunk is in-it is always on. It is also easy to remember which state the trunk ports are in-if the port is supposed to be a trunk, trunk mode is on.

Note: The default switchport mode for an interface on a Catalyst 2950 switch is dynamic desirable, but the default switchport mode for an interface on a Catalyst 2960 switch is dynamic auto. If S1 and S3 were Catalyst 2950 switches with interface F0/3 in default switchport mode, the link between S1 and S3 would become an active trunk.

Click the DTP Modes button in the figure to review the mode interactions.

For information on which Cisco switches support 802.1Q, ISL, and DTP, visit: http://www.cisco.com/en/US/tech/tk389/tk689/technologies_tech_note09186a008017f86a.shtml#topic1.

For information on how to support ISL on legacy networks, visit: http://www.cisco.com/en/US/tech/tk389/tk689/tsd_technology_support_troubleshooting_technotes_list.html.

Refer to **Packet Tracer Activity** for this chapter

Trunks carry the traffic of multiple VLANs through a single link, making them a vital part of communicating between switches with VLANs. This activity focuses on viewing switch configuration, trunk configuration, and VLAN tagging information. Detailed instructions are provided within the activity as well as in the PDF link below.

Activity Instructions (PDF)

3.3 Configure VLANs and Trunks

3.3.1 Configuring VLANs and Trunks Overview

Refer to **Figure** in online course

In this chapter, you have already seen examples of the commands used to configure VLANs and VLAN trunks. In this section, you will learn the key Cisco IOS commands needed to create, delete, and verify VLANs and VLAN trunks. Often these commands have many optional parameters that extend the capabilities of the VLAN and VLAN trunk technology. These optional commands are not presented; however, references are provided if you want to research these options. The focus of this section is to provide you with the necessary skills and knowledge to configure VLANs and VLAN trunks with their key features.

In this section, you are shown the configuration and verification syntax for one side of a VLAN or trunk. In the labs and activities, you will configure both sides and verify that the link (VLAN or VLAN trunk) is configured correctly.

Note: If you want to keep the newly configured running configuration, you must save it to the startup configuration.

3.3.2 Configure a VLAN

Refer to **Figure** in online course

Add a VLAN

In this topic, you will learn how to create a static VLAN on a Cisco Catalyst switch using VLAN global configuration mode. There are two different modes for configuring VLANs on a Cisco Catalyst switch, database configuration mode and global configuration mode. Although the Cisco documentation mentions VLAN database configuration mode, it is being phased out in favor of VLAN global configuration mode.

You will configure VLANs with IDs in the normal range. Recall there are two ranges of VLAN IDs. The normal range includes IDs 1 to 1001, and extended range consists of IDs 1006 to 4094. VLAN 1 and 1002 to 1005 are reserved ID numbers. When you configure normal range VLANs, the configuration details are stored automatically in flash memory on the switch in a file called vlan.dat. Because you often configure other aspects of a Cisco switch at the same time, it is good practice to save running configuration changes to the startup configuration.

Click the Command Syntax button in the figure.

The figure reviews the Cisco IOS commands used to add a VLAN to a switch.

Click the Example button in the figure.

The figure shows how the student VLAN, VLAN 20, is configured on switch S1. In the topology example, the student computer, PC2, is not in a VLAN yet it, but has an IP address of 172.17.20.22.

Click the Verification button in figure.

The figure shows an example of using the `show vlan brief` command to display the contents of the vlan.dat file. The student VLAN, VLAN 20, is highlighted in the screen capture. The default VLAN IDs 1 and 1002 to 1005 are shown in the screen output.

Note: In addition to entering a single VLAN ID, you can enter a series of VLAN IDs separated by commas, or a range of VLAN IDs separated by hyphens using the `vlan vlan-id` command, for example: switch(config)#**vlan 100,102,105-107**.

Refer to
Figure
in online course

Assign a Switch Port

After you have created a VLAN, assign one or more ports to the VLAN. When you manually assign a switch port to a VLAN, it is known as a static access port. A static access port can belong to only one VLAN at a time.

Click the Command Syntax button in the figure to review the Cisco IOS commands used to assign a static access port to VLAN.

Click the Example button in the figure to see how the student VLAN, VLAN 20, is statically assigned to port F0/18 on switch S1. Port F0/18 has been assigned to VLAN 20 so the student computer, PC2, is in VLAN 20. When VLAN 20 is configured on other switches, the network administrator knows to configure the other student computers to be in the same subnet as PC2: 172.17.20.0 /24.

Click the Verification button in the figure to confirm that the `show vlan brief` command displays the contents of the vlan.dat file. The student VLAN, VLAN 20, is highlighted in the screen capture.

3.3.3 Managing VLANs

Refer to
Figure
in online course

Verify VLANs and Port Memberships

After you configure the VLAN, you can validate the VLAN configurations using Cisco IOS `show` commands.

Click the Command Syntax button in the figure.

The command syntax for the various Cisco IOS `show` commands should be well known. You have used the `show vlan brief` command already. Examples of these commands can be seen by clicking the buttons in the figure.

Click the Show VLAN button in the figure.

In this example, you can see that the `show vlan name student` command does not produce very readable output. The preference here is to use the `show vlan brief` command. The `show vlan summary` command displays the count of all configured VLANs. The output shows six VLANs: 1, 1002-1005, and the student VLAN, VLAN 20.

Click the Interfaces VLAN button in the figure.

This command displays a lot of detail that is beyond the scope of this chapter. The key information appears on the second line of the screen capture, indicating that VLAN 20 is up.

Click the Interfaces Switchport button in the figure.

This command displays information that is useful to you. You can determine that the port F0/18 is assigned to VLAN 20 and that the native VLAN is VLAN 1. You have used this command to review the configuration of a voice VLAN.

For details on the `show vlan` command output fields, visit: http://www.cisco.com/en/US/docs/ios/lanswitch/command/reference/lsw_s2.html#wp1011412.

For details on the `show interfaces` command output fields, visit: http://www.cisco.com/en/US/docs/ios/12_0/interface/command/reference/irshowin.html#wp1017387.

Refer to
Figure
in online course

Manage Port Memberships

There are a number of ways to manage VLANs and VLAN port memberships. The figure shows the syntax for the `no switchport access vlan` command.

Click the Remove VLAN button in the figure.

Reassign a Port to VLAN 1

To reassign a port to VLAN 1, you can use the `no switchport access vlan` command in interface configuration mode. Examine the output in the `show vlan brief` command that immediately follows. Notice how VLAN 20 is still active. It has only been removed from interface F0/18. In the `show interfaces f0/18 switchport` command, you can see that the access VLAN for interface F0/18 has been reset to VLAN 1.

Click the Reassign VLAN button in the figure.

Reassign the VLAN to Another Port

A static access port can only have one VLAN. With Cisco IOS software, you do not need to first remove a port from a VLAN to change its VLAN membership. When you reassign a static access port to an existing VLAN, the VLAN is automatically removed from the previous port. In the example, port F0/11is reassigned to VLAN 20 .

Refer to
Figure
in online course

Delete VLANs

The figure provides an example of using the global configuration command `no vlan `*`vlan-id`* to remove VLAN 20 from the system. The `show vlan brief` command verifies that VLAN 20 is no longer in the vlan.dat file.

Alternatively, the entire vlan.dat file can be deleted using the command `delete flash:vlan.dat` from privileged EXEC mode. After the switch is reloaded, the previously configured VLANs will no longer be present. This effectively places the switch into is "factory default" concerning VLAN configurations.

Note: Before deleting a VLAN, be sure to first reassign all member ports to a different VLAN. Any ports that are not moved to an active VLAN are unable to communicate with other stations after you delete the VLAN.

3.3.4 Configure a Trunk

Refer to
Figure
in online course

Configure an 802.1Q Trunk

To configure a trunk on a switch port, use the `switchport mode trunk` command. When you enter trunk mode, the interface changes to permanent trunking mode, and the port enters into a DTP negotiation to convert the link into a trunk link even if the interface connecting to it does not agree to the change. In this course, you will configure a trunk using only the `switchport mode trunk` command. The Cisco IOS command syntax to specify a native VLAN other than VLAN 1 is shown in the figure. In the example, you configure VLAN 99 as the native VLAN.

Click the Topology button in the figure.

You are familiar with this topology. The VLANs 10, 20, and 30 will support the Faculty, Student, and Guest computers, PC1, PC2, and PC3. The F0/1 port on switch S1 will be configured as a trunk port and will forward traffic for VLANs 10, 20, and 30. VLAN 99 will be configured as the native VLAN.

Click the Example button in the figure.

The example configures port F0/1 on switch S1 as the trunk port. It reconfigures the native VLAN as VLAN 99.

A discussion on DTP and the details of how each switchport access mode option works is beyond the scope of the course. For details on all of the parameters associated with the `switchport mode` interface command, visit: http://www.cisco.com/en/US/docs/switches/lan/catalyst2960/software/ release/12.2_37_se/command/reference/cli3.html#wp1948171.

Refer to
Figure
in online course

Verify Trunk Configuration

The figure displays the configuration of switch port F0/1 on switch S1. The command used is the `show interfaces ` *interface-ID* ` switchport` command.

The first highlighted area shows that port F0/1 has its administrative mode set to Trunk-the port is in trunking mode. The next highlighted area verifies that the native VLAN is VLAN 99, the management VLAN. At the bottom of the output, the last highlighted area shows that the enabled trunking VLANs are VLANs 10, 20, and 30.

Refer to
Figure
in online course

Managing a Trunk Configuration

In the figure, the commands to reset the allowed VLANs and the native VLAN of the trunk to the default state are shown. The command to reset the switch port to an access port and, in effect, deleting the trunk port is also shown.

Click the Reset Example button in the figure.

In the figure, the commands used to reset all trunking characteristics of a trunking interface to the default settings are highlighted in the sample output. The `show interfaces f0/1 switchport` command reveals that the trunk has been reconfigured to a default state.

Click the Remove Example button in the figure.

In the figure, the sample output shows the commands used to remove the trunk feature from the F0/1 switch port on switch S1. The `show interfaces f0/1 switchport` command reveals that the F0/1 interface is now in static access mode.

Refer to **Packet
Tracer Activity**
for this chapter

VLANs are helpful in the administration of logical groups, allowing members of a group to be easily moved, changed, or added. This activity focuses on creating and naming VLANs, assigning access ports to specific VLANs, changing the native VLAN, and configuring trunk links. Detailed instructions are provided within the activity as well as in the PDF link below.

Activity Instructions (PDF)

3.4 Troubleshooting VLANs and Trunks

3.4.1 Common Problems with Trunks

Refer to
Figure
in online course

Common Problems with Trunks

In this topic, you learn about common VLAN and trunking issues, which usually are associated with incorrect configurations. When you are configuring VLANs and trunks on a switched infrastructure, these types of configuration errors are most common in the following order:

- *Native VLAN mismatches* - Trunk ports are configured with different native VLANs, for example, if one port has defined VLAN 99 as the native VLAN and the other trunk port has defined VLAN 100 as the native VLAN. This configuration error generates console notifications, causes control and management traffic to be misdirected and, as you have learned, poses a security risk.

- *Trunk mode mismatches* - One trunk port is configured with trunk mode "off" and the other with trunk mode "on". This configuration error causes the trunk link to stop working.

- *VLANs and IP Subnets* - End user devices configured with incorrect IP addresses will not have network connectivity. Each VLAN is a logically separate IP subnetwork. Devices within the VLAN must be configured with the correct IP settings.

- *Allowed VLANs on trunks* - The list of allowed VLANs on a trunk has not been updated with the current VLAN trunking requirements. In this situation, unexpected traffic or no traffic is being sent over the trunk.

If you have discovered an issue with a VLAN or trunk and do not know what the problem is, start your troubleshooting by examining the trunks for a native VLAN mismatch and then work down the list. The rest of this topic examines how to fix the common problems with trunks. The next topic presents how to identify and solve incorrectly configured VLAN and IP subnets.

Refer to
Figure
in online course

Native VLAN Mismatches

You are a network administrator and you get a call that the person using computer PC4 cannot connect to the internal web server, WEB/TFTP server in the figure. You learn that a new technician was recently configuring switch S3. The topology diagram seems correct, so why is there a problem? You decide to check the configuration on S3.

Click the Configurations button in the figure.

As soon as you connect to switch S3, the error message shown in the top highlighted area in the figure appears in your console window. You take a look at the interface using the `show interfaces f0/3 switchport` command. You notice that the native VLAN, the second highlighted area in the figure, has been set to VLAN 100 and it is inactive. As you scan further down the output, you see that the allowed VLANs are 10 and 99, shown in the bottom highlighted area.

Click the Solution button in the figure.

You need to reconfigure the native VLAN on the Fast Ethernet F0/3 trunk port to be VLAN 99. In the figure, the top highlighted area shows the command to configure the native VLAN to be VLAN 99. The next two highlighted areas confirm that the Fast Ethernet F0/3 trunk port has the native VLAN reset to VLAN 99.

The screen output for the computer PC4 shows that connectivity has been restored to the WEB/TFTP server found at IP address 172.17.10.30.

Refer to
Figure
in online course

Trunk Mode Mismatches

In this course, you have learned that trunk links are configured statically with the **switchport mode trunk** command. You have learned that the trunk ports use DTP advertisements to negotiate the state of the link with the remote port. When a port on a trunk link is configured with a trunk mode that is incompatible with the other trunk port, a trunk link fails to form between the two switches.

In this scenario, the same problem arises: the person using computer PC4 cannot connect to the internal web server. Again, the topology diagram has been maintained and shows a correct configuration. Why is there a problem?

Click the Configurations button in the figure.

The first thing you do is check the status of the trunk ports on switch S1 using the **show interfaces trunk** command. It reveals in the figure that there is not a trunk on interface F0/3 on switch S1. You examine the F0/3 interface to learn that the switch port is in dynamic auto mode, the first highlighted area in the top figure. An examination of the trunks on switch S3 reveals that are no active trunk ports. Further checking reveals that the F0/3 interface is also in dynamic auto mode, the first highlighted area in the bottom figure. Now you know why the trunk is down.

Click the Solution button in the figure.

You need to reconfigure the trunk mode of the Fast Ethernet F0/3 ports on switches S1 and S3. In the top left figure, the highlighted area shows that the port is now in trunking mode. The top right output from switch S3 shows the commands used to reconfigure the port and the results of the **show interfaces trunk** command, revealing that interface F0/3 has been reconfigured as a trunk. The output from computer PC4 indicates that PC4 has regained connectivity to the WEB/TFTP server found at IP address 172.17.10.30.

Refer to
Figure
in online course

Incorrect VLAN List

You have learned that for traffic from a VLAN to be transmitted across a trunk it has to be allowed access on the trunk. The command used to do this is the **switchport access trunk allowed vlan add** *vlan-id* command. In the figure, VLAN 20 (Student) and computer PC5 have been added to the network. The documentation has been updated to show that the VLANs allowed on the trunk are 10, 20, and 99.

In this scenario, the person using computer PC5 cannot connect to the student e-mail server shown in the figure.

Click the Configurations button in the figure.

Check the trunk ports on switch S1 using the **show interfaces trunk** command. The command reveals that the interface F0/3 on switch S3 is correctly configured to allow VLANs 10, 20, and 99. An examination of the F0/3 interface on switch S1 reveals that interfaces F0/1 and F0/3 only allow VLANs 10 and 99. It seems someone updated the documentation but forgot to reconfigure the ports on the S1 switch.

Click the Solution button in the figure.

You need to reconfigure the F0/1 and the F0/3 ports on switch S1 using the **switchport trunk allowed vlan 10,20,99** command. The top screen output in the figure shows that VLANs 10, 20, and 99 are now added to the F0/1 and F0/3 ports on switch S1. The **show interfaces trunk** command is an excellent tool for revealing common trunking problems. The bottom figure indicates that PC5 has regained connectivity to the student e-mail server found at IP address 172.17.20.10.

3.4.2 A Common Problem with VLAN Configurations

VLAN and IP Subnets

As you have learned, each VLAN must correspond to a unique IP subnet. If two devices in the same VLAN have different subnet addresses, they cannot communicate. This type of incorrect configuration is a common problem, and it is easy to solve by identifying the offending device and changing the *subnet address* to the correct one.

In this scenario, the person using computer PC1 cannot connect to the WEB/TFTP server shown in the figure.

Click the Configurations button in the figure.

In the figure, a check of the IP configuration settings of PC1 reveals the most common error in configuring VLANs: an incorrectly configured IP address. The PC1 computer is configured with an IP address of 172.172.10.21, but it should have been configured with 172.17.10.21.

Click the Solution button in the figure.

The screen capture of the PC1 Fast Ethernet configuration dialog box shows the updated IP address of 172.17.10.21. The bottom screen capture reveals that PC1 has regained connectivity to the WEB/TFTP server found at IP address 172.17.10.30.

In this activity, you will troubleshoot connectivity problems between PCs on the same VLAN. The activity is complete when you achieve 100% and the PCs can ping the other PCs on the same VLAN. Any solution you implement must conform to the topology diagram. Detailed instructions are provided within the activity as well as in the PDF link below.

Activity Instructions (PDF)

3.5 Chapter Labs

3.5.1 Basic VLAN Configuration

In a network it is essential to be able to limit the effects of network broadcasts. One way to do this is to break up a large physical network into a number of smaller logical or virtual networks. This is one of the goals of VLANs. This lab will teach you the basics of configuring VLANs.

This activity is a variation of Lab 3.5.1. Packet Tracer may not support all the tasks specified in the hands-on lab. This activity should not be considered equivalent to completing the hands-on lab. Packet Tracer is not a substitute for a hands-on lab experience with real equipment. Detailed instructions are provided within the activity as well as in the PDF link below.

Activity Instructions (PDF)

3.5.2 Challenge VLAN Configuration

Having set up VLANs once in the Basic lab, this lab will verify how much you learned. Attempt to do as much of the lab as possible without referring back to the Basic lab. Once you have completed as much of the lab as possible on your own, check your work with the answer key that your instructor will provide.

This activity is a variation of Lab 3.5.2. Packet Tracer may not support all the tasks specified in the hands-on lab. This activity should not be considered equivalent to completing the hands-on lab.

Packet Tracer is not a substitute for a hands-on lab experience with real equipment. Detailed instructions are provided within the activity as well as in the PDF link below.

Activity Instructions (PDF)

3.5.3 Troubleshooting VLAN Configurations

Refer to
Lab Activity
for this chapter

In this lab, you will practice troubleshooting a misconfigured VLAN environment. Load or have your instructor load the configurations below into your lab gear. Your objective is to locate and correct any and all errors in the configurations and establish end-to-end connectivity. Your final configuration should match the topology diagram and addressing table.

Refer to **Packet Tracer Activity**
for this chapter

In this activity, you will practice troubleshooting a misconfigured VLAN environment. The initial network has errors. Your objective is to locate and correct any and all errors in the configurations and establish end-to-end connectivity. Your final configuration should match the topology diagram and addressing table. Detailed instructions are provided within the activity as well as in the PDF link below.

Activity Instructions (PDF)

Refer to
Figure
in online course

Chapter Summary

In this chapter, we introduced VLANs. VLANs are used to segment broadcast domains in a switched LAN. This improves the performance and manageability of LANs. VLANs provides network administrators flexible control over traffic associated with devices in the LAN.

Refer to
Figure
in online course

There are several types of VLANs: a default VLAN, a management VLAN, native VLANs, user/data VLANs, and voice VLANs.

VLAN trunks facilitate inter-switch communication with multiple VLANs. IEEE 802.1Q frame tagging enables differentiation between Ethernet frames associated with distinct VLANs as they traverse common trunk links.

Refer to **Packet Tracer Activity** for this chapter

We discussed the configuration, verification, and troubleshooting of VLANs and trunks using the Cisco IOS CLI.

In this activity, you will connect and completely configure the Chapter 3 topology, including adding and connecting devices, and configuring security and VLANs. Detailed instructions are provided within the activity as well as in the PDF link below.

Activity Instructions (PDF)

Go to
the online course
to take the quiz.

Chapter Quiz

Take the chapter quiz to test your knowledge.

Your Chapter Notes

CHAPTER 4

VTP

Introduction

Refer to
Figure
in online course

As the size of the network for a small- or medium-sized business grows, the management involved in maintaining the network grows. In the previous chapter, you learned how to create and manage VLANs and trunks using Cisco IOS commands. The focus was on managing VLAN information on a single switch. But what if you have many switches to manage? How will you manage the VLAN database across many switches? In this chapter, you will explore how you can use the VLAN Trunking Protocol (VTP) of Cisco Catalyst switches to simplify management of the VLAN database across multiple switches.

4.1 VTP Concepts

4.1.1 What is VTP?

Refer to
Figure
in online course

The VLAN Management Challenge

As the number of switches increases on a small- or medium-sized business network, the overall administration required to manage VLANs and trunks in a network becomes a challenge.

Click Play to view an animation of the VLAN management challenge.

Small Network VLAN Management

In the animation, the figure shows a network manager adding a new VLAN, VLAN30. The network manager needs to update the three trunks to allow VLANs 10, 20, 30, and 99. Recall that a common error is forgetting to update the allowed list of VLANs on trunks.

Click the Larger Network button in the figure.

Larger Network VLAN Management

When you consider the larger network in the figure, the VLAN management challenge becomes clear. After you have manually updated this network a few times, you may want to know if there is a way for the switches to learn what the VLANs and trunks are so that you do not have to manually configure them. You are ready to learn about VLAN trunking protocol (VTP).

Refer to
Figure
in online course

What is VTP?

VTP allows a network manager to configure a switch so that it will propagate VLAN configurations to other switches in the network. The switch can be configured in the role of a VTP server or a VTP client. VTP only learns about normal-range VLANs (VLAN IDs 1 to 1005). Extended-range VLANs (IDs greater than 1005) are not supported by VTP.

Click Play in the figure to view an animation of an overview of how VTP works.

VTP Overview

VTP allows a network manager to makes changes on a switch that is configured as a VTP server. Basically, the VTP server distributes and synchronizes VLAN information to VTP-enabled switches throughout the switched network, which minimizes the problems caused by incorrect configurations and configuration inconsistencies. VTP stores VLAN configurations in the VLAN database called vlan.dat.

Click the Two Switches button in the figure.

Two Switches

Click Play in the figure to view an animation on the basic VTP interaction between a VTP server and a VTP client.

In the figure, a trunk link is added between switch S1, a VTP server, and S2, a VTP client. After a trunk is established between the two switches, VTP advertisements are exchanged between the switches. Both the server and client leverage advertisements from one another to ensure each has an accurate record of VLAN information. VTP advertisements will not be exchanged if the trunk between the switches is inactive. The details on how VTP works is explained in the rest of this chapter.

Refer to
Figure
in online course

Benefits of VTP

You have learned that VTP maintains VLAN configuration consistency by managing the addition, deletion, and renaming of VLANs across multiple Cisco switches in a network. VTP offers a number of benefits for network managers, as shown in the figure.

Refer to
Figure
in online course

VTP Components

There are number of key components that you need to be familiar with when learning about VTP. Here is a brief description of the components, which will be further explained as you go through the chapter.

- *VTP Domain-* Consists of one or more interconnected switches. All switches in a domain share VLAN configuration details using VTP advertisements. A router or Layer 3 switch defines the boundary of each domain.

- *VTP Advertisements-* VTP uses a hierarchy of advertisements to distribute and synchronize VLAN configurations across the network.

- *VTP Modes-* A switch can be configured in one of three modes: server, client, or transparent.

- *VTP Server-* VTP servers advertise the VTP domain VLAN information to other VTP-enabled switches in the same VTP domain. VTP servers store the VLAN information for the entire domain in NVRAM. The server is where VLANs can be created, deleted, or renamed for the domain.

- *VTP Client-* VTP clients function the same way as VTP servers, but you cannot create, change, or delete VLANs on a VTP client. A VTP client only stores the VLAN information for the entire domain while the switch is on. A switch reset deletes the VLAN information. You must configure VTP client mode on a switch.

- *VTP Transparent-* Transparent switches forward VTP advertisements to VTP clients and VTP servers. Transparent switches do not participate in VTP. VLANs that are created, renamed, or deleted on transparent switches are local to that switch only.

- *VTP Pruning-* VTP pruning increases network available bandwidth by restricting flooded traffic to those trunk links that the traffic must use to reach the destination devices. Without

VTP pruning, a switch floods broadcast, multicast, and unknown unicast traffic across all trunk links within a VTP domain even though receiving switches might discard them.

Roll over the key VTP components in the figure to see where they are in the network.

Refer to **Figure** in online course

Refer to **Figure** in online course

4.2 VTP Operation

4.2.1 Default VTP Configuration

In CCNA Exploration: Network Fundamentals, you learned that a Cisco switch comes from the factory with default settings. The default VTP settings are shown in the figure. The benefit of VTP is that it automatically distributes and synchronizes domain and VLAN configurations across the network. However, this benefit comes with a cost, you can only add switches that are in their default VTP configuration. If you add a VTP-enabled switch that is configured with settings that supersede existing network VTP configurations, changes that are difficult to fix are automatically propagated throughout the network. So make sure that you only add switches that are in their default VTP configuration. You will learn how to add switches to a VTP network later in this chapter.

VTP Versions

VTP has three versions, 1, 2, and 3. Only one VTP version is allowed in a VTP domain. The default is VTP version 1. A Cisco 2960 switch supports VTP version 2, but it is disabled. A discussion of VTP versions is beyond the scope of this course.

Click the Switch Output button in the figure to see the default VTP settings on switch S1.

Displaying the VTP Status

The figure shows how to view the VTP settings for a Cisco 2960 switch, S1. The Cisco IOS command **show VTP status** displays the VTP status. The output shows that switch S1 is in VTP server mode by default and that there is no VTP domain name assigned. The output also shows that the maximum VTP version available for the switch is version 2, and that VTP version 2 is disabled. You will use the **show VTP status** command frequently as you configure and manage VTP on a network. The following briefly describes the show VTP status parameters:

- *VTP Version-* Displays the VTP version the switch is capable of running. By default, the switch implements version 1, but can be set to version 2.
- *Configuration Revision-* Current configuration revision number on this switch. You will learn more about revisions numbers in this chapter.
- *Maximum VLANs Supported Locally-* Maximum number of VLANs supported locally.
- *Number of Existing VLANs-* Number of existing VLANs.
- *VTP Operating Mode-* Can be server, client, or transparent.
- *VTP Domain Name-* Name that identifies the administrative domain for the switch.
- *VTP Pruning Mode-* Displays whether pruning is enabled or disabled.
- *VTP V2 Mode-* Displays if VTP version 2 mode is enabled. VTP version 2 is disabled by default.
- *VTP Traps Generation-* Displays whether VTP traps are sent to a network management station.
- *MD5 Digest-* A 16-byte *checksum* of the VTP configuration.

■ *Configuration Last Modified-* Date and time of the last configuration modification. Displays the IP address of the switch that caused the configuration change to the database.

4.2.2 VTP Domains

Refer to
Figure
in online course

VTP Domains

VTP allows you to separate your network into smaller management domains to help reduce VLAN management. An additional benefit of configuring VTP domains is that it limits the extent to which configuration changes are propagated in the network if an error occurs. The figure shows a network with two VTP domains, cisco2 and cisco3. In this chapter, the three switches, S1, S2, and S3, will be configured for VTP.

A VTP domain consists of one switch or several interconnected switches sharing the same VTP domain name. Later in this chapter, you will learn how VTP-enabled switches acquire a common domain name. A switch can be a member of only one VTP domain at a time. Until the VTP domain name is specified you cannot create or modify VLANs on a VTP server, and VLAN information is not propagated over the network.

Click the Switch Output button in the figure to see switch S4 output.

Refer to
Figure
in online course

VTP Domain Name Propagation

For a VTP server or client switch to participate in a VTP-enabled network, it must be a part of the same domain. When switches are in different VTP domains, they do not exchange VTP messages. A VTP server propagates the VTP domain name to all switches for you. Domain name propagation uses three VTP components: servers, clients, and advertisements.

Click Play in the figure to see how a VTP server propagates the VTP domain name in a network.

The network in the figure shows three switches, S1, S2, and S3, in their default VTP configuration. They are configured as VTP servers. VTP domain names have not been configured on any of the switches.

The network manager configures the VTP domain name as **cisco1** on the VTP server switch S1. The VTP server sends out a VTP advertisement with the new domain name embedded inside. The S2 and S3 VTP server switches update their VTP configuration to the new domain name.

Note: Cisco recommends that access to the domain name configuration functions be protected by a password. The details of password configuration will be presented later in the course.

How does the domain name get placed into a VTP advertisement? What information is exchanged between VTP-enabled switches? In the next topic, you will learn about the details of VTP advertisements and find answers to these questions.

4.2.3 VTP Advertising

Refer to
Figure
in online course

VTP Frame Structure

VTP advertisements (or messages) distribute VTP domain name and VLAN configuration changes to VTP-enabled switches. In this topic, you will learn about the VTP frame structure and how the three types of advertisements enable VTP to distribute and synchronize VLAN configurations throughout the network.

Click the Overview button in the figure and then click Play to view an animation on the structure of a VTP frame.

VTP Frame *Encapsulation*

A VTP frame consists of a header field and a message field. The VTP information is inserted into the data field of an Ethernet frame. The Ethernet frame is then encapsulated as a 802.1Q trunk frame (or ISL frame). Each switch in the domain sends periodic advertisements out each trunk port to a reserved *multicast address*. These advertisements are received by neighboring switches, which update their VTP and VLAN configurations as necessary.

Click the VTP Frame Details button in the figure.

VTP Frame Details

In the figure, you can see the VTP frame structure in more detail. Keep in mind that a VTP frame encapsulated as an 802.1Q frame is not static. The contents of the VTP message determines which fields are present. The receiving VTP-enabled switch looks for specific fields and values in the 802.1Q frame to know what to process. The following key fields are present when a VTP frame is encapsulated as an 802.1Q frame:

Destination MAC address- This address is set to 01-00-0C-CC-CC-CC, which is the reserved multicast address for all VTP messages.

LLC field- Logical link control (*LLC*) field contains a destination service access point (*DSAP*) and a source service access point (*SSAP*) set to the value of AA.

SNAP field- Subnetwork Access Protocol (*SNAP*) field has an OUI set to AAAA and type set to 2003.

VTP header field- The contents vary depending on the VTP message type-summary, subset, or request, but it always contains these VTP fields:

- *Domain name*- Identifies the administrative domain for the switch.

- *Domain name length*- Length of the domain name.

- *Version*- Set to either VTP 1, VTP 2, or VTP 3. The Cisco 2960 switch only supports VTP 1 and VTP 2.

- *Configuration revision number*- The current configuration revision number on this switch.

VTP message field- Varies depending on the message type.

Click the VTP Message Contents button in the figure.

VTP Message Contents

VTP frames contain the following fixed-length global domain information:

- VTP domain name

- Identity of the switch sending the message, and the time it was sent

- MD5 digest VLAN configuration, including maximum transmission unit (*MTU*) size for each VLAN

- Frame format: ISL or 802.1Q

VTP frames contain the following information for each configured VLAN:

- VLAN IDs (IEEE 802.1Q)

- VLAN name

- VLAN type

- VLAN state

- Additional VLAN configuration information specific to the VLAN type

Note: A VTP frame is encapsulated in an 802.1Q Ethernet frame. The entire 802.1Q Ethernet frame is the VTP advertisement often called a VTP message. Often the terms frame, advertisement, and message are used interchangeably.

Refer to
Figure
in online course

VTP Revision Number

The configuration revision number is a 32-bit number that indicates the level of revision for a VTP frame. The default configuration number for a switch is zero. Each time a VLAN is added or removed, the configuration revision number is incremented. Each VTP device tracks the VTP configuration revision number that is assigned to it.

Note: A VTP domain name change does not increment the revision number. Instead, it resets the revision number to zero.

The configuration revision number determines whether the configuration information received from another VTP-enabled switch is more recent than the version stored on the switch. The figure shows a network manager adding three VLANs to switch S1.

Click the Switch Output button in the figure to see how the revision number has been changed.

The highlighted area shows that the revision number on switch S1 is 3, the number of VLANs is up to eight, because three VLANs have been added to the five default VLANs.

The revision number plays an important and complex role in enabling VTP to distribute and synchronize VTP domain and VLAN configuration information. To comprehend what the revision number does, you first need to learn about the three types of VTP advertisements and the three VTP modes.

Refer to
Figure
in online course

VTP Advertisements

Summary Advertisements

The summary advertisement contains the VTP domain name, the current revision number, and other VTP configuration details.

Summary advertisements are sent:

- Every 5 minutes by a VTP server or client to inform neighboring VTP-enabled switches of the current VTP configuration revision number for its VTP domain

- Immediately after a configuration has been made

Click the Summary button in the figure and then click Play to view an animation on the summary VTP advertisements.

Subset Advertisements

A subset advertisement contains VLAN information. Changes that trigger the subset advertisement include:

- Creating or deleting a VLAN

- Suspending or activating a VLAN

- Changing the name of a VLAN

- Changing the MTU of a VLAN

It may take multiple subset advertisements to fully update the VLAN information.

Click the Subset button in the figure and then click Play to view an animation on the subset VTP advertisements.

Request Advertisements

When a request advertisement is sent to a VTP server in the same VTP domain, the VTP server responds by sending a summary advertisement and then a subset advertisement.

Request advertisements are sent if:

- The VTP domain name has been changed
- The switch receives a summary advertisement with a higher configuration revision number than its own
- A subset advertisement message is missed for some reason
- The switch has been reset

Click the Request button in the figure and then click Play to view an animation on the request VTP advertisements.

Refer to **Figure** in online course

VTP Advertisements Details

VTP uses advertisements to distribute and synchronize information about domains and VLAN configurations. There are three main VTP advertisements.

Each type of VTP advertisement sends information about several parameters used by VTP. A description of the fields in each of the VTP advertisements are presented.

Click the Summary Details button in the figure.

Summary Advertisements

Summary advertisements comprise the majority of VTP advertisement traffic. Roll over the fields in the summary advertisement to view the descriptions.

Roll over the fields in the summary advertisement to view the descriptions.

Click the Subset Details button in the figure.

Subset Advertisements

The fields found in a subset advertisement are briefly described. The fields in the VLAN-info are not described.

Roll over the fields in the subset advertisement to view the descriptions.

Click the Request Details button in the figure.

Request Advertisements

The fields found in a request advertisement are briefly described.

Roll over the fields in the request advertisement to view the descriptions.

4.2.4 VTP Modes

Refer to **Figure** in online course

VTP Modes Overview

A Cisco switch, configured with Cisco IOS software, can be configured in either server, client, or transparent mode. These modes differ in how they are used to manage and advertise VTP domains and VLANs.

Server Mode

In server mode, you can create, modify, and delete VLANs for the entire VTP domain. VTP server mode is the default mode for a Cisco switch. VTP servers advertise their VLAN configurations to other switches in the same VTP domain and synchronize their VLAN configurations with other switches based on advertisements received over trunk links. VTP servers keep track of updates through a configuration revision number. Other switches in the same VTP domain compare their configuration revision number with the revision number received from a VTP server to see if they need to synchronize their VLAN database.

Client Mode

If a switch is in client mode, you cannot create, change, or delete VLANs. In addition, the VLAN configuration information that a VTP client switch receives from a VTP server switch is stored in a VLAN database, not in NVRAM. Consequently, VTP clients require less memory than VTP servers. When a VTP client is shut down and restarted, it sends a request advertisement to a VTP server for updated VLAN configuration information.

Switches configured as VTP clients are more typically found in larger networks, because in a network consisting of many hundreds of switches, it is harder to coordinate network upgrades. Often there are many network administrators working at different times of the day. Having only a few switches that are physically able to maintain VLAN configurations makes it easier to control VLAN upgrades and to track which network administrators performed them.

For large networks, having client switches is also more cost-effective. By default, all switches are configured to be VTP servers. This configuration is suitable for small scale networks in which the size of the VLAN information is small and the information is easily stored in NVRAM on the switches. In a large network of many hundreds of switches, the network administrator must decide if the cost of purchasing switches with enough NVRAM to store the duplicate VLAN information is too much. A cost-conscious network administrator could choose to configure a few well-equipped switches as VTP servers, and then use switches with less memory as VTP clients. Although a discussion of network redundancy is beyond the scope of this course, know that the number of VTP servers should be chosen to provide the degree of redundancy that is desired in the network.

Transparent Mode

Switches configured in transparent mode forward VTP advertisements that they receive on trunk ports to other switches in the network. VTP transparent mode switches do not advertise their VLAN configuration and do not synchronize their VLAN configuration with any other switch. Configure a switch in VTP transparent mode when you have VLAN configurations that have local significance and should not be shared with the rest of the network.

In transparent mode, VLAN configurations are saved in NVRAM (but not advertised to other switches), so the configuration is available after a switch reload. This means that when a VTP transparent mode switch reboots, it does not revert to a default VTP server mode, but remains in VTP transparent mode.

Refer to
Figure
in online course

VTP in Action

You will now see how the various VTP features come together to distribute and synchronize domain and VLAN configurations in a VTP-enabled network. The animation starts with three new switches, S1, S2, and S3, configured with their factory default settings, and finishes with all three switches configured and participating in a VTP-enabled network.

You can pause and rewind the animation to reflect and review this process.

Refer to
Figure
in online course

You have seen how VTP works with three switches. This animation examines in more detail how a switch configured in VTP transparent mode supports the functionality of VTP.

Click the Play button in the figure.

You can pause and rewind the animation to reflect and review this process.

4.2.5 VTP Pruning

Refer to
Figure
in online course

VTP pruning prevents unnecessary flooding of broadcast information from one VLAN across all trunks in a VTP domain. VTP pruning permits switches to negotiate which VLANs are assigned to ports at the other end of a trunk and, hence, prune the VLANs that are not assigned to ports on the remote switch. Pruning is disabled by default. VTP pruning is enabled using the `vtp pruning` global configuration command. You need to enable pruning on only one VTP server switch in the domain. In the figure, you would enable VTP pruning on switch S1. The figure shows a network with VLAN 10 and VLAN 20 configured. Switch S3 has VLAN 20 configured, and switch S2 has VLAN 10 and VLAN 20 configured. Examine the topology in the figure and then click to see the switch configurations.

Refer to
Figure
in online course

VTP Pruning in Action

Recall that a VLAN creates an isolated broadcast domain. A switch floods broadcast, multicast, and unknown unicast traffic across all trunk links within a VTP domain. When a computer or device broadcasts on a VLAN, for example, VLAN 10 in the figure, the broadcast traffic travels across all trunk links throughout the network to all ports on all switches in VLAN 10. In the figure, switches S1, S2, and S3 all receive broadcast frames from computer PC1. The broadcast traffic from PC1 consumes bandwidth on the trunk link between all 3 switches and consumes processor time on all 3 switches. The link between switches S1 and S3 does not carry any VLAN 10 traffic, so it is a candidate for VTP pruning.

Click the Play button in the figure to see the how VLAN flood traffic is handled on a network with no VTP pruning.

VTP Pruning

Click the VTP Pruning button and then click Play to see an animation on how VLAN flood traffic is handled on a network with VTP pruning.

The flood traffic is stopped from entering the trunk connecting switches S1 and S2. VTP pruning only prunes the egress port F0/1 on switch S2.

Refer to
Figure
in online course

VTP Pruning Enabled

The figure shows a network topology that has switches S1, S2, and S3 configured with VTP pruning. When VTP pruning is enabled on a network, it reconfigures the trunk links based on which ports are configured with which VLANs.

Click the Switch S1 button in the figure.

The highlighted area shows that the trunk on port F0/1 allows VLAN 10 traffic. VTP pruning only prunes the egress port.

Click the Switch S2 button in the figure.

The highlighted area shows that the trunk on port F0/1 does not allow VLAN 10 traffic. VLAN 10 is not listed. For more details on VTP pruning, visit: http://www.cisco.com/univercd/cc/td/doc/product/lan/cat5000/rel_4_2/config/vlans.htm#xtocid798016.

Refer to
Figure
in online course

4.3 Configure VTP

4.3.1 Configuring VTP

Refer to
Figure
in online course

VTP Configuration Guidelines

Now that you are familiar with the functionality of VTP, you are ready to learn how to configure a Cisco Catalyst switch to use VTP. The topology shows the reference topology for this chapter. VTP will be configured on this topology.

Click the Table button in the figure.

VTP Server Switches

Follow these steps and associated guidelines to ensure that you configure VTP successfully:

- Confirm that all of the switches you are going to configure have been set to their default settings.

- Always reset the configuration revision number before installing a previously configured switch into a VTP domain. Not resetting the configuration revision number allows for potential disruption in the VLAN configuration across the rest of the switches in the VTP domain.

- Configure at least two VTP server switches in your network. Because only server switches can create, delete, and modify VLANs, you should make sure that you have one backup VTP server in case the primary VTP server becomes disabled. If all the switches in the network are configured in VTP client mode, you cannot create new VLANs on the network.

- Configure a VTP domain on the VTP server. Configuring the VTP domain on the first switch enables VTP to start *advertising* VLAN information. Other switches connected through trunk links receive the VTP domain information automatically through VTP advertisements.

- If there is an existing VTP domain, make sure that you match the name exactly. VTP domain names are case-sensitive.

- If you are configuring a VTP password, ensure that the same password is set on all switches in the domain that need to be able to exchange VTP information. Switches without a password or with the wrong password reject VTP advertisements.

- Ensure that all switches are configured to use the same VTP protocol version. VTP version 1 is not compatible with VTP version 2. By default, Cisco Catalyst 2960 switches run version 1 but are capable of running version 2. When the VTP version is set to version 2, all version 2 capable switches in the domain autoconfigure to use version 2 through the VTP announcement process. Any version 1-only switches cannot participate in the VTP domain after that point.

- Create the VLAN after you have enabled VTP on the VTP server. VLANs created before you enable VTP are removed. Always ensure that trunk ports are configured to interconnect switches in a VTP domain. VTP information is only exchanged on trunk ports.

VTP Client Switches

- As on the VTP server switch, confirm that the default settings are present.

- Configure VTP client mode. Recall that the switch is not in VTP client mode by default. You have to configure this mode.

- Configure trunks. VTP works over trunk links.

- Connect to a VTP server. When you connect to a VTP server or another VTP-enabled switch, it takes a few moments for the various advertisements to make their way back and forth to the VTP server.

Refer to
Figure
in online course

- Verify VTP status. Before you begin configuring the access ports, confirm that the revision mode and number of VLANs have been updated.

- Configure access ports. When a switch is in VTP client mode, you cannot add new VLANs. You can only assign access ports to existing VLANs.

Configuring VTP Step 1 - Configure the VTP Server

The next three topics will show you how to configure a VTP server and two VTP clients. Initially none of the devices are connected.

The topology highlights switch S1. You will configure this switch to be a VTP server. The commands to configure the trunk ports are provided for interface F0/1.

Click the Confirm Details button in the figure.

The output of the `show vtp status` command confirms that the switch is by default a VTP server. Since no VLANs have yet been configured, the revision number is still set to 0 and the switch does not belong to VTP domain.

If the switch was not already configured as a VTP server, you could configure it using the the `vtp mode {server}` command.

Click the Configure Domain Name button in the figure.

The domain name is configured using the the `vtp domain` *domain-name* command. In the figure, switch S1 has been configured with the domain name **cisco1**.

For security reasons, a password could be configured using the `vtp password` *password* command.

Click the Configure Version button in the figure.

Refer to
Figure
in online course

Most switches can support VTP version 1 and 2. However, the default setting for Catalyst 2960 switches is version 1. When the `vtp version 1` command is entered on the switch, it informs us that the switch is already configured to be in version 1.

Click the Add VLANs and Trunks button in the figure.

Assume that three VLANs have been configured and have been assigned VLANs names. The output in the figure is displaying the result of these changes.

You can use the **no** version of the commands.

The topology highlights switches S2 and S3. You will be shown the VTP client configuration for S2. To configure S3 as a VTP client, you will follow the same procedure.

Click the Confirm Defaults button to verify the switch status.

Before configuring a switch as a VTP client, verify its current VTP status. Once you've confirmed status, you will configure the switch to operate in VTP client mode.

Click the Enable VTP Client Mode button to see how to configure a switch for VTP client mode.

Configure VTP client mode using the following Cisco IOS command syntax:

Enter global configuration mode with the `configure terminal` command.

Configure the switch in client mode with the `vtp mode` {*client*} command.

If you need to reset the VTP configuration to the default values, you can use the **no** version of the commands.

Refer to
Figure
in online course

Click the Verify VTP Status button to see the rest of VTP client configuration.

Configuring VTP Step 3 - Confirm and Connect

After configuring the main VTP server and the VTP clients, you will connect the VTP client switch S2 to the switch S1 VTP server.

The topology highlights the trunks that will be added to this topology. In the figure, switch S2 will be connected to switch S1. Then switch S2 will be configured to support the computers, PC1 to PC3. The same procedure will be applied to switch S3, although the commands for S3 are not shown.

Confirm VTP Operation

Click the Confirm VTP Operation button in the figure.

There are two Cisco IOS commands for confirming that VTP domain and VLAN configurations have been transferred to switch S2. Use the show VTP status command to verify the following:

- Configuration revision number has been incremented to 6.

- There are now three new VLANs indicated by the existing number of VLANs showing 8.

- Domain name has been changed to cisco1.

Use the `show vtp counters` command to confirm that the advertisements took place.

Configure Access Ports

Click the Configure Access Ports button in the figure.

The top highlight in the screen output confirms that the switch S2 is in VTP client mode. The task now is to configure the port F0/18 on switch S2 to be in VLAN 20. The bottom highlighted area shows the Cisco IOS command used to configure port F0/18 on switch S2 to be in VLAN 20.

4.3.2 Troubleshooting VTP Configurations

Refer to
Figure
in online course

Troubleshooting VTP Connections

You have learned how VTP can be used to simplify managing a VLAN database across multiple switches. In this topic, you will learn about common VTP configuration problems. This information, combined with your VTP configuration skills, will help you when troubleshooting VTP configuration problems.

The figure lists the common VTP configuration issues that will be explored in this topic.

Refer to
Figure
in online course

Incompatible VTP Versions

VTP versions 1 and 2 are incompatible with each other. Modern Cisco Catalyst switches, such as the 2960, are configured to use VTP version 1 by default. However, older switches may only support VTP version 1. Switches that only support version 1 cannot participate in the VTP domain along with version 2 switches. If your network contains switches that support only version 1, you need to manually configure the version 2 switches to operate in version 1 mode.

Click the VTP Version Solution button in the figure.

VTP Password Issues

When using a VTP password to control participation in the VTP domain, ensure that the password is set correctly on all switches in the VTP domain. Forgetting to set a VTP password is a very common problem. If a password is used, it must be configured on each switch in the domain. By default, a Cisco switch does not use a VTP password. The switch does not automatically set the password parameter, unlike other parameters that are set automatically when a VTP advertisement is received.

Click the VTP Password Solution button in the figure.

Refer to
Figure
in online course

Incorrect VTP Domain Name

The VTP domain name is a key parameter that is set on a switch. An improperly configured VTP domain affects VLAN synchronization between switches. As you learned earlier, if a switch receives the wrong VTP advertisement, the switch discards the message. If the discarded message contains legitimate configuration information, the switch does not synchronize its VLAN database as expected.

Click Play in the figure to see an animation of this issue.

Click the VTP Domain Solution button in the figure.

Solution

To avoid incorrectly configuring a VTP domain name, only set the VTP domain name on one VTP server switch. All other switches in the same VTP domain will accept and automatically configure their VTP domain name when they receive the first VTP summary advertisement.

Refer to
Figure
in online course

Switches Set to VTP Client Mode

It is possible to change the operating mode of all switches to VTP client. By doing so, you lose all ability to create, delete, and manage VLANs within your network environment. Because the VTP client switches do not store the VLAN information in NVRAM, they need to refresh the VLAN information after a reload.

Click Play in the figure to see an animation of this issue.

Click the Solution button in the figure.

Solution

To avoid losing all VLAN configurations in a VTP domain by accidentally reconfiguring the only VTP server in the domain as a VTP client, you can configure a second switch in the same domain as a VTP server. It is not uncommon for small networks that use VTP to have all the switches in VTP server mode. If the network is being managed by a couple of network administrators, it is unlikely that conflicting VLAN configurations will arise.

Refer to
Figure
in online course

Incorrect Revision Number

Even after you have configured the switches in your VTP domain correctly, there are other factors that can adversely affect the functionality of VTP.

Configuration Revision Number Issues

The topology in the figure is configured with VTP. There is one VTP server switch, S1, and two VTP client switches, S2 and S3.

Click the Incorrect Revision Number button in the figure to play an animation showing how the addition of a switch with a higher configuration revision number affects the rest of the switches in the VTP domain.

S4, which has been previously configured as a VTP client, is added to the network. The revision number of the switch S4 is 35, which is higher than the revision number of 17 in the existing network. S4 comes preconfigured with two VLANs, 30 and 40, that are not configured in the existing network. The existing network has VLANs 10 and 20.

When switch S4 is connected to switch S3, VTP summary advertisements announce the arrival of a VTP-enabled switch with the highest revision number in the network. The animation shows how switch S3, switch S1, and finally switch S2 all reconfigure themselves to the configuration found in switch S4. As each switch reconfigures itself with VLANs that are not supported in the network, the ports no longer forward traffic from the computers because they are configured with VLANs that no longer exist on the newly reconfigured switches.

Click the Reset Revision Number button in the figure.

Solution

The solution to the problem is to reset each switch back to an earlier configuration and then reconfigure the correct VLANs, 10 and 20, on switch S1. To prevent this problem in the first place, reset the configuration revision number on previously configured switches being added to a VTP-enabled network. The figure shows the commands needed to reset switch S4 back to the default revision number.

Click Verify Revision Number button in the figure to see that switch S4 has had its revision number reset.

4.3.3 Managing VLANs on a VTP Server

Refer to
Figure
in online course

Managing VLANs on a VTP Server

You have learned about VTP and how it can be used to simplify managing VLANs in a VTP-enabled network. Consider the topology in the figure. When a new VLAN, for example, VLAN 10, is added to the network, the network manager adds the VLAN to the VTP server, switch S1 in the figure. As you know, VTP takes care of propagating the VLAN configuration details to the rest of the network. It does not have any effect on which ports are configured in VLAN 10 on switches S1, S2, and S3.

Click the Configure New VLANs and Ports button in the figure.

The figure displays the commands used to configure VLAN 10 and the port F0/11 on switch S1. The commands to configure the correct ports for switches S2 and S3 are not shown.

After you have configured the new VLAN on switch S1 and configured the ports on switches S1, S2, and S3 to support the new VLAN, confirm that VTP updated the VLAN database on switches S2 and S3.

Click the `show vtp status` button in the figure.

The output of the command is used to verify the configuration on switch S2. The verification for S3 is not shown.

Click the `show interfaces trunk` button in the figure.

The output confirms that the new VLAN has been added to F0/1 on switch S2. The highlighted area shows that VLAN 10 is now active in the VTP management domain.

Refer to **Packet
Tracer Activity**
for this chapter

In this activity, you will practice configuring VTP. When Packet Tracer first opens, the switches already contain a partial configuration.

Detailed instructions are provided within the activity as well as in the PDF link below.

Activity Instructions (PDF)

4.4 Chapter Labs

4.4.1 Basic VTP Configuration

Refer to **Lab Activity** for this chapter

Imagine a network with 50 switches with a total of 12 identical VLANs each. If you had to manually type in the commands to each switch, it would be a huge undertaking. It would be so much easier if you could configure those 12 VLANs once, and then allow those VLANs to be propagated automatically to the other 49 switches. VTP configuration makes this possible.

Refer to **Packet Tracer Activity** for this chapter

This activity is a variation of Lab 4.4.1. Packet Tracer may not support all the tasks specified in the hands-on lab. This activity should not be considered equivalent to completing the hands-on lab. Packet Tracer is not a substitute for a hands-on lab experience with real equipment.

Detailed instructions are provided within the activity as well as in the PDF link below.

Activity Instructions (PDF)

4.4.2 VTP Configuration Challenge

Refer to **Lab Activity** for this chapter

How much of the basics of VTP configuration do you remember? Let's see how much you can configure from memory having completed the Basic VTP lab. Be sure to check your work with the answer key that your instructor will provide.

Refer to **Packet Tracer Activity** for this chapter

This activity is a variation of Lab 4.4.2. Packet Tracer may not support all the tasks specified in the hands-on lab. This activity should not be considered equivalent to completing the hands-on lab. Packet Tracer is not a substitute for a hands-on lab experience with real equipment.

Detailed instructions are provided within the activity as well as in the PDF link below.

Activity Instructions (PDF)

4.4.3 Troubleshooting VTP Configuration

Refer to **Lab Activity** for this chapter

In this lab, you will use the supplied scripts to configure S1 as a VTP server, and S2 and S3 as VTP clients. However, there are a number of errors in this configuration that you must troubleshoot and correct before end-to-end connectivity within the VLAN is restored.

You will have successfully resolved all errors when the same VLANs are configured on all three switches, and you can ping between any two hosts in the same VLAN or between any two switches.

Refer to **Packet Tracer Activity** for this chapter

This activity is a variation of Lab 4.4.3. Packet Tracer may not support all the tasks specified in the hands-on lab. This activity should not be considered equivalent to completing the hands-on lab. Packet Tracer is not a substitute for a hands-on lab experience with real equipment.

Detailed instructions are provided within the activity as well as in the PDF link below.

Activity Instructions (PDF)

Refer to
Figure
in online course

Chapter Summary

In this chapter, we discussed the VLAN trunking protocol. VTP is a Cisco-proprietary protocol used to exchange VLAN information across trunk links, reducing VLAN administration and configuration errors. VTP allows you to create a VLAN once within a VTP domain and have that VLAN propagated to all other switches in the VTP domain.

Refer to
Figure
in online course

There are three VTP operating modes: server, client, and transparent. VTP client mode switches are more prevalent in large networks, where there definition reduces the administration of VLAN information. In small networks, network managers can more easily keep track of network changes, so switches are often left in the default VTP server mode.

Refer to **Packet
Tracer Activity**
for this chapter

VTP pruning limits the unnecessary propagation of VLAN traffic across a LAN. VTP determines which trunk ports forward which VLAN traffic. VTP pruning improves overall network performance by restricting the unnecessary flooding of traffic across trunk links. Pruning only permits VLAN traffic for VLANs that are assigned to some switch port of a switch on the other end of a trunk link. By reducing the total amount of flooded traffic on the network, bandwidth is freed up for other network traffic.

We discussed VTP configuration and preventative measures to take to avoid common problematic VTP issues.

In this activity, you will configure switches including basic configuration, port security, trunking and VLANs. You will use VTP to advertise the VLAN configurations to other switches.

Activity Instructions (PDF)

Go to
the online course
to take the quiz.

Chapter Quiz

Take the chapter quiz to test your knowledge.

Your Chapter Notes

Chapter Introduction

Refer to
Figure
in online course

It is clear that computer networks are critical components of most small- and medium-sized businesses. Consequently IT administrators have to implement redundancy in their hierarchical networks. However adding extra links to switches and routers in the network introduces traffic loops that need to be managed in a dynamic way; when a switch connection is lost, another link needs to quickly take its place without introducing new traffic *loops*. In this chapter you will learn how spanning-tree protocol (*STP*) prevents loop issues in the network and how STP has evolved into a protocol that rapidly calculates which ports should be blocked so that a VLAN-based network is kept free of traffic loops.

5.1 Redundant Layer 2 Topologies

5.1.1 Redundancy

Refer to
Figure
in online course

Redundancy in a hierarchical network

The hierarchical design model was introduced in Chapter 1. The hierarchical design model addresses issues found in the flat model network topologies. One of the issues is redundancy. Layer 2 redundancy improves the availability of the network by implementing alternate network paths by adding equipment and cabling. Having multiple paths for data to traverse the network allows for a single path to be disrupted without impacting the connectivity of devices on the network.

As you can see in the animation:

Step 1. PC1 is communicating with PC4 over a redundantly configured network topology.

Step 2. When the network link between switch S1 and switch S2 is disrupted, the path between PC1 and PC4 is automatically adjusted to compensate for the disruption.

Step 3. When the network connection between S1 and S2 is restored, the path is then readjusted to route traffic directly from S2 through S1 to get to PC4.

As businesses become increasingly dependent on the network, the availability of the network infrastructure becomes a critical business concern that must be addressed. Redundancy is the solution for achieving the necessary availability.

Refer to
Figure
in online course

Examine a redundant design

In a hierarchical design, redundancy is achieved at the distribution and core layers through additional hardware and alternate paths through the additional hardware.

Click the Starting Point Access to Distribution Layer button in the figure.

In this example, there is a hierarchical network with access, distribution, and core layers. Each access layer switch is connected to two different distribution layer switches. Also, each distribution layer switch is connected to both core layer switches. By having multiple paths to get between

PC1 and PC4, there is redundancy that can accommodate a single point of failure between the access and distribution layer, and between the distribution and core layer.

STP is enabled on all switches. STP is the topic of this chapter and will be explained at length. For now, notice that STP has placed some switch ports in forwarding state and other switch ports in blocking state. This is to prevent loops in the Layer 2 network. STP will only use a redundant link if there is a failure on the primary link.

In the example, PC1 can communicate with PC4 over the identified path.

Click the Path Failure Access to Distribution Layer button in the figure.

The link between switch S1 and switch D1 has been disrupted, preventing the data from PC1 that is destined for PC4 from reaching switch D1 on its original path. However, because switch S1 has a second path to PC4 through switch D2, the path is updated and the data is able to reach PC4.

Click the Path Failure Distribution to Core Layer button in the figure.

The link between switch D1 and switch C2 has been disrupted, preventing the data from PC1 that is destined for PC4 from reaching switch C2 on its original path. However, because switch D1 has a second path to PC4 through switch C1, the path is updated and the data is able to reach PC4.

Click the Switch Failure Distribution Layer button in the figure.

Switch D1 has now failed preventing the data from PC1, destined for PC4 from reaching switch C2 on its original path. However, since switch S1 has a second path to PC4 through switch D2, the path is updated and the data is able to reach PC4.

Click the Switch Failure Core Layer button in the figure.

Switch C2 has now failed, preventing the data from PC1 that is destined for PC4 from reaching switch D4 on its original path. However, because switch D1 has a second path to PC4 through switch C1, the path is updated and the data is able to reach PC4.

Redundancy provides a lot of flexibility in path choices on a network, allowing data to be transmitted regardless of a single path or device failing in the distribution or core layers. Redundancy does have some complications that need to be addressed before it can be safely deployed on a hierarchical network.

5.1.2   Issues with Redundancy

Layer 2 Loops

Refer to
Figure
in online course

Redundancy is an important part of the hierarchical design. Although it is important for availability, there are some considerations that need to be addressed before redundancy is even possible on a network.

When multiple paths exist between two devices on the network and STP has been disabled on those switches, a Layer 2 loop can occur. If STP is enabled on these switches, which is the default, a Layer 2 loop would not occur.

Ethernet frames do not have a time to live (*TTL*) like IP packets traversing routers. As a result, if they are not terminated properly on a switched network, they continue to bounce from switch to switch endlessly or until a link is disrupted and breaks the loop.

Broadcast frames are forwarded out all switch ports, except the originating port. This ensures that all devices in the broadcast domain are able to receive the frame. If there is more than one path for the frame to be forwarded out, it can result in an endless loop.

Click the Play button in the figure to start the animation.

In the animation:

Step 1. PC1 sends out a broadcast frame to switch S2.

Step 2. When S2 receives the broadcast frame it updates its MAC address table to record that PC1 is available on port F0/11.

Step 3. Because it is a broadcast frame, S2 forwards the frame out all switch ports, including Trunk1 and Trunk2.

Step 4. When the broadcast frame arrives at switches S3 and S1, they update their MAC address tables to indicate that PC1 is available out port F0/1 on S1 and port F0/2 on S3.

Step 5. Because it is a broadcast frame, S3 and S1 forward it out all switch ports, except the one they received the frame on.

Step 6. S3 then sends the frame to S1 and vice versa. Each switch updates its MAC address table with the incorrect port for PC1.

Step 7. Each switch again forwards the broadcast frame out all of its ports, except the one it came in on, resulting in both switches forwarding the frame to S2.

Step 8. When S2 receives the broadcast frames from S3 and S1, the MAC address table is updated once again, this time with the last entry received from the other two switches.

This process repeats over and over again until the loop is broken by physically disconnecting the connections causing the loop, or turning the power off on one of the switches in the loop.

Loops result in high CPU load on all switches caught in the loop. Because the same frames are constantly being forwarded back and forth between all switches in the loop, the CPU of the switch ends up having to process a lot of data. This slows down performance on the switch when legitimate traffic arrives.

A host caught in a network loop is not accessible to other hosts on the network. Because the MAC address table is constantly changing with the updates from the broadcast frames, the switch does not know which port to forward the unicast frames out to reach the final destination. The unicast frames end up looping around the network as well. As more and more frames end up looping on the network, a broadcast storm occurs.

Refer to
Figure
in online course

Broadcast Storms

A broadcast storm occurs when there are so many broadcast frames caught in a Layer 2 loop that all available bandwidth is consumed. Consequently, no bandwidth is available bandwidth for legitimate traffic, and the network becomes unavailable for data communication.

A broadcast storm is inevitable on a looped network. As more devices send broadcasts out on the network, more and more traffic gets caught in the loop, eventually creating a broadcast storm that causes the network to fail.

There are other consequences for broadcast storms. Because broadcast traffic is forwarded out every port on a switch, all connected devices have to process all broadcast traffic that is being flooded endlessly around the looped network. This can cause the end device to malfunction because of the high processing requirements for sustaining such a high traffic load on the *network interface card*.

Click the Play button in the figure to start the animation.

In the animation:

Step 1. PC1 sends a broadcast frame out onto the looped network.

Step 2. The broadcast frame ends up looping between all the interconnected switches on the network.

Step 3. PC4 also sends a broadcast frame out on to the looped network.

Step 4. The PC4 broadcast frame also gets caught in the loop and ends up looping between all the interconnected switches, just like the PC1 broadcast frame.

Step 5. As more and more broadcast frames are sent out onto the network by other devices, more traffic gets caught in the loop, eventually resulting in a broadcast storm.

Step 6. When the network is fully saturated with broadcast traffic looping between the switches, new traffic is discarded by the switch because it is unable to process it.

Because devices connected to a network are constantly sending out broadcast frames, such as ARP requests, a broadcast storm can develop in seconds. As a result, when a loop is created, the network quickly becomes disabled.

Refer to **Figure** in online course

Duplicate Unicast Frames

Broadcast frames are not the only type of frames that are affected by loops. Unicast frames sent onto a looped network can result in duplicate frames arriving at the destination device.

Click the Play button in the figure to start the animation.

In the animation:

Step 1. PC1 sends a unicast frame destined for PC4.

Step 2. Switch S2 does not have an entry for PC4 in its MAC table, so it floods the unicast frame out all switch ports in an attempt to find PC4.

Step 3. The frame arrives at switches S1 and S3.

Step 4. S1 does have a MAC address entry for PC4, so it forwards the frame out to PC4.

Step 5. S3 also has an entry in its MAC address table for PC4, so it forwards the unicast frame out Trunk3 to S1.

Step 6. S1 receives the duplicate frame and once again forwards the frame out to PC4.

Step 7. PC4 has now received the same frame twice.

Most upper layer protocols are not designed to recognize or cope with duplicate transmissions. In general, protocols that make use of a sequence-numbering mechanism assume that the transmission has failed and that the *sequence number* has recycled for another communication session. Other protocols attempt to hand the duplicate transmission to the appropriate upper layer protocol to be processed and possibly discarded.

Fortunately, switches are capable of detecting loops on a network. The Spanning Tree Protocol (STP) eliminates these loop issues. You will learn about STP in the next section.

5.1.3 Real-world Redundancy Issues

Refer to **Figure** in online course

Loops in the Wiring Closet

Redundancy is an important component of a highly available hierarchical network topology, but loops can arise as a result of the multiple paths configured on the network. You can prevent loops using the Spanning Tree Protocol (STP). However, if STP has not been implemented in preparation for a redundant topology, loops can occur unexpectedly.

Network wiring for small to medium-sized businesses can get very confusing. Network cables between access layer switches, located in the wiring closets, disappear into the walls, floors, and ceilings where they are run back to the distribution layer switches on the network. If the network cables are not properly labeled when they are terminated in the *patch panel* in the wiring closet, it is difficult to determine where the destination is for the patch panel port on the network. Network loops that are a result of accidental duplicate connections in the wiring closets are a common occurrence.

Click the Loop from two connections to the same switch button in the figure.

The example displays a loop that occurs if two connections from the same switch are connected to another switch. The loop is localized to the switches that are interconnected. However, the loop affects the rest of the network because of high broadcast forwarding that reaches all the other switches on the network. The impact on the other switches may not be enough to disrupt legitimate communications, but it could noticeably affect the overall performance of the other switches.

This type of loop is common in the wiring closet. It happens when an administrator mistakenly connects a cable to the same switch it is already connected to. This usually occurs when network cables are not labeled or mislabeled or when the administrator has not taken the time to verify where the cables are connected.

There is an exception to this problem. An EtherChannel is a grouping of Ethernet ports on a switch that act as a single logical network connection. Because the switch treats the ports configured for the EtherChannel as a single network link, loops are not possible. Configuring EtherChannels is beyond the scope of this course. If you would like to learn more about EtherChannels, visit: http://www.cisco.com/en/US/tech/tk389/tk213/technologies_white_paper09186a0080092944.shtml

Click the Loop from a connection to a second switch on the same network button in the figure.

The example displays a loop that occurs if a switch is connected to two different switches on a network that are both also interconnected. The impact of this type of loop is much greater because it affects more switches directly.

Loops in the Cubicles

Because of insufficient network data connections, some end users have a personal hub or switch located in their working environment. Rather than incur the costs of running additional network data connections to the workspace, a simple hub or switch is connected to an existing network data connection allowing all devices connected to the personal hub or switch to gain access to the network.

Wiring closets are typically secured to prevent unauthorized access, so often the network administrator is the only one who has full control over how and what devices are connected to the network. Unlike the wiring closet, the administrator is not in control of how personal hubs and switches are being used or connected, so the end user can accidentally interconnect the switches or hubs.

Click the Loop from two interconnected hubs button in the figure.

In the example, the two user hubs are interconnected resulting in a network loop. The loop disrupts communication between all devices connected to switch S1.

In this activity, you will examine how STP operates by default. Switches have been added to the network "out of the box." Cisco switches can be plugged in and connected to a network without any additional action by the network administrator. Therefore, these switches are not yet configured.

Detailed instructions are provided within the activity as well as in the PDF link below.

Activity Instructions (PDF)

5.2 Introduction to STP

5.2.1 The Spanning Tree Algorithm

Refer to
Figure
in online course

STP Topology

Redundancy increases the availability of the network topology by protecting the network from a single point of failure, such as a failed network cable or switch. When redundancy is introduced into a Layer 2 design, loops and duplicate frames can occur. Loops and duplicate frames can have severe consequences on a network. The Spanning Tree Protocol (STP) was developed to address these issues.

STP ensures that there is only one logical path between all destinations on the network by intentionally *blocking* redundant paths that could cause a loop. A port is considered blocked when network traffic is prevented from entering or leaving that port. This does not include bridge protocol data unit (*BPDU*) frames that are used by STP to prevent loops. You will learn more about STP BPDU frames later in the chapter. Blocking the redundant paths is critical to preventing loops on the network. The physical paths still exist to provide redundancy, but these paths are disabled to prevent the loops from occurring. If the path is ever needed to compensate for a network cable or switch failure, STP recalculates the paths and unblocks the necessary ports to allow the redundant path to become active.

Click the Play button in the figure to start the animation.

In the example, all switches have STP enabled:

Step 1. PC1 sends a broadcast out onto the network.

Step 2. Switch S3 is configured with STP and has set the port for Trunk2 to a blocking state. The blocking state prevents ports from being used to forward switch traffic, preventing a loop from occurring. Switch S2 forwards a broadcast frame out all switch ports, except the originating port from PC1, and the port on Trunk2, which leads to the blocked port on S3.

Step 3. Switch S1 receives the broadcast frame and forwards it out all of its switch ports, where it reaches PC4 and S3. S3 does not forward the frame back to S2 over Trunk2 because of the blocked port. The Layer 2 loop is prevented.

Click the STP compensates for network failure button in the figure and click Play to start the animation.

In this example:

Step 1. PC1 sends a broadcast out onto the network.

Step 2. The broadcast is then forwarded around the network, just as in the previous animation.

Step 3. The trunk link between switch S2 and switch S1 fails, resulting in the previous path being disrupted.

Step 4. Switch S3 unblocks the previously blocked port for Trunk2 and allows the broadcast traffic to traverse the alternate path around the network, permitting communication to continue. If this link comes back up, STP reconverges and the port on S3 is again blocked.

STP prevents loops from occurring by configuring a loop-free path through the network using strategically placed blocking state ports. The switches running STP are able to compensate for failures by dynamically unblocking the previously blocked ports and permitting traffic to traverse the alternate paths. The next topic describes how STP accomplishes this process automatically.

Refer to
Figure
in online course

STP Algorithm

STP uses the Spanning Tree Algorithm (*STA*) to determine which switch ports on a network need to be configured for blocking to prevent loops from occurring. The STA designates a single switch as the *root bridge* and uses it as the reference point for all path calculations. In the figure the root bridge, switch S1, is chosen through an election process. All switches participating in STP exchange BPDU frames to determine which switch has the lowest bridge ID (BID) on the network. The switch with the lowest BID automatically becomes the root bridge for the STA calculations. The root bridge election process will be discussed in detail later in this chapter.

The BPDU is the message frame exchanged by switches for STP. Each BPDU contains a BID that identifies the switch that sent the BPDU. The BID contains a priority value, the MAC address of the sending switch, and an optional extended system ID. The lowest BID value is determined by the combination of these three fields. You will learn more about the root bridge, BPDU, and BID in later topics.

After the root bridge has been determined, the STA calculates the shortest path to the root bridge. Each switch uses the STA to determine which ports to block. While the STA determines the best paths to the root bridge for all destinations in the broadcast domain, all traffic is prevented from forwarding through the network. The STA considers both path and port costs when determining which path to leave unblocked. The *path costs* are calculated using port cost values associated with port speeds for each switch port along a given path. The sum of the port cost values determines the overall path cost to the root bridge. If there is more than one path to choose from, STA chooses the path with the lowest path cost. You will learn more about path and port costs in later topics.

When the STA has determined which paths are to be left available, it configures the switch ports into distinct port roles. The port roles describe their relation in the network to the root bridge and whether they are allowed to forward traffic.

Root ports - Switch ports closest to the root bridge. In the example, the root port on switch S2 is F0/1 configured for the trunk link between switch S2 and switch S1. The root port on switch S3 is F0/1, configured for the trunk link between switch S3 and switch S1.

Designated ports - All non-root ports that are still permitted to forward traffic on the network. In the example, switch ports F0/1 and F0/2 on switch S1 are designated ports. Switch S2 also has its port F0/2 configured as a designated port.

Non-designated ports - All ports configured to be in a blocking state to prevent loops. In the example, the STA configured port F0/2 on switch S3 in the non-designated role. Port F0/2 on switch S3 is in the blocking state.

You will learn more about port roles and states in a later topic.

Refer to
Figure
in online course

The Root Bridge

Every spanning-tree instance (switched LAN or broadcast domain) has a switch designated as the root bridge. The root bridge serves as a reference point for all spanning-tree calculations to determine which redundant paths to block.

An election process determines which switch becomes the root bridge.

Click the BID Fields button in the figure.

The figure shows the BID fields. The details of each BID field are discussed later, but it is useful to know now that the BID is made up of a priority value, an extended system ID, and the MAC address of the switch.

All switches in the broadcast domain participate in the election process. After a switch boots, it sends out BPDU frames containing the switch BID and the root ID every 2 seconds. By default, the root ID matches the local BID for all switches on the network. The root ID identifies the root bridge on the network. Initially, each switch identifies itself as the root bridge after bootup.

As the switches forward their BPDU frames, adjacent switches in the broadcast domain read the root ID information from the BPDU frame. If the root ID from the BPDU received is lower than the root ID on the receiving switch, the receiving switch updates its root ID identifying the adjacent switch as the root bridge. Note: It may not be an adjacent switch, but any other switch in the broadcast domain. The switch then forwards new BPDU frames with the lower root ID to the other adjacent switches. Eventually, the switch with the lowest BID ends up being identified as the root bridge for the spanning-tree instance.

Best Paths to the Root Bridge

Refer to **Figure** in online course

When the root bridge has been designated for the spanning-tree instance, the STA starts the process of determining the best paths to the root bridge from all destinations in the broadcast domain. The path information is determined by summing up the individual port costs along the path from the destination to the root bridge.

The default port costs are defined by the speed at which the port operates. In the table, you can see that 10-Gb/s Ethernet ports have a port cost of 2, 1-Gb/s Ethernet ports have a port cost of 4, 100-Mb/s Fast Ethernet ports have a port cost of 19, and 10-Mb/s Ethernet ports have a port cost of 100.

Note: IEEE defines the port cost values used by STP. As newer, faster Ethernet technologies enter the marketplace, the path cost values may change to accommodate the different speeds available. The non-linear numbers accommodate some improvements to the Ethernet standard but be aware that the numbers can be changed by IEEE if needed. In the table, the values have already been changed to accommodate the newer 10-Gb/s Ethernet standard.

Although switch ports have a default port cost associated with them, the port cost is configurable. The ability to configure individual port costs gives the administrator the flexibility to control the spanning-tree paths to the root bridge.

Click the Configuring Port Costs button in the figure.

To configure the port cost of an interface, enter the `spanning-tree cost` *value* command in interface configuration mode. The *range* `value` can be between 1 and 200,000,000.

In the example, switch port F0/1 has been configured with a port cost of 25 using the `spanning-tree cost 25` interface configuration command on the F0/1 interface.

To revert the port cost back to the default value, enter the `no spanning-tree cost` interface configuration command.

Click the Path Costs button in the figure.

Path cost is the sum of all the port costs along the path to the root bridge. The paths with the lowest path cost become the preferred path, and all other redundant paths are blocked. In the example, the path cost from switch S2 to the root bridge switch S1, over path 1 is 19 (based on the IEEE-specified individual port cost), while the path cost over path 2 is 38. Because path 1 has a lower overall path cost to the root bridge, it is the preferred path. STP then configures the redundant path to be blocked, preventing a loop from occurring.

Click the Verify Port and Path Costs button in the figure.

To verify the port and path cost to the root bridge, enter the `show spanning-tree` privileged EXEC mode command. The Cost field in the output is the total path cost to the root bridge. This value changes depending on how many switch ports need to be traversed to get to the root bridge. In the output, each interface is also identified with an individual port cost of 19.

Another command to explore is the `show spanning-tree detail` privileged EXEC mode command.

5.2.2 STP BPDU

Refer to
Figure
in online course

The BPDU Fields

In the previous topic, you learned that STP determines a root bridge for the spanning-tree instance by exchanging BPDUs. In this topic, you will learn the details of the BPDU frame and how it facilitates the spanning-tree process.

The BPDU frame contains 12 distinct fields that are used to convey path and priority information that STP uses to determine the root bridge and paths to the root bridge.

Roll over the BPDU fields in the figure to learn what they contain.

- The first four fields identify the protocol, version, message type, and status flags.

- The next four fields are used to identify the root bridge and the cost of the path to the root bridge.

- The last four fields are all timer fields that determine how frequently BPDU messages are sent, and how long the information received through the BPDU process (next topic) is retained. The role of the timer fields will be covered in more detail later in this course.

Click the BPDU Example button in the figure.

The example in the figure was captured using Wireshark. In the example, the BPDU frame contains more fields than previously described. The BPDU message is encapsulated in an Ethernet frame when it is transmitted across the network. The 802.3 header indicates the source and destination addresses of the BPDU frame. This frame has a destination MAC address of 01:80:C2:00:00:00, which is a multicast address for the spanning-tree group. When a frame is addressed with this MAC address, each switch that is configured for spanning tree accepts and reads the information from the frame. By using this multicast group address, all other devices on the network that receive this frame disregard it.

In the example, the root ID and the BID are the same in the captured BPDU frame. This indicates that the frame was captured from a root bridge switch.

The timers are all set to the default values.

Refer to
Figure
in online course

The BPDU Process

Each switch in the broadcast domain initially assumes that it is the root bridge for the spanning-tree instance, so the BPDU frames sent contain the BID of the local switch as the root ID. By default, BPDU frames are sent every 2 seconds after a switch is booted; that is, the default value of the hello timer specified in the BPDU frame is 2 seconds. Each switch maintains local information about its own BID, the root ID, and the path cost to the root.

When adjacent switches receive a BPDU frame, they compare the root ID from the BPDU frame with the local root ID. If the root ID in the BPDU is lower than the local root ID, the switch updates the local root ID and the ID in its BPDU messages. These messages serve to indicate the new root bridge on the network. Also, the path cost is updated to indicate how far away the root bridge is. For example, if the BPDU was received on a Fast Ethernet switch port, the path cost would be set to 19. If the local root ID is lower than the root ID received in the BPDU frame, the BPDU frame is discarded.

After a root ID has been updated to identify a new root bridge, all subsequent BPDU frames sent from that switch contain the new root ID and updated path cost. That way, all other adjacent switches are able to see the lowest root ID identified at all times. As the BPDU frames pass between other adjacent switches, the path cost is continually updated to indicate the total path cost to the root bridge. Each switch in the spanning tree uses its path costs to identify the best possible path to the root bridge.

Click each step in the figure to learn about the BPDU process.

The following summarizes the BPDU process:

Note: Priority is the initial deciding factor when choosing a root bridge. If the priority of all the switches was the same, the MAC address would be the deciding factor.

Step 1. Initially, each switch identifies itself as the root bridge. Switch S2 forwards BPDU frames out all switch ports.

Step 2. When switch S3 receives a BPDU from switch S2, S3 compares its root ID with the BPDU frame it received. The priorities are equal, so the switch is forced to examine the MAC address portion to determine which MAC address has a lower value. Because S2 has a lower MAC address value, S3 updates its root ID with the S2 root ID. At that point, S3 considers S2 as the root bridge.

Step 3. When S1 compares its root ID with the one in the received BPDU frame, it identifies the local root ID as the lower value and discards the BPDU from S2.

Step 4. When S3 sends out its BPDU frames, the root ID contained in the BPDU frame is that of S2.

Step 5. When S2 receives the BPDU frame, it discards it after verifying that the root ID in the BPDU matched its local root ID.

Step 6. Because S1 has a lower priority value in its root ID, it discards the BPDU frame received from S3.

Step 7. S1 sends out its BPDU frames.

Step 8. S3 identifies the root ID in the BPDU frame as having a lower value and therefore updates its root ID values to indicate that S1 is now the root bridge.

Step 9. S2 identifies the root ID in the BPDU frame as having a lower value and therefore updates its root ID values to indicate that S1 is now the root bridge.

5.2.3 Bridge ID

Refer to
Figure
in online course

BID Fields

The bridge ID (BID) is used to determine the root bridge on a network. This topic describes what makes up a BID and how to configure the BID on a switch to influence the election process to ensure that specific switches are assigned the role of root bridge on the network.

The BID field of a BPDU frame contains three separate fields: bridge priority, extended system ID, and MAC address. Each field is used during the root bridge election.

Bridge Priority

The bridge priority is a customizable value that you can use to influence which switch becomes the root bridge. The switch with the lowest priority, which means lowest BID, becomes the root bridge (the lower the priority value, the higher the priority). For example, to ensure that a specific switch is always the root bridge, you set the priority to a lower value than the rest of the switches on the network. The default value for the priority of all Cisco switches is 32768. The priority range is between 1 and 65536; therefore, 1 is the highest priority.

Extended System ID

As shown in the example, the extended system ID can be omitted in BPDU frames in certain configurations. The early implementation of STP was designed for networks that did not use VLANs. There was a single common spanning tree across all switches. When VLANs started to become common for network infrastructure segmentation, STP was enhanced to include support for VLANs. As a result, the extended system ID field contains the ID of the VLAN with which the BPDU is associated.

When the extended system ID is used, it changes the number of bits available for the bridge priority value, so the increment for the bridge priority value changes from 1 to 4096. Therefore, bridge priority values can only be multiples of 4096.

The extended system ID value is added to the bridge priority value in the BID to identify the priority and VLAN of the BPDU frame.

You will learn about per VLAN spanning tree (PVST) in a later section of this chapter.

MAC Address

When two switches are configured with the same priority and have the same extended system ID, the switch with the MAC address with the lowest hexadecimal value has the lower BID. Initially, all switches are configured with the same default priority value. The MAC address is then the deciding factor on which switch is going to become the root bridge. This results in an unpredictable choice for the root bridge. It is recommended to configure the desired root bridge switch with a lower priority to ensure that it is elected root bridge. This also ensures that the addition of new switches to the network does not trigger a new spanning-tree election, which could disrupt network communication while a new root bridge is being selected.

Click the Priority-based decision button in the figure.

In the example, S1 has a lower priority than the other switches; therefore, it is preferred as the root bridge for that spanning-tree instance.

Click the MAC Address-based decision button in the figure.

When all switches are configured with the same priority, as is the case with all switches kept in the default configuration with a priority of 32768, the MAC address becomes the deciding factor for which switch becomes the root bridge.

Note: In the example, the priority of all the switches is 32769. The value is based on the 32768 default priority and the VLAN 1 assignment associated with each switch (1+32768).

The MAC address with the lowest hexadecimal value is considered to be the preferred root bridge. In the example, S2 has the lowest value for its MAC address and is therefore designated as the root bridge for that spanning-tree instance.

Refer to **Figure** in online course

Configure and Verify the BID

When a specific switch is to become a root bridge, the bridge priority value needs to be adjusted to ensure it is lower than the bridge priority values of all the other switches on the network. There are two different configuration methods that you can use to configure the bridge priority value on a Cisco Catalyst switch.

Method 1 - To ensure that the switch has the lowest bridge priority value, use the `spanning-tree vlan` *vlan-id* `root primary` command in global configuration mode. The priority for the switch is set to the predefined value of 24576 or to the next 4096 decrement value below the lowest bridge priority detected on the network.

If an alternate root bridge is desired, use the `spanning-tree vlan` *vlan-id* `root secondary` global configuration mode command. This command sets the priority for the switch to the predefined value of 28672. This ensures that this switch becomes the root bridge if the primary root bridge fails and a new root bridge election occurs and assuming that the rest of the switches in the network have the default 32768 priority value defined.

In the example, switch S1 has been assigned as the primary root bridge using the `spanning-tree vlan 1 root primary` global configuration mode command, and switch S2 has been configured as the secondary root bridge using the `spanning-tree vlan 1 root secondary` global configuration mode command.

Method 2 - Another method for configuring the bridge priority value is using the `spanning-tree vlan` *vlan-id* `priority` *value* global configuration mode command. This command gives you more granular control over the bridge priority value. The priority value is configured in increments of 4096 between 0 and 65536.

In the example, switch S3 has been assigned a bridge priority value of 24576 using the `spanning-tree vlan 1 priority 24576` global configuration mode command.

Click the Verification button in the figure.

To verify the bridge priority of a switch, use the show spanning-tree privileged EXEC mode command. In the example, the priority of the switch has been set to 24576. Also notice that the switch is designated as the root bridge for the spanning-tree instance.

5.2.4 Port Roles

Refer to
Figure
in online course

Port Roles

The root bridge is elected for the spanning-tree instance. The location of the root bridge in the network topology determines how port roles are calculated. This topic describes how the switch ports are configured for specific roles to prevent the possibility of loops on the network.

There are four distinct port roles that switch ports are automatically configured for during the spanning-tree process.

Root Port

The root port exists on non-root bridges and is the switch port with the best path to the root bridge. Root ports forward traffic toward the root bridge. The source MAC address of frames received on the root port are capable of populating the MAC table. Only one root port is allowed per bridge.

In the example, switch S1 is the root bridge and switches S2 and S3 have root ports defined on the trunk links connecting back to S1.

Designated Port

The designated port exists on root and non-root bridges. For root bridges, all switch ports are designated ports. For non-root bridges, a designated port is the switch port that receives and forwards frames toward the root bridge as needed. Only one designated port is allowed per segment. If multiple switches exist on the same segment, an election process determines the designated switch, and the corresponding switch port begins forwarding frames for the segment. Designated ports are capable of populating the MAC table.

In the example, switch S1 has both sets of ports for its two trunk links configured as designated ports. Switch S2 also has a designated port configured on the trunk link going toward switch S3.

Non-designated Port

The non-designated port is a switch port that is blocked, so it is not forwarding data frames and not populating the MAC address table with source addresses. A non-designated port is not a root port or a designated port. For some variants of STP, the non-designated port is called an alternate port.

In the example, switch S3 has the only non-designated ports in the topology. The non-designated ports prevent the loop from occurring.

Disabled Port

The disabled port is a switch port that is administratively shut down. A disabled port does not function in the spanning-tree process. There are no disabled ports in the example.

Refer to
Figure
in online course

Port Roles

The STA determines which port role is assigned to each switch port.

When determining the root port on a switch, the switch compares the path costs on all switch ports participating in the spanning tree. The switch port with the lowest overall path cost to the root is automatically assigned the root port role because it is closest to the root bridge. In a network topology, all switches that are using spanning tree, except for the root bridge, have a single root port defined.

When there are two switch ports that have the same path cost to the root bridge and both are the lowest path costs on the switch, the switch needs to determine which switch port is the root port. The switch uses the customizable port priority value, or the lowest port ID if both port priority values are the same.

The port ID is the interface ID of the switch port. For example, the figure shows four switches. Port F0/1 and F0/2 on switch S2 have the same path cost value back to the root bridge. However, port F0/1 on switch S2 is the preferred port because it has a lower port ID value.

The port ID is appended to the port priority. For example, switch port F0/1 has a default port priority value of 128.1, where 128 is the configurable port priority value, and .1 is the port ID. Switch port F0/2 has a port priority value of 128.2, by default.

Refer to
Figure
in online course

Configure Port Priority

You can configure the port priority value using the `spanning-tree port-priority` *value* interface configuration mode command. The port priority values range from 0 - 240, in increments of 16. The default port priority value is 128. As with bridge priority, lower port priority values give the port higher priority.

In the example, the port priority for port F0/1 has been set to 112, which is below the default port priority of 128. This ensures that the port is the preferred port when competing with another port for a specific port role.

When the switch decides to use one port over another for the root port, the other is configured as a non-designated port to prevent a loop from occurring.

Refer to
Figure
in online course

Port Role Decisions

In the example, switch S1 is the root bridge. Switches S2 and S3 have root ports configured for the ports connecting back to S1.

After a switch has determined which of its ports is configured in the root port role, it needs to decide which ports have the designated and non-designated roles.

The root bridge automatically configures all of its switch ports in the designated role. Other switches in the topology configure their non-root ports as designated or non-designated ports.

Designated ports are configured for all LAN segments. When two switches are connected to the same LAN segment, and root ports have already been defined, the two switches have to decide which port gets to be configured as a designated port and which one is left as the non-designated port.

Refer to
Figure
in online course

The switches on the LAN segment in question exchange BPDU frames, which contain the switch BID. Generally, the switch with the lower BID has its port configured as a designated port, while the switch with the higher BID has its port configured as a non-designated port. However, keep in mind that the first priority is the lowest path cost to the root bridge and that only if the port costs are equal, is the BID of the sender used.

As a result, each switch determines which port roles are assigned to each of its ports to create the loop-free spanning tree.

Click each step in the figure to learn about how port roles are determined.

Verifying Port Roles and Port Priority

Now that spanning tree has determined the logical loop-free network topology, you may want to confirm which port roles and port priorities are configured for the various switch ports in the network.

To verify the port roles and port priorities for the switch ports, use the `show spanning-tree` privileged EXEC mode command.

In the example, the `show spanning-tree` output displays all switch ports and their defined roles. Switch port F0/1 and F0/2 are configured as designated ports. The output also displays the port priority of each switch port. Switch port F0/1 has a port priority of 128.1.

5.2.5 STP Port States and BPDU Timers

Port States

Refer to
Figure
in online course

STP determines the logical loop-free path throughout the broadcast domain. The spanning tree is determined through the information learned by the exchange of the BPDU frames between the interconnected switches. To facilitate the learning of the logical spanning tree, each switch port transitions through five possible port states and three BPDU timers.

The spanning tree is determined immediately after a switch is finished booting up. If a switch port were to transition directly from the blocking to the forwarding state, the port could temporarily create a data loop if the switch was not aware of all topology information at the time. For this reason, STP introduces five port states. The table summarizes what each port state does. The following provides some additional information on how the port states ensure that no loops are created during the creation of the logical spanning tree.

- *Blocking -* The port is a non-designated port and does not participate in frame forwarding. The port receives BPDU frames to determine the location and root ID of the root bridge switch and what port roles each switch port should assume in the final active STP topology.

- *Listening -* STP has determined that the port can participate in frame forwarding according to the BPDU frames that the switch has received thus far. At this point, the switch port is not only receiving BPDU frames, it is also transmitting its own BPDU frames and informing adjacent switches that the switch port is preparing to participate in the active topology.

- *Learning -* The port prepares to participate in frame forwarding and begins to populate the MAC address table.

- *Forwarding -* The port is considered part of the active topology and forwards frames and also sends and receives BPDU frames.

- *Disabled -* The Layer 2 port does not participate in spanning tree and does not forward frames. The disabled state is set when the switch port is administratively disabled.

Refer to
Figure
in online course

BPDU Timers

The amount of time that a port stays in the various port states depends on the BPDU timers. Only the switch in the role of root bridge may send information through the tree to adjust the timers. The following timers determine STP performance and state changes:

- Hello time
- Forward delay
- Maximum age

Click the Roles and Timers button in the figure.

When STP is enabled, every switch port in the network goes through the blocking state and the transitory states of listening and learning at power up. The ports then stabilize to the forwarding or blocking state, as seen in the example. During a topology change, a port temporarily implements the listening and learning states for a specified period called the *forward delay interval*.

These values allow adequate time for convergence in a network with a switch diameter of seven. To review, switch diameter is the number of switches a frame has to traverse to travel from the two farthest points on the broadcast domain. A seven-switch diameter is the largest diameter that STP permits because of convergence times. Convergence in relation to spanning tree is the time it takes to recalculate the spanning tree if a switch or a link fails. You will learn how convergence works in the next section.

Click the Configure Network Diameter button in the figure.

It is recommended that the BPDU timers not be adjusted directly because the values have been optimized for the seven-switch diameter. Adjusting the spanning-tree diameter value on the root bridge to a lower value automatically adjusts the forward delay and maximum age timers proportionally for the new diameter. Typically, you do not adjust the BPDU timers nor reconfigure the network diameter. However, if after research, a network administrator determined that the convergence time of the network could be optimized, the administrator would do so by reconfiguring the network diameter, not the BPDU timers.

To configure a different network diameter for STP, use the `spanning-tree vlan` *vlan id* `root primary diameter` *value* global configuration mode command on the root bridge switch.

In the example, the `spanning-tree vlan 1 root primary diameter 5` global configuration mode command was entered to adjust the spanning tree diameter to five switches.

Refer to **Figure** in online course

Cisco PortFast Technology

PortFast is a Cisco technology. When a switch port configured with PortFast is configured as an access port, that port transitions from blocking to forwarding state immediately, bypassing the typical STP listening and learning states. You can use PortFast on access ports, which are connected to a single workstation or to a server, to allow those devices to connect to the network immediately rather than waiting for spanning tree to converge. If an interface configured with PortFast receives a BPDU frame, spanning tree can put the port into the blocking state using a feature called BPDU guard. Configuring BPDU guard is beyond the scope of this course.

Note: Cisco PortFast technology can be used to support DHCP. Without PortFast, a PC can send a DHCP request before the port is in forwarding state, denying the host from getting a usable IP address and other information. Because PortFast immediately changes the state to forwarding, the PC always gets a usable IP address.

For more information on configuring BPDU guard, see:

http://www.cisco.com/en/US/tech/tk389/tk621/technologies_tech_note09186a008009482f.shtml.

Note: Because the purpose of PortFast is to minimize the time that access ports must wait for spanning tree to converge, it should be used only on access ports. If you enable PortFast on a port connecting to another switch, you risk creating a spanning-tree loop.

Click the Configure PortFast button in the figure.

To configure PortFast on a switch port, enter the `spanning-tree portfast` interface configuration mode command on each interface that PortFast is to be enabled.

To disable PortFast, enter the `no spanning-tree portfast` interface configuration mode command on each interface that PortFast is to be disabled.

Click the Verify PortFast button in the figure.

To verify that PortFast has been enabled for a switch port, use the `show running-config` privileged EXEC mode command. The absence of the `spanning-tree portfast` command in the running configuration for an interface indicates that PortFast has been disabled for that interface. PortFast is disabled on all interfaces by default.

Refer to **Packet Tracer Activity** for this chapter

In this activity, the switches are "out of the box" without any configuration. You will manipulate the root bridge election so that the core switches are chosen before the distribution or access layer switches.

Detailed instructions are provided within the activity as well as in the PDF link below.

Activity Instructions (PDF)

5.3 STP Convergence

5.3.1 STP Convergence

Refer to **Figure** in online course

STP Convergence Steps

The previous section described the components that enable STP to create the logical loop-free network topology. In this section, you will examine the whole STP process from start to finish.

Convergence is an important aspect of the spanning-tree process. Convergence is the time it takes for the network to determine which switch is going to assume the role of the root bridge, go through all the different port states, and set all switch ports to their final spanning-tree port roles where all potential loops are eliminated. The convergence process takes time to complete because of the different timers used to coordinate the process.

To understand the convergence process more thoroughly, it has been broken down into three distinct steps:

Step 1. Elect a root bridge

Step 2. Elect root ports

Step 3. Elect designated and non-designated ports

The remainder of this section explores each step in the convergence process.

5.3.2 Step 1. Electing A Root Bridge

Refer to **Figure** in online course

Step 1. Electing a Root Bridge

The first step of the spanning-tree convergence process is to elect a root bridge. The root bridge is the basis for all spanning-tree path cost calculations and ultimately leads to the assignment of the different port roles used to prevent loops from occurring.

A root bridge election is triggered after a switch has finished booting up, or when a path failure has been detected on a network. Initially, all switch ports are configured for the blocking state, which by default lasts 20 seconds. This is done to prevent a loop from occurring before STP has had time to calculate the best root paths and configure all switch ports to their specific roles. While the switch ports are in a blocking state, they are still able to send and receive BPDU frames so that the spanning-tree root election can proceed. Spanning tree supports a maximum network diameter of seven switch hops from end to end. This allows the entire root bridge election process to occur within 14 seconds, which is less than the time the switch ports spend in the blocking state.

Immediately after the switches have finished booting up, they start sending BPDU frames advertising their BID in an attempt to become the root bridge. Initially, all switches in the network assume that they are the root bridge for the broadcast domain. The flood of BPDU frames on the network have the root ID field matching the BID field, indicating that each switch considers itself the root bridge. These BPDU frames are sent every 2 seconds based on the default hello timer value.

As each switch receives the BPDU frames from its neighboring switches, they compare the root ID from the received BPDU frame with the root ID configured locally. If the root ID from the received BPDU frame is lower than the root ID it currently has, the root ID field is updated indicating the new best candidate for the root bridge role.

After the root ID field is updated on a switch, the switch then incorporates the new root ID in all future BPDU frame transmissions. This ensures that the lowest root ID is always conveyed to all other adjacent switches in the network. The root bridge election ends once the lowest bridge ID populates the root ID field of all switches in the broadcast domain.

Even though the root bridge election process has completed, the switches continue to forward their BPDU frames advertising the root ID of the root bridge every 2 seconds. Each switch is configured with a max age timer that determines how long a switch retains the current BPDU configuration in the event it stops receiving updates from its neighboring switches. By default, the max age timer is set to 20 seconds. Therefore, if a switch fails to receive 10 consecutive BPDU frames from one of its neighbors, the switch assumes that a logical path in the spanning tree has failed and that the BPDU information is no longer valid. This triggers another spanning-tree root bridge election.

Click the Play button in the figure to review the steps STP uses to elect a root bridge.

As you review how STP elects a root bridge, recall that the root bridge election process occurs with all switches sending and receiving BPDU frames simultaneously. Performing the election process simultaneously allows the switches to determine which switch is going to become the root bridge much faster.

Refer to
Figure
in online course

Verify Root Bridge Election

When the root bridge election is completed, you can verify the identity of the root bridge using the `show spanning-tree` privileged EXEC mode command

In the topology example, switch S1 has the lowest priority value of the three switches, so we can assume it will become the root bridge.

Click the Switch S1 Output button in the figure.

In the example, the `show spanning-tree` output for switch S1 reveals that it is the root bridge. You can see that the BID matches the root ID, confirming that S1 is the root bridge.

Click the Switch S2 Output button in the figure.

In the example, the show `show spanning-tree` output for switch S2 shows that the root ID matches the expected root ID of switch S1, indicating that S2 considers S1 the root bridge.

Click the Switch S3 Output button in the figure.

In the example, the **show spanning-tree** output for switch S3 shows that the root ID matches the expected root ID of switch S1, indicating that S3 considers S1 the root bridge.

5.3.3 Step 2. Elect Root Ports

Refer to
Figure
in online course

Step 2. Elect Root Ports

Now that the root bridge has been determined, the switches start configuring the port roles for each of their switch ports. The first port role that needs to be determined is the root port role.

Every switch in a spanning-tree topology, except for the root bridge, has a single root port defined. The root port is the switch port with the lowest path cost to the root bridge. Normally path cost alone determines which switch port becomes the root port. However, additional port characteristics determine the root port when two or more ports on the same switch have the same path cost to the root. This can happen when redundant links are used to uplink one switch to another switch when an EtherChannel configuration is not used. Recall that Cisco EtherChannel technology allows you to configure multiple physical Ethernet type links as one logical link.

Switch ports with equivalent path costs to the root use the configurable port priority value. They use the port ID to break a tie. When a switch chooses one equal path cost port as a root port over another, the losing port is configured as the non-designated to avoid a loop.

The process of determining which port becomes a root port happens during the root bridge election BPDU exchange. Path costs are updated immediately when BPDU frames arrive indicating a new root ID or redundant path. At the time the path cost is updated, the switch enters decision mode to determine if port configurations need to be updated. The port role decisions do not wait until all switches settle on which switch is going to be the final root bridge. As a result, the port role for a given switch port may change multiple times during convergence, until it finally settles on its final port role after the root ID changes for the last time.

Click each step in the figure to learn about electing root ports.

Refer to
Figure
in online course

Verify the Root Port

When the root bridge election has completed, you can verify the configuration of the root ports using the **show spanning-tree** privileged EXEC mode command.

In the topology example, switch S1 has been identified as the root bridge. The switch S2 F0/1 port and switch S3 F0/1 port are the two closest ports to the root bridge and, therefore, should be configured as root ports. You can confirm the port configuration using the **show spanning-tree** privileged EXEC mode command.

Click the Switch S1 Output button in the figure.

In the example, the **show spanning-tree** output for switch S1 reveals that it is the root bridge and consequently does not have any root ports configured.

Click the Switch S2 output button in the figure.

In the example, the **show spanning-tree** output for switch S2 shows that switch port F0/1 is configured as a root port. The Root ID shows the Priority and MAC Address of switch S1.

Click the Switch S3 output button in the figure.

In the example, the **show spanning-tree** output for switch S3 shows that switch port F0/1 is configured as a root port. The Root ID shows the Priority and MAC Address of switch S1.

5.3.4 Step 3. Electing Designated Ports and Non-Designated Ports

Refer to
Figure
in online course

Step 3. Electing Designated Ports and Non-Designated Ports

After a switch determines which of its ports is the root port, the remaining ports must be configured as either a designated port (DP) or a non-designated port (non-DP) to finish creating the logical loop-free spanning tree.

Each segment in a switched network can have only one designated port. When two non-root port switch ports are connected on the same LAN segment, a competition for port roles occurs. The two switches exchange BPDU frames to sort out which switch port is designated and which one is non-designated.

Generally, when a switch port is configured as a designated port, it is based on the BID. However, keep in mind that the first priority is the lowest path cost to the root bridge and that only if the port costs are equal, is the BID of the sender.

When two switches exchange their BPDU frames, they examine the sending BID of the received BPDU frame to see if it is lower than its own. The switch with the lower BID wins the competition and its port is configured in the designated role. The losing switch configures its switch port to be non-designated and, therefore, in the blocking state to prevent the loop from occurring.

The process of determining the port roles happens concurrently with the root bridge election and root port designation. As a result, the designated and non-designated roles may change multiple times during the convergence process until the final root bridge has been determined. The entire process of electing the root bridge, determining the root ports, and determining the designated and non-designated ports happens within the 20-second blocking port state. This convergence time is based on the 2-second hello timer for BPDU frame transmission and the seven-switch diameter supported by STP. The max age delay of 20 seconds provides enough time for the seven-switch diameter with the 2-second hello timer between BPDU frame transmissions.

Click each step in the figure to learn about electing designated ports and non-designated ports.

Refer to
Figure
in online course

Verify DP and Non-DP

After the root ports have been assigned, the switches determine which remaining ports are configured as designated and non-designated ports. You can verify the configuration of the designated and non-designated ports using the **show spanning-tree** privileged EXEC mode command.

In the topology:

Step 1. Switch S1 is identified as the root bridge and therefore configures both of its switch ports as designated ports.

Step 2. The switch S2 F0/1 port and switch S3 F0/1 port are the two closest ports to the root bridge and are configured as root ports.

Step 3. The remaining switch S2 F0/2 port and switch S3 F0/2 port need to decide which of the two remaining ports will be the designated port and which will be the non-designated port.

Step 4. Switch S2 and switch S3 compare their BID values to determine which one is lower The one with the lower BID is configured as the designated port.

Step 5. Because both switches have the same priority, the MAC address becomes the deciding factor.

Step 6. Because switch S2 has a lower MAC address, it configures its F0/2 port as a designated port.

Step 7. Switch S3 consequently configures its F0/2 port as a non-designated port to prevent the loop from occurring.

You can confirm the port configuration using the show spanning-tree privileged EXEC mode command.

Click the Switch S1 Output button in the figure.

In the example, the `show spanning-tree` output for switch S1 reveals that it is the root bridge and consequently has both of its ports configured as designated ports.

Click the Switch S2 Output button in the figure.

In the example, the `show spanning-tree` output for switch S2 shows that switch port F0/2 is configured as a designated port.

Click the Switch S3 Output button in the figure.

In the example, the `show spanning-tree` output for switch S3 shows that switch port F0/2 is configured as a non-designated port.

5.3.5 STP Topology Change

Refer to
Figure
in online course

STP Topology Change Notification Process

A switch considers it has detected a topology change either when a port that was forwarding is going down (blocking for instance) or when a port transitions to forwarding and the switch has a designated port. When a change is detected, the switch notifies the root bridge of the spanning tree. The root bridge then broadcasts the information into the whole network.

In normal STP operation, a switch keeps receiving configuration BPDU frames from the root bridge on its root port. However, it never sends out a BPDU toward the root bridge. To achieve that, a special BPDU called the topology change notification (TCN) BPDU was introduced. When a switch needs to signal a topology change, it starts to send TCNs on its root port. The TCN is a very simple BPDU that contains no information and is sent out at the hello time interval. The receiving switch is called the designated bridge and it acknowledges the TCN by immediately sending back a normal BPDU with the topology change acknowledgement (TCA) bit set. This exchange continues until the root bridge responds.

For example, in the figure switch S2 experiences a topology change. It sends a TCN to its designated bridge, which in this case is switch D1. Switch D1 receives the TCN, acknowledges it back to switch S2 with a TCA. Switch D1 generates a TCN, and forwards it to its designated bridge, which in this case is the root bridge.

Click the Broadcast Notification button in the figure.

Broadcast Notification

Once the root bridge is aware that there has been a topology change event in the network, it starts to send out its configuration BPDUs with the topology change (TC) bit set. These BPDUs are relayed by every switch in the network with this bit set. As a result, all switches become aware of the topology change and can reduce their aging time to forward delay. Switches receive topology change BPDUs on both forwarding and blocking ports.

The TC bit is set by the root for a period of max age + forward delay seconds, which is 20+15=35 seconds by default.

5.4 PVST+, RSTP and Rapid-PVST+

5.4.1 Cisco and STP Variants

Refer to
Figure
in online course

Like many networking standards, the evolution of STP has been driven by the need to create industry-wide specifications when proprietary protocols become *de facto standards*. When a proprietary protocol becomes so prevalent that all competitors in the market need to support it, agencies like the IEEE step in and create a public specification. The evolution of STP has followed this same path, as seen in the table.

When you read about STP on the Cisco.com site, you notice that there are many types or variants of STP. Some of these variants are Cisco proprietary and others are IEEE standards. You will learn more details on some of these STP variants, but to get started you need to have a general knowledge of what the key STP variants are. The table summarizes the following descriptions of the key Cisco and IEEE STP variants.

Cisco Proprietary

Per-VLAN spanning tree protocol (PVST) - Maintains a spanning-tree instance for each VLAN configured in the network. It uses the Cisco proprietary ISL trunking protocol that allows a VLAN trunk to be forwarding for some VLANs while blocking for other VLANs. Because PVST treats each VLAN as a separate network, it can *load balance* traffic at Layer 2 by forwarding some VLANs on one trunk and other VLANs on another trunk without causing a loop. For PVST, Cisco developed a number of proprietary extensions to the original IEEE 802.1D STP, such as Backbone-Fast, UplinkFast, and PortFast. These Cisco STP extensions are not covered in this course. To learn more about these extensions, visit: http://www.cisco.com/en/US/docs/switches/lan/catalyst4000/7.4/configuration/guide/stp_enha.html.

Per-VLAN spanning tree protocol plus (PVST+) - Cisco developed PVST+ to provide support for IEEE 802.1Q trunking. PVST+ provides the same functionality as PVST, including the Cisco proprietary STP extensions. PVST+ is not supported on non-Cisco devices. PVST+ includes the PortFast enhancement called BPDU guard, and root guard. To learn more about BPDU guard, visit: http://www.cisco.com/en/US/tech/tk389/tk621/technologies_tech_note09186a008009482f.shtml.

To learn more about root guard, visit: http://www.cisco.com/en/US/tech/tk389/tk621/technologies_tech_note09186a00800ae96b.shtml.

Rapid per-VLAN spanning tree protocol (rapid PVST+) - Based on the IEEE 802.1w standard and has a faster convergence than STP (standard 802.1D). Rapid PVST+ includes Cisco-proprietary extensions such as BackboneFast, UplinkFast, and PortFast.

IEEE Standards

Rapid spanning tree protocol (RSTP) - First introduced in 1982 as an evolution of STP (802.1D standard). It provides faster spanning-tree convergence after a topology change. RSTP implements the Cisco-proprietary STP extensions, BackboneFast, UplinkFast, and PortFast, into the public standard. As of 2004, the IEEE has incorporated RSTP into 802.1D, identifying the specification as IEEE 802.1D-2004. So when you hear STP, think RSTP. You will learn more about RSTP later in this section.

Multiple STP (MSTP) - Enables multiple VLANs to be mapped to the same spanning-tree instance, reducing the number of instances needed to support a large number of VLANs. MSTP was inspired by the Cisco-proprietary Multiple Instances STP (MISTP) and is an evolution of STP and RSTP. It was introduced in IEEE 802.1s as amendment to 802.1Q, 1998 edition. Standard IEEE 802.1Q-2003 now includes MSTP. MSTP provides for multiple forwarding paths for data traffic and enables load balancing. A discussion of MSTP is beyond the scope of this course. To learn more about MSTP, visit: http://www.cisco.com/en/US/docs/switches/lan/catalyst2950/software/release/ 12.1_19_ea1/configuration/guide/swmstp.html.

5.4.2 PVST+

Refer to Figure in online course

PVST+

Cisco developed PVST+ so that a network can run an STP instance for each VLAN in the network. With PVST+, more than one trunk can block for a VLAN and load sharing can be implemented. However, implementing PVST+ means that all switches in the network are engaged in converging the network, and the switch ports have to accommodate the additional bandwidth used for each PVST+ instance to send its own BPDUs.

In a Cisco PVST+ environment, you can tune the spanning-tree parameters so that half of the VLANs forward on each uplink trunk. In the figure, port F0/3 on switch S2 is the forwarding port for VLAN 20, and F0/2 on switch S2 is the forwarding port for VLAN 10. This is accomplished by configuring one switch to be elected the root bridge for half of the total number of VLANs in the network, and a second switch to be elected the root bridge for the other half of the VLANs. In the figure, switch S3 is the root bridge for VLAN 20, and switch S1 is the root bridge for VLAN 10. Creating different STP root switches per VLAN creates a more redundant network.

Refer to Figure in online course

PVST+ Bridge ID

As you recall, in the original 802.1D standard, an 8-byte BID is composed of a 2-byte bridge priority and a 6-byte MAC address of the switch. There was no need to identify a VLAN because there was only one spanning tree in a network. PVST+ requires that a separate instance of spanning tree run for each VLAN. To support PVST+, the 8-byte BID field is modified to carry a VLAN ID (VID). In the figure, the bridge priority field is reduced to 4 bits and a new 12-bit field, the extended system ID field, contains the VID. The 6-byte MAC address remains unchanged.

The following provides more details on the PVST+ fields:

- Bridge priority - A 4-bit field carries the bridge priority. Because of the limited bit count, the priority is conveyed in discrete values in increments of 4096 rather than discreet values in increments of 1, as they would be if the full 16-bit field was available. The default priority, in accordance with IEEE 802.1D, is 32,768, which is the midrange value.

- Extended system ID - A 12-bit field carrying the VID for PVST+.

- MAC address - A 6-byte field with the MAC address of a single switch.

The MAC address is what makes a BID unique. When the priority and extended system ID are prepended to the switch MAC address, each VLAN on the switch can be represented by a unique BID.

Click on the PVST+ Bridge ID Example button in the figure.

In the figure, the values for priority, VLAN, and MAC address for switch S1 are shown. They are combined to form the BID.

Caution: If no priority has been configured, every switch has the same default priority, and the election of the root bridge for each VLAN is based on the MAC address. Therefore, to ensure that you get the root bridge you want, it is advisable to assign a lower priority value to the switch that should serve as the root bridge.

Refer to Figure in online course

The table shows the default spanning-tree configuration for a Cisco Catalyst 2960 series switch. Notice that the default spanning-tree mode is PVST+.

Refer to
Figure
in online course

Configure PVST+

The topology shows three switches with 802.1Q trunks connecting them. There are two VLANs, 10 and 20, which are being trunked across these links. This network has not been configured for spanning tree. The goal is to configure S3 as the root bridge for VLAN 20 and S1 as the root bridge for VLAN 10. Port F0/3 on S2 is the forwarding port for VLAN 20 and the blocking port for VLAN 10. Port F0/2 on S2 is the forwarding port for VLAN 10 and the blocking port for VLAN 20. The steps to configure PVST+ on this example topology are:

Step 1. Select the switches you want for the primary and secondary root bridges for each VLAN.

Step 2. Configure the switch to be a primary bridge for one VLAN, for example switch S3 is a primary bridge for VLAN 20.

Step 3. Configure the switch to be a secondary bridge for the other VLAN, for example, switch S3 is a secondary bridge for VLAN 10.

Optionally, set the spanning-tree priority to be low enough on each switch so that it is selected as the primary bridge.

Click the Primary and Secondary Root Bridges button in the figure.

Configure the Primary Root Bridges

The goal is to configure switch S3 as the primary root bridge for VLAN 20 and configure switch S1 as the primary root bridge for VLAN 10. To configure a switch to become the root bridge for a specified VLAN, use the `spanning-tree vlan vlan-ID root primary` global configuration mode command. Recall that you are starting with a network that has not been configured with spanning tree, so assume that all the switches are in their default configuration. In this example, switch S1, which has VLAN 10 and 20 enabled, retains its default STP priority.

Configure the Secondary Root Bridges

A secondary root is a switch that may become the root bridge for a VLAN if the primary root bridge fails. To configure a switch as the secondary root bridge, use the `spanning-tree vlan vlan-ID root secondary` global configuration mode command. Assuming the other bridges in the VLAN retain their default STP priority, this switch becomes the root bridge if the primary root bridge fails. This command can be executed on more than one switch to configure multiple backup root bridges.

The graphic shows the Cisco IOS command syntax to specify switch S3 as the primary root bridge for VLAN 20 and as the secondary root bridge for VLAN 10. Also, switch S1 becomes the primary root bridge for VLAN 10 and the secondary root bridge for VLAN 20. This configuration permits spanning tree load balancing, with VLAN 10 traffic passing through switch S1 and VLAN 20 traffic passing through switch S3.

Click the PVST+ Switch Priority button in the figure.

PVST+ Switch Priority

Earlier in this chapter you learned that the default settings used to configure spanning tree are adequate for most networks. This is true for Cisco PVST+ as well. There are a number of ways to tune PVST+. A discussion on how to tune a PVST+ implementation is beyond the scope of this course. However, you can set the switch priority for the specified spanning-tree instance. This setting affects the likelihood that this switch is selected as the root switch. A lower value increases the probability that the switch is selected. The range is 0 to 61440 in increments of 4096. For example, a valid priority value is 4096x2 = 8192. All other values are rejected.

The examples show the Cisco IOS command syntax.

Click the Verify button in the figure.

The privileged EXEC command `show spanning tree active` shows spanning-tree configuration details for the active interfaces only. The output shown is for switch S1 configured with PVST+. There are a lot of Cisco IOS command parameters associated with the `show spanning tree` command. For a complete description, visit: http://www.cisco.com/en/US/docs/switches/lan/catalyst2960/software/release/12.2_37_se/command/reference/cli2.html#wpxref47293.

Click the `show run` button in the figure.

You can see in the output that the priority for VLAN 10 is 4096, the lowest of the three VLAN priorities. This priority setting ensures that this switch is the primary root bridge for VLAN 10.

5.4.3 RSTP

Refer to
Figure
in online course

What is RSTP?

RSTP (IEEE 802.1w) is an evolution of the 802.1D standard. The 802.1w STP terminology remains primarily the same as the IEEE 802.1D STP terminology. Most parameters have been left unchanged, so users familiar with STP can rapidly configure the new protocol.

In the figure, a network shows an example of RSTP. Switch S1 is the root bridge with two designated ports in a forwarding state. RSTP supports a new port type. Port F0/3 on switch S2 is an alternate port in discarding state. Notice that there are no blocking ports. RSTP does not have a blocking port state. RSTP defines port states as discarding, learning, or forwarding. You will learn more about port types and states later in the chapter.

Click the RSTP Characteristics button in the figure.

RSTP Characteristics

RSTP speeds the recalculation of the spanning tree when the Layer 2 network topology changes. RSTP can achieve much faster convergence in a properly configured network, sometimes in as little as a few hundred milliseconds. RSTP redefines the type of ports and their state. If a port is configured to be an alternate or a backup port it can immediately change to a forwarding state without waiting for the network to converge. The following briefly describes RSTP characteristics:

- RSTP is the preferred protocol for preventing Layer 2 loops in a switched network environment. Many of the differences were informed by Cisco-proprietary enhancements to 802.1D. These enhancements, such as BPDUs carrying and sending information about port roles only to neighboring switches, require no additional configuration and generally perform better than the earlier Cisco-proprietary versions. They are now transparent and integrated in the protocol's operation.

- Cisco-proprietary enhancements to 802.1D, such as UplinkFast and BackboneFast, are not compatible with RSTP.

- RSTP (802.1w) supersedes STP (802.1D) while retaining backward compatibility. Much of the STP terminology remains, and most parameters are unchanged. In addition, 802.1w is capable of reverting back to 802.1D to interoperate with legacy switches on a per-port basis. For example, the RSTP spanning-tree algorithm elects a root bridge in exactly the same way as 802.1D.

- RSTP keeps the same BPDU format as IEEE 802.1D, except that the version field is set to 2 to indicate RSTP, and the flags field uses all 8 bits. The RSTP BPDU is discussed later.

- RSTP is able to actively confirm that a port can safely transition to the forwarding state without having to rely on any timer configuration.

Refer to
Figure
in online course

RSTP BPDU

RSTP (802.1w) uses type 2, version 2 BPDUs, so an RSTP bridge can communicate 802.1D on any shared link or with any switch running 802.1D. RSTP sends BPDUs and populates the flag byte in a slightly different manner than in 802.1D:

- Protocol information can be immediately aged on a port if hellos are not received for three consecutive hello times, 6 seconds by default, or if the max age timer expires.

- Because BPDUs are used as a keepalive mechanism, three consecutively missed BPDUs indicate lost connectivity between a bridge and its neighboring root or designated bridge. The fast aging of the information allows failures to be detected quickly.

Note: Like STP, an RSTP bridge sends a BPDU with its current information every hello time period (2 seconds by default), even if the RSTP bridge does not receive any BPDUs from the root bridge.

RSTP uses the flag byte of version 2 BPDU as shown in the figure:

- Bits 0 and 7 are used for topology change and *acknowledgment* as they are in 802.1D.

- Bits 1 and 6 are used for the Proposal Agreement process (used for rapid convergence).

- Bits 2-5 encode the role and state of the port originating the BPDU.

- Bits 4 and 5 are used to encode the port role using a 2-bit code.

5.4.4 Edge Ports

Refer to
Figure
in online course

Edge Ports

An RSTP edge port is a switch port that is never intended to be connected to another switch device. It immediately transitions to the forwarding state when enabled.

The edge port concept is well known to Cisco spanning-tree users, because it corresponds to the PortFast feature in which all ports directly connected to end stations anticipate that no switch device is connected to them. The PortFast ports immediately transition to the STP forwarding state, thereby skipping the time-consuming listening and learning stages. Neither edge ports nor PortFast-enabled ports generate topology changes when the port transitions to a disabled or enabled status.

Unlike PortFast, an RSTP edge port that receives a BPDU loses its edge port status immediately and becomes a normal spanning-tree port.

The Cisco RSTP implementation maintains the PortFast keyword using the `spanning-tree port-fast` command for edge port configuration. Therefore making an overall network transition to RSTP more seamless. Configuring an edge port to be attached to another switch can have negative implications for RSTP when it is in sync state because a temporary loop can result, possibly delaying the convergence of RSTP due to BPDU contention with loop traffic.

5.4.5 Link Types

Refer to
Figure
in online course

Link Types

The link type provides a categorization for each port participating in RSTP. The link type can predetermine the active role that the port plays as it stands by for immediate transition to forwarding state if certain conditions are met. These conditions are different for edge ports and non-edge ports. Non-edge ports are categorized into two link types, point-to-point and shared. The link type is automatically determined, but can be overwritten with an explicit port configuration.

Edge ports, the equivalent of PortFast-enabled ports, and point-to-point links are candidates for rapid transition to a forwarding state. However, before the link type parameter is considered, RSTP must determine the port role. You will learn about port roles next, but for now know that:

- Root ports do not use the link type parameter. Root ports are able to make a rapid transition to the forwarding state as soon as the port is in sync.

- Alternate and backup ports do not use the link type parameter in most cases.

- Designated ports make the most use of the link type parameter. Rapid transition to the forwarding state for the designated port occurs only if the link type parameter indicates a point-to-point link.

5.4.6 RSTP Port States and Port Roles

Refer to
Figure
in online course

RSTP Port States

RSTP provides rapid convergence following a failure or during re-establishment of a switch, switch port, or link. An RSTP topology change causes a transition in the appropriate switch ports to the forwarding state through either explicit handshakes or a proposal and agreement process and synchronization. You will learn more about the proposal and agreement process later.

With RSTP, the role of a port is separated from the state of a port. For example, a designated port could be in the discarding state temporarily, even though its final state is to be forwarding. The figure shows the three possible RSTP port states: discarding, learning, and forwarding.

Click the Descriptions button in the figure.

The table in the figure describes the characteristics of each of the three RSTP port states. In all port states, a port accepts and processes BPDU frames.

Click the STP and RSTP Ports button in the figure.

The table in the figure compares STP and RSTP port states. Recall how the ports in the STP blocking, listening and disabled port states do not forward any frames. These port states have been merged into the RSTP discarding port state.

Refer to
Figure
in online course

RSTP Port Roles

The port role defines the ultimate purpose of a switch port and how it handles data frames. Port roles and port states are able to transition independently of each other. Creating the additional port roles allows RSTP to define a standby switch port before a failure or topology change. The alternate port moves to the forwarding state if there is a failure on the designated port for the segment.

Roll over the port roles in the figure to learn more about each RSTP port role.

Refer to
Figure
in online course

RSTP Proposal and Agreement Process

In IEEE 802.1D STP, when a port has been selected by spanning tree to become a designated port, it must wait two times the forward delay before transitioning the port to the forwarding state. RSTP significantly speeds up the recalculation process after a topology change, because it converges on a link-by-link basis and does not rely on timers expiring before ports can transition. Rapid transition to the forwarding state can only be achieved on edge ports and point-to-point links. In RSTP, this condition corresponds to a designated port in the discarding state.

Click the Play button in the figure to start the animation.

5.4.7 Configuring Rapid-PVST+

Refer to
Figure
in online course

Rapid-PVST+ is a Cisco implementation of RSTP. It supports spanning tree for each VLAN and is the rapid STP variant to use in Cisco-based networks. The topology in the figure has two VLANs: 10 and 20. The final configuration will implement rapid-PVST+ on switch S1, which is the root bridge.

Configuration Guidelines

It is useful to review some of the spanning tree configuration guidelines. If you would like to review the default spanning-tree configuration on a Cisco 2960 switch, see the Default Switch Configuration section earlier in this chapter. Keep these guidelines in mind when you implement rapid-PVST+.

Rapid-PVST+ commands control the configuration of VLAN spanning-tree instances. A spanning-tree instance is created when an interface is assigned to a VLAN and is removed when the last interface is moved to another VLAN. As well, you can configure STP switch and port parameters before a spanning-tree instance is created. These parameters are applied when a loop is created and a spanning-tree instance is created. However, ensure that at least one switch on each loop in the VLAN is running spanning tree, otherwise a broadcast storm can result.

The Cisco 2960 switch supports PVST+, rapid-PVST+, and MSTP, but only one version can be active for all VLANs at any time.

For details on configuring the STP software features on a Cisco 2960 series switch visit this Cisco site:

http://www.cisco.com/en/US/products/ps6406/
products_configuration_guide_chapter09186a0080875377.html.

Click the Configuration Commands button in the figure.

The figure shows the Cisco IOS command syntax needed to configure rapid-PVST+ on a Cisco switch. There are other parameters that can also be configured.

Note: If you connect a port configured with the spanning-tree link-type point-to-point command to a remote port through a point-to-point link and the local port becomes a designated port, the switch negotiates with the remote port and rapidly changes the local port to the forwarding state.

Note: When a port is configured with the clear spanning-tree detected-protocols command and that port is connected to a port on a legacy IEEE 802.1D switch, the Cisco IOS software restarts the protocol migration process on the entire switch. This step is optional, though recommended as a standard practice, even if the designated switch detects that this switch is running rapid-PVST+.

For complete details on all the parameters associated with specific Cisco IOS commands, visit:
http://www.cisco.com/en/US/docs/switches/lan/catalyst2960/software/release/12.2_37_se/command/reference/cli3.html.

Click the Example Configuration button in the figure.

The example configuration shows the rapid-PVST+ commands being enabled on switch S1.

Click the Verify button in the figure.

The `show spanning-tree vlan` *vlan-id* command shows the configuration of VLAN 10 on switch S1. Notice that the BID priority is set to 4096. The BID was set using the `spanning-tree vlan` *vlan-id* `priority` *priority-number* command.

Click the `show run` button in the figure.

In this example, the `show running-configuration` command has been used to verify the rapid-PVST+ configuration on S1.

5.4.8 Design STP for Trouble Avoidance

Refer to
Figure
in online course

Know Where the Root Is

You now know that the primary function of the STA is to break loops that redundant links create in bridge networks. STP operates at Layer 2 of the OSI model. STP can fail in some specific cases. Troubleshooting the problem can be very difficult and depends on the design of the network. That is why it is recommended that you perform the most important part of the troubleshooting before the problem occurs.

Very often information about the location of the root is not available at troubleshooting time. Do not leave it up to the STP to decide which bridge is root. For each VLAN, you can usually identify which switch can best serve as root. Generally, choose a powerful bridge in the middle of the network. If you put the root bridge in the center of the network with a direct connection to the servers and routers, you reduce the average distance from the clients to the servers and routers.

The figure shows:

- If switch S2 is the root, the link from S1 to S3 is blocked on S1 or S3. In this case, hosts that connect to switch S2 can access the server and the router in two hops. Hosts that connect to bridge S3 can access the server and the router in three hops. The average distance is two and one-half hops.

- If switch S1 is the root, the router and the server are reachable in two hops for both hosts that connect on S2 and S3. The average distance is now two hops.

The logic behind this simple example transfers to more complex topologies.

Note: For each VLAN, configure the root bridge and the backup root bridge using lower priorities.

Refer to
Figure
in online course

To make it easier to solve STP problems, plan the organization of your redundant links. In non-hierarchical networks you might need to tune the STP cost parameter to decide which ports to block. However, this tuning is usually not necessary if you have a hierarchical design and a root bridge in a good location.

Note: For each VLAN, know which ports should be blocking in the stable network. Have a network diagram that clearly shows each physical loop in the network and which blocked ports break the loops.

Knowing the location of redundant links helps you identify an accidental bridging loop and the cause. Also, knowing the location of blocked ports allows you to determine the location of the error.

Minimize the Number of Blocked Ports

The only critical action that STP takes is the blocking of ports. A single blocking port that mistakenly transitions to forwarding can negatively impact a large part of the network. A good way to limit the risk inherent in the use of STP is to reduce the number of blocked ports as much as possible.

VTP Pruning

You do not need more than two redundant links between two nodes in a switched network. However, a configuration shown in the figure is common. Distribution switches are dual-attached to two core switches, switches, C1 and C2. Users on switches S1 and S2 that connect on distribution switches are only in a subset of the VLANs available in the network. In the figure, users that connect on switch D1 are all in VLAN 20; switch D2 only connects users in VLAN 30. By default, trunks carry all the VLANs defined in the VTP domain. Only switch D1 receives unnecessary broadcast and multicast traffic for VLAN 20, but it is also blocking one of its ports for VLAN 30. There are three redundant paths between core switch C1 and core switch C2. This redundancy results in more blocked ports and a higher likelihood of a loop.

Note: Prune any VLAN that you do not need off your trunks.

Click the Manual Pruning button in the figure.

Manual Pruning

VTP pruning can help, but this feature is not necessary in the core of the network. In this figure, only an access VLAN is used to connect the distribution switches to the core. In this design, only one port is blocked per VLAN. Also, with this design, you can remove all redundant links in just one step if you shut down C1 or C2.

Refer to
Figure
in online course

Use Layer 3 Switching

Layer 3 switching means routing approximately at the speed of switching. A router performs two main functions:

- It builds a forwarding table. The router generally exchanges information with peers by way of routing protocols.

- It receives packets and forwards them to the correct interface based on the destination address.

High-end Cisco Layer 3 switches are now able to perform this second function, at the same speed as the Layer 2 switching function. In the figure:

- There is no speed penalty with the routing *hop* and an additional segment between C1 and C2.

- Core switch C1 and core switch C2 are Layer 3 switches. VLAN 20 and VLAN 30 are no longer bridged between C1 and C2, so there is no possibility for a loop.

Redundancy is still present, with a reliance on Layer 3 routing protocols. The design ensures a convergence that is even faster than convergence with STP.

- STP no longer blocks any single port, so there is no potential for a bridging loop.

- Leaving the VLAN by Layer 3 switching is as fast as bridging inside the VLAN.

Refer to
Figure
in online course

Final Points

Keep STP Even If It Is Unnecessary

Assuming you have removed all the blocked ports from the network and do not have any physical redundancy, it is strongly suggested that you do not disable STP.

STP is generally not very processor intensive; packet switching does not involve the CPU in most Cisco switches. Also, the few BPDUs that are sent on each link do not significantly reduce the available bandwidth. However, if a technician makes a connection error on a patch panel and accidentally creates a loop, the network will be negatively impacted. Generally, disabling STP in a switched network is not worth the risk.

Keep Traffic off the Administrative VLAN and Do Not Have a Single VLAN Span the Entire Network

A Cisco switch typically has a single IP address that binds to a VLAN, known as the administrative VLAN. In this VLAN, the switch behaves like a generic IP host. In particular, every broadcast or multicast packet is forwarded to the CPU. A high rate of broadcast or multicast traffic on the administrative VLAN can adversely impact the CPU and its ability to process vital BPDUs. Therefore, keep user traffic off the administrative VLAN.

Until recently, there was no way to remove VLAN 1 from a trunk in a Cisco implementation. VLAN 1 generally serves as an administrative VLAN, where all switches are accessible in the same IP subnet. Though useful, this setup can be dangerous because a bridging loop on VLAN 1 affects all trunks, which can bring down the whole network. Of course, the same problem exists no matter which VLAN you use. Try to segment the bridging domains using high-speed Layer 3 switches.

Note: As of Cisco IOS Software Release 12.1(11b)E, you can remove VLAN 1 from trunks. VLAN 1 still exists, but it blocks traffic, which prevents any loop possibility.

5.4.9 Troubleshoot STP Operation

Switch or Link Failure

Refer to Figure in online course

In the animation you see that when a port fails in a network configured with STP, a broadcast storm may result.

In the intial state of the STP failure scenario, switch S3 has a lower BID than S2 consequently the designated port between S3 and S2 is port F0/1 on switch S3. Switch S3 is considered to have a "better BPDU" than switch S2.

Click the Play button in the figure to see STP fail.

Refer to Figure in online course

Troubleshoot a Failure

Unfortunately, there is no systematic procedure to troubleshoot an STP issue. This section summarizes some of the actions that are available to you. Most of the steps apply to troubleshooting bridging loops in general. You can use a more conventional approach to identify other failures of STP that lead to a loss of connectivity. For example, you can explore the path being taken by the traffic that is experiencing a problem.

Note: In-band access may not be available during a bridging loop. For example, during a broadcast storm you may not be able to Telnet to the infrastructure devices. Therefore, *out-of-band* connectivity, such as console access may be required.

Before you troubleshoot a bridging loop, you need to know at least these items:

- Topology of the bridge network
- Location of the root bridge
- Location of the blocked ports and the redundant links

This knowledge is essential. To know what to fix in the network, you need to know how the network looks when it works correctly. Most of the troubleshooting steps simply use **show** commands to try to identify error conditions. Knowledge of the network helps you focus on the critical ports on the key devices.

The rest of this topic briefly looks at two common spanning tree problems, a PortFast configuration error and network diameter issues. To learn about other STP issues, visit: http://www.cisco.com/en/US/tech/tk389/tk621/technologies_tech_note09186a00800951ac.shtml.

Refer to Figure in online course

PortFast Configuration Error

You typically enable PortFast only for a port or interface that connects to a host. When the link comes up on this port, the bridge skips the first stages of the STA and directly transitions to the forwarding mode.

Caution: Do not use PortFast on switch ports or interfaces that connect to other switches, hubs, or routers. Otherwise, you may create a network loop.

In this example, port F0/1 on switch S1 is already forwarding. Port F0/2 has erroneously been configured with the PortFast feature. Therefore, when a second connection from switch S2 is connected to F0/2 on S1, the port automatically transitions to forwarding mode and creates a loop.

Eventually, one of the switches will forward a BPDU and one of these switches will transition a port into blocking mode.

However, there is a problem with this kind of transient loop. If the looped traffic is very intensive, the switch can have trouble successfully transmitting the BPDU that stops the loop. This problem can delay the convergence considerably or in some extreme cases can actually bring down the network.

Even with a PortFast configuration, the port or interface still participates in STP. If a switch with a lower bridge priority than that of the current active root bridge attaches to a PortFast-configured port or interface, it can be elected as the root bridge. This change of root bridge can adversely affect the active STP topology and can render the network suboptimal. To prevent this situation, most Catalyst switches that run Cisco IOS software have a feature called BPDU guard. BPDU guard disables a PortFast-configured port or interface if the port or interface receives a BPDU.

For more information on using PortFast on switches that run Cisco IOS software, refer to the document "Using PortFast and Other Commands to Fix Workstation Startup Connectivity Delays," available at: http://www.cisco.com/en/US/products/hw/switches/ps700/products_tech_note09186a00800b1500.shtml.

For more information on using the BPDU guard feature on switches that run Cisco IOS software, visit: http://www.cisco.com/en/US/tech/tk389/tk621/technologies_tech_note09186a008009482f.shtml.

Refer to
Figure
in online course

Network Diameter Issues

Another issue that is not well known relates to the diameter of the switched network. The conservative default values for the STP timers impose a maximum network diameter of seven. In the figure this design creates a network diameter of eight. The maximum network diameter restricts how far away swtiches in the network can be from each other. In this case, two distinct switches cannot be more than seven hops away. Part of this restriction comes from the age field that BPDUs carry.

When a BPDU propagates from the root bridge toward the leaves of the tree, the age field increments each time the BPDU goes though a switch. Eventually, the switch discards the BPDU when the age field goes beyond maximum age. If the root is too far away from some switches of the network, BPDUs will be dropped. This issue affects convergence of the spanning tree.

Take special care if you plan to change STP timers from the default value. There is danger if you try to get faster convergence in this way. An STP timer change has an impact on the diameter of the network and the stability of the STP. You can change the switch priority to select the root bridge, and change the port cost or priority parameter to control redundancy and load balancing.

Refer to
Figure
in online course

5.5 Chapter Labs

5.5.1 Basic Spanning Tree Protocol

Refer to
Lab Activity
for this chapter

One of the design goals of any network is redundancy. If a network link fails, is there a backup link that can immediately switch the traffic that was previously going over the down link? Physical redundancy in the network is necessary to prevent network outages or down time. However that same physical redundancy in the network creates a logical problem. If there is physical redundancy in the switch network, how do you prevent Layer 2 loops from occuring? Spanning Tree Protocol (STP) was written to solve this problem. In this lab we will learn how to configure STP.

5.5.2 Challenge Spanning Tree Protocol

Refer to
Lab Activity
for this chapter

A strong understanding of how to configure Spanning Tree Protocol is fundamental to implementing switched networks. This lab will give you additional practice in configuring it.

Refer to **Packet Tracer Activity**
for this chapter

This activity is a variation of Lab 5.5.2. Packet Tracer may not support all the tasks specified in the hands-on lab. This activity should not be considered equivalent to completing the hands-on lab. Packet Tracer is not a substitute for a hands-on lab experience with real equipment.

Detailed instructions are provided within the activity as well as in the PDF link below.

Activity Instructions (PDF)

5.5.3 Troubleshooting Spanning Tree Protocol

Refer to
Lab Activity
for this chapter

You are responsible for the operation of the redundant switched LAN shown in the topology diagram. You and your users have been observing increased latency during peak usage times, and your analysis points to congested trunks. You recognize that of the six trunks configured, only three are forwarding packets in the default STP configuration currently running. The solution to this problem requires more effective use of the available trunks. The PVST+ feature of Cisco switches provides the required flexibility to distribute the inter-switch traffic using all six trunks.

This lab is complete when all wired trunks are carrying traffic, and all three switches are participating in per-VLAN load balancing for the three user VLANs.

Refer to **Packet Tracer Activity**
for this chapter

This activity is a variation of Lab 5.5.3. Packet Tracer may not support all the tasks specified in the hands-on lab. This activity should not be considered equivalent to completing the hands-on lab. Packet Tracer is not a substitute for a hands-on lab experience with real equipment.

Detailed instructions are provided within the activity as well as in the PDF link below.

Activity Instructions (PDF)

Chapter Summary

Refer to
Figure
in online course

Implementing redundancy in a hierarchical network introduces physical loops that result in Layer 2 issues which impact network availability. To prevent problems resulting from physical loops introduced to enhance redundancy, the spanning-tree protocol was developed. The spanning-tree protocol uses the spanning-tree algorithm to compute a loop-free logical topology for a broadcast domain.

The spanning-tree process uses different port states and timers to logically prevent loops by constructing a loop-free topology. The determination of the spanning-tree topology is constructed in terms of the distance from the root bridge. The distance is determined by the exchange of BPDUs and spanning-tree algorithm. In the process, port roles are determined: designated ports, non-designated ports, and root ports.

Using the original IEEE 802.1D spanning-tree protocol involves a convergence time of up to 50 seconds. This time delay is unacceptable in modern switched networks, so the IEEE 802.1w rapid spanning-tree protocol was developed. The per-VLAN Cisco implementation of IEEE 802.1D is called PVST+ and the per-VLAN Cisco implementation of rapid spanning-tree protocol is rapid PVST+. RSTP reduces convergence time to approximately 6 seconds or less.

We discussed point-to-point and shared link types with RSTP, as well as edge ports. We also discussed the new concepts of alternate ports and backup ports used with RSTP.

Refer to
Figure
in online course

Rapid PVST+ is the preferred spanning-tree protocol implementation used in a switched network running Cisco Catalyst switches.

Refer to **Packet Tracer Activity** for this chapter

In this activity, you will configure a redundant network with VTP, VLANs, and STP. In addition, you will design an addressing scheme based on user requirements. The VLANs in this activity are different than what you have seen in previous chapters. It is important for you to know that the management and default VLAN does not have to be 99. It can be any number you choose. Therefore, we use VLAN 5 in this activity.

Detailed instructions are provided within the activity as well as in the PDF link below.

Activity Instructions (PDF)

Chapter Quiz

Go to
the online course
to take the quiz.

Take the chapter quiz to test your knowledge.

Your Chapter Notes

CHAPTER 6

Inter-VLAN Routing

Chapter Introduction

Refer to
Figure
in online course

In the previous chapters of this course, we discussed how you can use VLANs and trunks to segment a network. Limiting the scope of each broadcast domain on the LAN through VLAN segmentation provides better performance and security across the network. You also learned how VTP is used to share the VLAN information across multiple switches in a LAN environment to simplify management of VLANs. Now that you have a network with many different VLANs, the next question is, "How do we permit devices on separate VLANs to communicate?"

In this chapter, you will learn about inter-VLAN routing and how it is used to permit devices on separate VLANs to communicate. You will learn different methods for accomplishing inter-VLAN routing, and the advantages and disadvantages of each. You will also learn how different router interface configurations facilitate inter-VLAN routing. Finally, you will explore the potential issues faced when implementing inter-VLAN routing, and how to identify and correct them.

6.1 Inter-VLAN Routing

6.1.1 Introducing Inter-VLAN Routing

Refer to
Figure
in online course

Now that you know how to configure VLANs on a network switch, the next step is to allow devices connected to the various VLANs to communicate with each other. In a previous chapter, you learned that each VLAN is a unique broadcast domain, so computers on separate VLANs are, by default, not able to communicate. There is a way to permit these end stations to communicate; it is called inter-VLAN routing. In this topic, you will learn what inter-VLAN routing is and some of the different ways to accomplish inter-VLAN routing on a network.

In this chapter, we focus on one type of inter-VLAN routing using a separate router connected to the switch infrastructure. We define inter-VLAN routing as a process of forwarding network traffic from one VLAN to another VLAN using a router. VLANs are associated with unique IP subnets on the network. This subnet configuration facilitates the routing process in a multi-VLAN environment. When using a router to facilitate inter-VLAN routing, the router interfaces can be connected to separate VLANs. Devices on those VLANs send traffic through the router to reach other VLANs.

As you can see in the figure, traffic from PC1 on VLAN10 is routed through router R1 to reach PC3 on VLAN30.

Refer to
Figure
in online course

Traditionally, LAN routing has used routers with multiple physical interfaces. Each interface needed to be connected to a separate network and configured for a different subnet.

In a traditional network that uses multiple VLANs to segment the network traffic into logical broadcast domains, routing is performed by connecting different physical router interfaces to different physical switch ports. The switch ports connect to the router in access mode; in access mode, different static VLANs are assigned to each port interface. Each switch interface would be assigned to a different static VLAN. Each router interface can then accept traffic from the VLAN associated with the switch interface that it is connected to, and traffic can be routed to the other VLANs connected to the other interfaces.

Click the Play button in the figure to view traditional inter-VLAN routing.

As you can see in the animation:

Step 1. PC1 on VLAN10 is communicating with PC3 on VLAN30 through router R1.

Step 2. PC1 and PC3 are on different VLANs and have IP addresses on different subnets.

Step 3. Router R1 has a separate interface configured for each of the VLANs.

Step 4. PC1 sends unicast traffic destined for PC3 to switch S2 on VLAN10, where it is then forwarded out the trunk interface to switch S1.

Step 5. Switch S1 then forwards the unicast traffic to router R1 on interface F0/0.

Step 6. The router routes the unicast traffic through to its interface F0/1, which is connected to VLAN30.

Step 7. The router forwards the unicast traffic to switch S1 on VLAN 30.

Step 8. Switch S1 then forwards the unicast traffic to switch S2 through the trunk link, after which switch S2 can then forward the unicast traffic to PC3 on VLAN30.

In this example, the router was configured with two separate physical interfaces to interact with the different VLANs and perform the routing.

Traditional inter-VLAN routing requires multiple physical interfaces on both the router and the switch. However, not all inter-VLAN routing configurations require multiple physical interfaces. Some router software permits configuring router interfaces as trunk links. This opens up new possibilities for inter-VLAN routing.

Refer to
Figure
in online course

"Router-on-a-stick" is a type of router configuration in which a single physical interface routes traffic between multiple VLANs on a network. As you can see in the figure, the router is connected to switch S1 using a single, physical network connection.

The router interface is configured to operate as a trunk link and is connected to a switch port configured in trunk mode. The router performs the inter-VLAN routing by accepting VLAN tagged traffic on the trunk interface coming from the adjacent switch and internally routing between the VLANs using *subinterfaces*. The router then forwards the routed traffic-VLAN tagged for the destination VLAN-out the same physical interface.

Subinterfaces are multiple virtual interfaces, associated with one physical interface. These subinterfaces are configured in software on a router that is independently configured with an IP address and VLAN assignment to operate on a specific VLAN. Subinterfaces are configured for different subnets corresponding to their VLAN assignment to facilitate logical routing before the data frames are VLAN tagged and sent back out the physical interface. You will learn more about interfaces and subinterfaces in the next topic.

Click the Play button in the figure to view how a router-on-a-stick performs its routing function.

As you can see in the animation:

Step 1. PC1 on VLAN10 is communicating with PC3 on VLAN30 through router R1 using a single, physical router interface.

Step 2. PC1 sends its unicast traffic to switch S2.

Step 3. Switch S2 then tags the unicast traffic as originating on VLAN10 and forwards the unicast traffic out its trunk link to switch S1.

Step 4. Switch S1 forwards the tagged traffic out the other trunk interface on port F0/5 to the interface on router R1.

Step 5. Router R1 accepts the tagged unicast traffic on VLAN10 and routes it to VLAN30 using its configured subinterfaces.

Step 6. The unicast traffic is tagged with VLAN30 as it is sent out the router interface to switch S1.

Step 7. Switch S1 forwards the tagged unicast traffic out the other trunk link to switch S2.

Step 8. Switch S2 removes the VLAN tag of the unicast frame and forwards the frame out to PC3 on port F0/6.

Refer to **Figure** in online course

Some switches can perform Layer 3 functions, replacing the need for dedicated routers to perform basic routing on a network. Multilayer switches are capable of performing inter-VLAN routing.

Click the Play button in the figure to see how switch-based inter-VLAN routing occurs.

As you can see in the animation:

Step 1. PC1 on VLAN10 is communicating with PC3 on VLAN30 through switch S1 using VLAN interfaces configured for each VLAN.

Step 2. PC1 sends its unicast traffic to switch S2.

Step 3. Switch S2 tags the unicast traffic as originating on VLAN10 as it forwards the unicast traffic out its trunk link to switch S1.

Step 4. Switch S1 removes the VLAN tag and forwards the unicast traffic to the VLAN10 interface.

Step 5. Switch S1 routes the unicast traffic to its VLAN30 interface.

Step 6. Switch S1 then retags the unicast traffic with VLAN30 and forwards it out the trunk link back to switch S2.

Step 7. Switch S2 removes the VLAN tag of the unicast frame and forwards the frame out to PC3 on port F0/6.

To enable a multilayer switch to perform routing functions, VLAN interfaces on the switch need to be configured with the appropriate IP addresses that match the subnet that the VLAN is associated with on the network. The multilayer switch also must have IP routing enabled. Multilayer switching is complex and beyond the scope of this course. For a good overview of multilayer switching, visit: http://cisco.com/en/US/docs/ios/12_0/switch/configuration/guide/xcmls.html.

Configuring inter-VLAN routing on a multilayer switch is beyond the scope of this course. However, the CCNP curriculum covers the concept comprehensively. Also, to explore additional information, visit: http://www.cisco.com/en/US/tech/tk389/tk815/technologies_configuration_example09186a008019e74e.shtml.

6.1.2 Interfaces and Subinterfaces

Refer to **Figure** in online course

As we discussed, there are various inter-VLAN routing options to choose from. Each uses a different router configuration to accomplish the task of routing between VLANs. In this topic, we will look at how each type of router interface configuration routes between VLANs, and the advantages and disadvantages. We will begin by reviewing the traditional model.

Using the Router as a Gateway

Traditional routing requires routers to have multiple physical interfaces to facilitate inter-VLAN routing. The router accomplishes the routing by having each of its physical interfaces connected to a unique VLAN. Each interface is also configured with an IP address for the subnet associated with the particular VLAN that it is connected to. By configuring the IP addresses on the physical interfaces, network devices connected to each of the VLANs can communicate with the router using the physical interface connected to the same VLAN. In this configuration, network devices can use the router as a *gateway* to access the devices connected to the other VLANs.

The routing process requires the source device to determine if the destination device is local or remote to the local subnet. The source device accomplishes this by comparing the source and destination addresses against the subnet mask. Once the destination address has been determined to be on a remote network, the source device has to identify where it needs to forward the packet to reach the destination device. The source device examines the local *routing table* to determine where it needs to send the data. Typically, devices use their default gateway as the destination for all traffic that needs to leave the local subnet. The default gateway is the route that the device uses when it has no other explicitly defined route to the destination network. The router interface on the local subnet acts as the default gateway for the sending device.

Once the source device has determined that the packet must travel through the local router interface on the connected VLAN, the source device sends out an ARP request to determine the MAC address of the local router interface. Once the router sends its ARP reply back to the source device, the source device can use the MAC address to finish framing the packet before it sends it out on the network as unicast traffic.

Since the Ethernet frame has the destination MAC address of the router interface, the switch knows exactly which switch port to forward the unicast traffic out of to reach the router interface on that VLAN. When the frame arrives at the router, the router removes the source and destination MAC address information to examine the destination IP address of the packet. The router compares the destination address to entries in its routing table to determine where it needs to forward the data to reach its final destination. If the router determines that the destination network is a locally connected network, as would be the case in inter-VLAN routing, the router sends an ARP request out the interface physically connected to the destination VLAN. The destination device responds back to the router with its MAC address, which the router then uses to frame the packet. The router then sends the unicast traffic to the switch, which forwards it out the port where the destination device is connected.

Click the Play button in the figure to view how traditional routing is accomplished.

Even though there are many steps in the process of inter-VLAN routing when two devices on different VLANs communicate through a router, the entire process happens in a fraction of a second.

Refer to
Figure
in online course

Interface Configuration

Click the Interface Configuration button in the figure to see an example of router interfaces being configured.

Router interfaces are configured similarly to configuring VLAN interfaces on switches. In global configuration mode, switch to interface configuration mode for the specific interface you want to configure.

As you see in the example, interface F0/0 is configured with IP address 172.17.10.1 and subnet mask 255.255.255.0 using the `ip address 172.17.10.1 255.255.255.0` command.

To enable a router interface, the `no shutdown` command needs to be entered for the interface. Notice also that interface F0/1 has been configured. After both IP addresses are assigned to each of the physical interfaces, the router is capable of performing routing.

Click the Routing Table button in the figure to see an example of a routing table on a Cisco router.

Routing Table

As you can see in the example, the routing table has two entries, one for network 172.17.10.0 and the other for network 172.17.30.0. Notice the letter **C** to the left of each route entry. This letter indicates that the route is local for a connected interface, which is also identified in the route entry. Using the output in this example, if traffic was destined for the 172.17.30.0 subnet, the router would forward the traffic out interface F0/1.

Traditional inter-VLAN routing using physical interfaces does have a limitation. As the number of VLANs increases on a network, the physical approach of having one router interface per VLAN quickly becomes hindered by the physical hardware limitations of a router. Routers have a limited number of physical interfaces that they can use to connect to different VLANs. Large networks with many VLANs must use VLAN trunking to assign multiple VLANs to a single router interface to work within the hardware constraints of dedicated routers.

Refer to
Figure
in online course

To overcome the hardware limitations of inter-VLAN routing based on router physical interfaces, virtual subinterfaces and trunk links are used, as in the router-on-a-stick example described earlier. Subinterfaces are software-based virtual interfaces that are assigned to physical interfaces. Each subinterface is configured with its own IP address, subnet mask, and unique VLAN assignment, allowing a single physical interface to simultaneously be part of multiple logical networks. This is useful when performing inter-VLAN routing on networks with multiple VLANs and few router physical interfaces.

When configuring inter-VLAN routing using the router-on-a-stick model, the physical interface of the router must be connected to a trunk link on the adjacent switch. Subinterfaces are created for each unique VLAN/subnet on the network. Each subinterface is assigned an IP address specific to the subnet that it will be part of and configured to VLAN tag frames for the VLAN that the interface is to interact with. That way, the router can keep the traffic from each subinterface separated as it traverses the trunk link back to the switch.

Functionally, the router-on-a-stick model for inter-VLAN routing is the same as using the traditional routing model, but instead of using the physical interfaces to perform the routing, subinterfaces of a single interface are used.

Let's explore an example. In the figure, PC1 wants to communicate with PC3. PC1 is on VLAN10, and PC3 is on VLAN30. For PC1 to communicate with PC3, PC1 needs to have its data routed through router R1 using configured subinterfaces.

Click the Play button in the figure to see how subinterfaces are used to route between VLANs.

Refer to
Figure
in online course

Subinterface Configuration

Configuring router subinterfaces is similar to configuring physical interfaces, except that you need to create the subinterface and assign it to a VLAN.

In the example, create the router subinterface by entering the `interface f0/0.10` command in global configuration mode. The syntax for the subinterface is always the physical interface, in this case **f0/0**, followed by a period and a subinterface number. The subinterface number is configurable, but it is typically associated to reflect the VLAN number. In the example, the subinterfaces use **10** and **30** as subinterface numbers to make it easier to remember which VLANs they are associated with. The physical interface is specified because there could be multiple interfaces in the router, each of which could be configured to support many subinterfaces.

Before assigning an IP address to a subinterface, the subinterface needs to be configured to operate on a specific VLAN using the **encapsulation dot1q** *vlan id* command. In the example, subinterface Fa0/0.10 is assigned to VLAN10. After the VLAN has been assigned, the **ip address 172.17.10.1 255.255.255.0** command assigns the subinterface to the appropriate IP address for that VLAN.

Unlike a typical physical interface, subinterfaces are not enabled with the **no shutdown** command at the subinterface configuration mode level of the Cisco IOS software. Instead, when the physical interface is enabled with the **no shutdown** command, all the configured subinterfaces are enabled. Likewise, if the physical interface is disabled, all subinterfaces are disabled.

Click the Routing Table button in the figure to see an example of a routing table when subinterfaces are configured.

Router Table Output

As you see in the figure, the routes defined in the routing table indicate that they are associated with specific subinterfaces, rather than separate physical interfaces.

One advantage of using a trunk link is that the number of router and switch ports used are reduced. Not only can this save money, it can also reduce configuration complexity. Consequently, the router subinterface approach can scale to a much larger number of VLANs than a configuration with one physical interface per VLAN design.

As we just discussed, both physical interfaces and subinterfaces are used to perform inter-VLAN routing. There are advantages and disadvantage to each method.

Refer to
Figure
in online course

Port Limits

Physical interfaces are configured to have one interface per VLAN on the network. On networks with many VLANs, using a single router to perform inter-VLAN routing is not possible. Routers have physical limitations that prevent them from containing large numbers of physical interfaces. Instead, you could use multiple routers to perform inter-VLAN routing for all VLANs if avoiding the use of subinterfaces is a priority.

Subinterfaces allow a router to scale to accommodate more VLANs than the physical interfaces permit. Inter-VLAN routing in large environments with many VLANs can usually be better accommodated by using a single physical interface with many subinterfaces.

Performance

Because there is no contention for bandwidth on separate physical interfaces, physical interfaces have better performance when compared to using subinterfaces. Traffic from each connected VLAN has access to the full bandwidth of the physical router interface connected to that VLAN for inter-VLAN routing.

When subinterfaces are used for inter-VLAN routing, the traffic being routed competes for bandwidth on the single physical interface. On a busy network, this could cause a bottleneck for communication. To balance the traffic load on a physical interface, subinterfaces are configured on multiple physical interfaces resulting in less contention between VLAN traffic.

Access Ports and Trunk Ports

Connecting physical interfaces for inter-VLAN routing requires that the switch ports be configured as access ports. Subinterfaces require the switch port to be configured as a trunk port so that it can accept VLAN tagged traffic on the trunk link. Using subinterfaces, many VLANs can be routed over a single trunk link rather than a single physical interface for each VLAN.

Cost

Financially, it is more cost-effective to use subinterfaces over separate physical interfaces. Routers that have many physical interfaces cost more than routers with a single interface. Additionally, if you have a router with many physical interfaces, each interface is connected to a separate switch port, consuming extra switch ports on the network. Switch ports are an expensive resource on high performance switches. By consuming additional ports for inter-VLAN routing functions, both the switch and the router drive up the overall cost of the inter-VLAN routing solution.

Complexity

Using subinterfaces for inter-VLAN routing results in a less complex physical configuration than using separate physical interfaces, because there are fewer physical network cables interconnecting the router to the switch. With fewer cables, there is less confusion about where the cable is connected on the switch. Because the VLANs are being trunked over a single link, it is easier to troubleshoot the physical connections.

On the other hand, using subinterfaces with a trunk port results in a more complex software configuration, which can be difficult to troubleshoot. In the router-on-a-stick model, only a single interface is used to accommodate all the different VLANs. If one VLAN is having trouble routing to other VLANs, you cannot simply trace the cable to see if the cable is plugged into the correct port. You need to check to see if the switch port is configured to be a trunk and verify that the VLAN is not being filtered on any of the trunk links before it reaches the router interface. You also need to check that the router subinterface is configured to use the correct VLAN ID and IP address for the subnet associated with that VLAN.

6.2 Configuring Inter-VLAN Routing

6.2.1 Configure Inter-VLAN Routing

Refer to
Figure
in online course

In this topic, you will learn how to configure a Cisco IOS router for inter-VLAN routing, as well as review the commands needed to configure a switch to support inter-VLAN routing.

Before configuring the router, configure the switch that it will be connected to. As you see in the figure, Router R1 is connected to switch ports F0/4 and F0/5, which have been configured for VLANs 10 and 30, respectively.

Click the Switch Configuration button in the figure to see the example switch configuration.

To review, VLANs are created in global configuration mode using the `vlan vlan id` command. In this example, VLANs 10 and 30 were created on switch S1.

After the VLANs have been created, they are assigned to the switch ports that the router will be connecting to. To accomplish this task, the `switchport access vlan vlan id` command is executed from interface configuration mode on the switch for each interface that the router will connect to.

In this example, interfaces F0/4 and F0/11 has been configured on VLAN 10 using the `switchport access vlan 10` command. The same process is used to assign VLAN 30 to interface F0/5 and F0/6 on switch S1.

Finally, to protect the configuration so that it is not lost after a reload of the switch, the `copy running-config startup-config` command is executed in privileged EXEC mode to back up the running configuration to the startup configuration.

Click the Router Interface Configuration button in the figure to see the example router configuration.

Next, the router can be configured to perform the inter-VLAN routing.

As you see in the figure, each interface is configured with an IP address using the `ip address` `ip_address subnet_mask` command in interface configuration mode.

Router interfaces are disabled by default and need to be enabled using the `no shutdown` command before they are used.

In this example, interface F0/0 has been assigned the IP address of 172.17.10.1 using the `ip address 172.17.10.1 255.255.255.0` command. You will also notice that after the `no shutdown` interface configuration mode command has been executed a notification is displayed indicating that the interface state has changed to up. This indicates that the interface is now enabled.

The process is repeated for all router interfaces. Each router interface needs to be assigned to a unique subnet for routing to occur. In this example, the other router interface, F0/1, has been configured to use IP address 172.17.30.1, which is on a different subnet than interface F0/0.

By default, Cisco routers are configured to route traffic between the local interfaces. As a result, routing does not specifically need to be enabled. However, if multiple routers are being configured to perform inter-VLAN routing, you may want to enable a dynamic routing protocol to simplify routing table management. If you have not taken the course CCNA Exploration: Routing Protocols and Concepts, you can learn more at this Cisco site: http://www.cisco.com/en/US/products/sw/iosswrel/ps1835/products_configuration_guide_chapter09186a00800ca760.html.

Routing Table

> Refer to
> **Figure**
> in online course

Now examine the routing table using the `show ip route` privileged EXEC mode command.

In the example, there are two routes in the routing table. One route is to the 172.17.10.0 subnet, which is attached to the local interface F0/0. The other route is to the 172.17.30.0 subnet, which is attached to the local interface F0/1. The router uses this routing table to determine where to send the traffic it receives. For example, if the router receives a packet on interface F0/0 destined for the 172.17.30.0 subnet, the router would identify that it should send the packet out interface F0/1 to reach hosts on the 172.17.30.0 subnet.

Click the Verify Router Configuration button in the figure to see an example router configuration.

Verify Router Configuration

To verify the router configuration, use the `show running-config` privileged EXEC mode command. This command displays the current operating configuration of the router. You can see which IP addresses have been configured for each of the router interfaces, as well as the operational status of the interface.

In this example, notice that interface F0/0 is configured correctly with the 172.17.10.1 IP address. Also, notice the absence of the `shutdown` command below the F0/0 interface. The absence of the `shutdown` command confirms that the `no shutdown` command has been issued and that the interface is enabled.

You can get more detailed information about the router interfaces, such as diagnostic information, status, MAC address, and transmit or receive errors, using the `show interface` command in privileged EXEC mode.

6.2.2 Configure Router-on-a-Stick Inter-VLAN Routing

> Refer to
> **Figure**
> in online course

Before configuring the router, configure the switch that it will be connected to.

As you see in the figure, Router R1 is connected to switch S1 on trunk port F0/5. VLANs 10 and 30 have also been added to switch S1.

Click the Switch Configuration button in the figure to see the example switch configuration.

To review, VLANs are created in global configuration mode using the `vlan vlan id` command. In this example, VLANs 10 and 30 were created on switch S1 using the `vlan 10` and `vlan 30` commands.

Because switch port F0/5 will be configured as a trunk port, you do not have to assign any VLANs to the port. To configure switch port F0/5 as a trunk port, execute the `switchport mode trunk` command in interface configuration mode on the F0/5 interface. You cannot use the `switchport mode dynamic auto` or `switchport mode dynamic desirable` commands because the router does not support dynamic trunking protocol.

Finally, to protect the configuration so that it is not lost after a reload of the switch, the `copy running-config startup-config` command is executed in privileged EXEC mode to back up the running configuration to the startup configuration.

Click the Router Configuration button in the figure to see the example router configuration.

Router Configuration

Next, the router can be configured to perform the inter-VLAN routing.

As you see in the figure, the configuration of multiple subinterfaces is different than when physical interfaces are used.

Each subinterface is created using the `interface interface_id.Subinterface_id` global configuration mode command. In this example, the subinterface Fa0/0.10 is created using the `interface fa0/0.10` global configuration mode command. After the subinterface has been created, the VLAN ID is assigned using the `encapsulation dot1q vlan_id` subinterface configuration mode command.

Next, assign the IP address for the subinterface using the `ip address ip_address subnet_mask` subinterface configuration mode command. In this example, subinterface F0/0.10 is assigned the IP address 172.17.10.1 using the `ip address 172.17.10.1 255.255.255.0` command. You do not need to execute a `no shutdown` command at the subinterface level because it does not enable the physical interface.

This process is repeated for all the router subinterfaces that are needed to route between the VLANs configured on the network. Each router subinterface needs to be assigned an IP address on a unique subnet for routing to occur. In this example, the other router subinterface, F0/0.30, is configured to use IP address 172.17.30.1, which is on a different subnet from subinterface F0/0.10.

Once all subinterfaces have been configured on the router physical interface, the physical interface is enabled. In the example, interface F0/0 has the `no shutdown` command executed to enable the interface, which enables all of the configured subinterfaces.

By default, Cisco routers are configured to route traffic between the local subinterfaces. As a result, routing does not specifically need to be enabled.

Refer to
Figure
in online course

Routing Table

Next, examine the routing table using the `show ip route` command from privileged EXEC mode. In the example, there are two routes in the routing table. One route is to the 172.17.10.0 subnet, which is attached to the local subinterface F0/0.10. The other route is to the 172.17.30.0 subnet, which is attached to the local subinterface F0/0.30. The router uses this routing table to determine where to send the traffic it receives. For example, if the router received a packet on subinterface F0/0.10 destined for the 172.17.30.0 subnet, the router would identify that it should send the packet out subinterface F0/0.30 to reach hosts on the 172.17.30.0 subnet.

Click the Verify Router Configuration button in the figure to see an example router configuration.

Verify Router Configuration

To verify the router configuration, use the `show running-config` command in privileged EXEC mode. The `show running-config` command displays the current operating configuration of the router. Notice which IP addresses have been configured for each router subinterface, as well as whether the physical interface has been left disabled or enabled using the `no shutdown` command.

In this example, notice that interface F0/0.10 has been configured correctly with the 172.17.10.1 IP address. Also, notice the absence of the `shutdown` command below the F0/0 interface. The absence of the `shutdown` command confirms that the `no shutdown` command has been issued and the interface is enabled.

You can get more detailed information about the router interfaces, such as diagnostic information, status, MAC address, and transmit or receive errors, using the `show interface` command in privileged EXEC mode.

Refer to
Figure
in online course

After the router and switch have been configured to perform the inter-VLAN routing, the next step is to verify that the router is functioning correctly. You can test access to devices on remote VLANs using the `ping` command.

For the example shown in the figure, you would initiate a `ping` and a `tracert` from PC1 to the destination address of PC3.

The Ping Test

The `ping` command sends an *ICMP* echo request to the destination address. When a host receives an ICMP echo request, it responds with an ICMP echo reply to confirm that it received the ICMP echo request. The `ping` command calculates the elapsed time using the difference between the time the ping was sent and the time the echo reply was received. This elapsed time is used to determine the latency of the connection. Successfully receiving a reply confirms that there is a path between the sending device and the receiving device.

The Tracert Test

Tracert is a useful utility for confirming the routed path taken between two devices. On *UNIX* systems, the utility is specified by `traceroute`. Tracert also uses ICMP to determine the path taken, but it uses ICMP echo requests with specific time-to-live values defined on the frame.

The time-to-live value determines exactly how many router hops away the ICMP echo is allowed to reach. The first ICMP echo request is sent with a time-to-live value set to expire at the first router on route to the destination device.

When the ICMP echo request times out on the first route, a confirmation is sent back from the router to the originating device. The device records the response from the router and proceeds to send out another ICMP echo request, but this time with a greater time-to-live value. This allows the ICMP echo request to traverse the first router and reach the second device on route to the final destination. The process repeats until finally the ICMP echo request is sent all the way to the final destination device. After the tracert utility finishes running, you are presented with a list of every router interface that the ICMP echo request reached on its way to the destination.

Click the Device Outputs button in the figure to see a sample ping and tracert command output.

In the example, the ping utility was able to send an ICMP echo request to the IP address of PC3. Also, the tracert utility confirms that the path to PC3 is through the 172.17.10.1 subinterface IP address of router R1.

Refer to **Packet Tracer Activity** for this chapter

In this activity, you will configure traditional inter-VLAN routing simply by configuring the Fast Ethernet interface on a router. R1 has two connections to S1, one for each of the two VLANs. S1 and R1 already have basic configurations. You will complete the configuration by adding VLANs to S1 and assigning VLANs to the correct ports. Then you will configure R1 with IP addressing. In traditional inter-VLAN routing, there are no additional VLAN-related configurations needed on R1.

Detailed instructions are provided within the activity as well as in the PDF link below.

Activity Instructions (PDF)

Refer to **Packet Tracer Activity** for this chapter

In this activity, you will configure Router-on-a-Stick inter-VLAN routing. R1 has one connection to S1. S1 and R1 already have basic configurations. You will complete the configuration by adding VLANs to S1 and assigning VLANs to the correct ports. Then you will configure R1 with subinterfaces, 802.1Q encapsulation, and IP addressing.

Detailed instructions are provided within the activity as well as in the PDF link below.

Activity Instructions (PDF)

6.3 Troubleshooting Inter-VLAN Routing

6.3.1 Switch Configuration Issues

Refer to **Figure** in online course

In this topic, we discuss the challenges associated with configuring multiple VLANs on a network. This topic explores common issues and describes troubleshooting methods to identify and correct those issues.

When using the traditional routing model for inter-VLAN routing, ensure that the switch ports that connect to the router interfaces are configured on the correct VLANs. If the switch ports are not configured on the correct VLAN, devices configured on that VLAN cannot connect to the router interface, and therefore, are unable to route to the other VLANs.

Click the Topology 1 button in the figure.

As you can see in Topology 1, PC1 and router R1 interface F0/0 are configured to be on the same logical subnet, as indicated by their IP address assignment. However, the switch port F0/4 that connects to router R1 interface F0/0 has not been configured and remains in the default VLAN. Because router R1 is on a different VLAN than PC1, they are unable to communicate.

To correct this problem, execute the `switchport access vlan 10` interface configuration command on switch port F0/4 on switch S1. When the switch port is configured for the correct VLAN, PC1 can communicate with router R1 interface F0/0, which allows it to access the other VLANs connected to router R1.

Click the Topology 2 button in the figure to see another switch configuration issue.

In Topology 2, the router-on-a-stick routing model has been chosen. However, the F0/5 interface on switch S1 is not configured as a trunk and subsequently left in the default VLAN for the port. As a result, the router is not able to function correctly because each of its configured subinterfaces is unable to send or receive VLAN tagged traffic. This prevents all configured VLANs from routing through router R1 to reach the other VLANs.

To correct this problem, execute the `switchport mode trunk` interface configuration command on switch port F0/5 on switch S1. This converts the interface to a trunk, allowing the trunk to successfully establish a connection with router R1. When the trunk is successfully established, devices connected to each of the VLANs are able to communicate with the subinterface assigned to their VLAN, allowing inter-VLAN routing to occur.

Click the Topology 3 button in the figure to see another switch configuration issue.

In Topology 3, the trunk link between switch S1 and switch S2 is down. Because there is no redundant connection or path between the devices, all devices connected to switch S2 are unable to reach router R1. As a result, all devices connected to switch S2 are unable to route to other VLANs through router R1.

To reduce the risk of a failed inter-switch link disrupting inter-VLAN routing, redundant links and alternate paths should be configured between switch S1 and switch S2. Redundant links are configured in the form of an EtherChannel that protects against a single link failure. Cisco EtherChannel technology enables you to aggregate multiple physical links into one logical link. This can provide up to 80 Gb/s of aggregate bandwidth for with 10 Gigabit EtherChannel.

Additionally, alternate paths through other interconnected switches could be configured. This approach is dependent on the Spanning Tree Protocol (STP) to prevent the possibility of loops within the switch environment. There would also be a slight disruption in router access while STP determines whether the current link is down and finds an alternate route.

The CCNP curriculum addresses EtherChannel technology; also, to learn more about Cisco EtherChannel technology, visit: http://www.cisco.com/en/US/tech/tk389/tk213/ technologies_white_paper09186a0080092944.shtml.

To learn more about configuring EtherChannel on a Cisco Catalyst 2960 switch, visit: http://www.cisco.com/en/US/products/ps6406/products_configuration_guide_chapter09186a00808752d9.html.

Refer to
Figure
in online course

Switch Cisco IOS Commands

When you suspect that there is a problem with a switch configuration, use the various verification commands to examine the configuration and identify the problem.

Click the Incorrect VLAN Assignment button in the figure.

The screen output shows the results of the `show interface interface-id switchport` command. Assume that you have issued these commands because you suspect that VLAN 10 has not been assigned to port F0/4 on switch S1. The top highlighted area shows that port F0/4 on switch S1 is in access mode, but it does not show that it has been directly assigned to VLAN 10. The bottom highlighted area confirms that port F0/4 is still set to the default VLAN. The `show running-config` and the `show interface interface-id switchport` commands are useful for identifying VLAN assignment and port configuration issues.

Click the Incorrect Access Mode button in the figure.

After device configuration has changed, communication between router R1 and switch S1 has stopped. The link between the router and the switch is supposed to be a trunk link. The screen output shows the results of the `show interface interface-id switchport` and the `show running-config` commands. The top highlighted area confirms that port F0/4 on switch S1 is in access mode, not trunk mode. The bottom highlighted area also confirms that port F0/4 has been configured for access mode.

6.3.2 Router Configuration Issues

Refer to
Figure
in online course

One of the most common inter-VLAN router configuration errors is to connect the physical router interface to the wrong switch port, placing it on the incorrect VLAN and preventing it from reaching the other VLANs.

As you can see in Topology 1, router R1 interface F0/0 is connected to switch S1 port F0/9. Switch port F0/9 is configured for Default VLAN, not VLAN10. This prevents PC1 from being able to communicate with the router interface, and it is therefore unable to route to VLAN30.

To correct this problem, physically connect router R1 interface F0/0 to switch S1 port F0/4. This puts the router interface on the correct VLAN and allows inter-VLAN routing to function. Alternatively, you could change the VLAN assignment of switch port F0/9 to be on VLAN10. This also allows PC1 to communicate with router R1 interface F0/0.

Click the Topology 2 button in the figure to see another router configuration issue.

In Topology 2, router R1 has been configured to use the wrong VLAN on subinterface F0/0.10, preventing devices configured on VLAN10 from communicating with subinterface F0/0.10. This subsequently prevents those devices from being able to route to other VLANs on the network.

To correct this problem, configure subinterface F0/0.10 to be on the correct VLAN using the **encapsulation dot1q 10** subinterface configuration mode command. When the subinterface has been assigned to the correct VLAN, it is accessible by devices on that VLAN and can perform inter-VLAN routing.

Verify Router Configuration

In this troubleshooting scenario, you suspect a problem with the router R1. The subinterface F0/0.10 should allow access to VLAN 10 traffic, and the subinterface F0/0.30 should allow VLAN 30 traffic. The screen capture shows the results of running the **show interface** and the **show running-config** commands.

The top highlighted section shows that the subinterface F0/0.10 on router R1 uses VLAN 100. The **show interface** command produces a lot of output, making it sometimes hard to see the problem.

The **show running-config** confirms that the subinterface F0/0.10 on router R1 has been configured to allow access to VLAN 100 traffic and not VLAN 10. Perhaps this was a typing mistake.

With proper verification, router configuration problems are quickly addressed, allowing for inter-VLAN routing to function again properly. Recall that the VLANs are directly connected, which is how they enter the routing table.

6.3.3 IP Addressing Issues

As we have discussed, subnets are the key to implementing inter-VLAN routing. VLANs correspond to unique subnets on the network. For inter-VLAN routing to operate, a router needs to be connected to all VLANs, either by separate physical interfaces or trunked subinterfaces. Each interface, or subinterface, needs to be assigned an IP address that corresponds to the subnet for which it is connected. This permits devices on the VLAN to communicate with the router interface and enable the routing of traffic to other VLANs connected to the router.

Let's examine some common errors.

As you can see in Topology 1, router R1 has been configured with an incorrect IP address on interface F0/0. This prevents PC1 from being able to communicate with router R1 on VLAN10.

To correct this problem, assign the correct IP address to router R1 interface F0/0 using the **ip address 172.17.10.1 255.255.255.0** interface command in configuration mode. After the router interface has been assigned the correct IP address, PC1 can use the interface as a default gateway for accessing other VLANs.

Click the Topology 2 button in the figure to see another IP address configuration issue.

In Topology 2, PC1 has been configured with an incorrect IP address for the subnet associated with VLAN10. This prevents PC1 from being able to communicate with router R1 on VLAN10.

To correct this problem, assign the correct IP address to PC1. Depending on the type of PC being used, the configuration details may be different.

Click the Topology 3 button in figure to see another IP address configuration issue.

In Topology 3, PC1 has been configured with the incorrect subnet mask. According to the subnet mask configured for PC1, PC1 is on the 172.17.0.0 network. This results in PC1 determining that PC3, with IP address 172.17.30.23, is on the local subnet. As a result, PC1 does not forward traffic destined for PC3 to router R1 interface F0/0. Therefore, the traffic never reaches PC3.

To correct this problem, change the subnet mask on PC1 to 255.255.255.0. Depending on the type of PC being used, the configuration details may be different.

Verification Commands

Refer to
Figure
in online course

Earlier you learned that each interface, or subinterface, needs to be assigned an IP address that corresponds to the subnet for which it is connected. A common error is to incorrectly configure an IP address for a subinterface. The screen capture shows the results of the `show running-config` command. The highlighted area shows that the subinterface F 0/0.10 on router R1 has an IP address of 172.17.20.1. The VLAN for this subinterface should allow VLAN 10 traffic. There is an IP address that has been incorrectly configured. The `show ip interface` is another useful command. The second highlight shows the incorrect IP address.

Click PC IP Addressing Issue button.

Sometimes it is the end-user device, such as a personal computer, that is the culprit. In the screen output configuration of the computer PC1, the IP address is 172.17.20.21, with a subnet mask of 255.255.255.0. But in this scenario, PC1 should be in VLAN10, with an address of 172.17.10.21 and a subnet mask of 255.255.255.0.

Refer to **Packet Tracer Activity** for this chapter

In this activity, you will troubleshoot connectivity problems between PC1 and PC3. The activity is complete when you achieve 100% and the two PCs can ping each other. Any solution you implement must conform to the topology diagram.

Detailed instructions are provided within the activity as well as in the PDF link below.

Activity Instructions (PDF)

6.4 Chapter Labs

6.4.1 Basic Inter-VLAN Routing

Refer to
Lab Activity
for this chapter

It is necessary to break up large broadcast domains created by the physical topology of a switched network using VLANs. It is also necessary for users on one VLAN to be able to communicate with each other. This communication is possible because of Inter-VLAN routing. This lab will teach you how to configure it.

Refer to **Packet Tracer Activity** for this chapter

This activity is a variation of Lab 6.4.1. Packet Tracer may not support all the tasks specified in the hands-on lab. This activity should not be considered equivalent to completing the hands-on lab. Packet Tracer is not a substitute for a hands-on lab experience with real equipment.

Detailed instructions are provided within the activity as well as in the PDF link below.

Activity Instructions (PDF)

6.4.2 Challenge Inter-VLAN Routing

Refer to **Lab Activity** for this chapter

Given a network topology and a set of requirements, are you able to set up Inter-VLAN routing? This lab will test your abilities. Be sure to verify your answers with your instructor.

Refer to **Packet Tracer Activity** for this chapter

This activity is a variation of Lab 6.4.2. Packet Tracer may not support all the tasks specified in the hands-on lab. This activity should not be considered equivalent to completing the hands-on lab. Packet Tracer is not a substitute for a hands-on lab experience with real equipment.

Detailed instructions are provided within the activity as well as in the PDF link below.

Activity Instructions (PDF)

6.4.3 Troubleshooting Inter-VLAN Routing

Refer to **Lab Activity** for this chapter

The network has been designed and configured to support five VLANs and a separate server network. Inter-VLAN routing is being provided by an external router in a router-on-a-stick configuration, and the server network is routed across a separate Fast Ethernet interface. However, it is not working as designed, and complaints from your users have not given much insight into the source of the problems. You must first define what is not working as expected, and then analyze the existing configurations to determine and correct the source of the problems.

This lab is complete when you can demonstrate IP connectivity between each of the user VLANs and the external server network, and between the switch management VLAN and the server network.

Refer to **Packet Tracer Activity** for this chapter

This activity is a variation of Lab 6.4.3. Packet Tracer may not support all the tasks specified in the hands-on lab. This activity should not be considered equivalent to completing the hands-on lab. Packet Tracer is not a substitute for a hands-on lab experience with real equipment.

Detailed instructions are provided within the activity as well as in the PDF link below.

Activity Instructions (PDF)

Refer to
Figure
in online course

Chapter Summary

Inter-VLAN routing is the process of routing traffic between different VLANs, using either a dedicated router or a multilayer switch. Inter-VLAN routing facilitates communication between devices isolated by VLAN boundaries.

Refer to
Figure
in online course

The inter-VLAN routing topology using an external router with subinterfaces trunked to a Layer 2 switch is called router-on-a-stick. With this option, it is important to configure an IP address on each logical subinterface as well as the associated VLAN number.

Modern switched networks use switch virtual interfaces on multilayer switches to enable inter-VLAN routing.

Refer to **Packet Tracer Activity** for this chapter

Catalyst 2960 switches can be used in a router-on-a-stick scenario, while Catalyst 3560 switches can be used for the multilayer switching option for inter-VLAN routing.

In this activity, you will demonstrate and reinforce your ability to configure switches and routers for inter-VLAN communication. Among the skills you will demonstrate are configuring VLANs, VTP, and trunking on switches. You will also administer STP on switches and configure a router-on-a-stick using subinterfaces.

Detailed instructions are provided within the activity as well as in the PDF link below.

Activity Instructions (PDF)

Go to
the online course
to take the quiz.

Chapter Quiz

Take the chapter quiz to test your knowledge.

Your Chapter Notes

CHAPTER 7

Basic Wireless Concepts and Configuration

Chapter Introduction

Refer to
Figure
in online course

In the previous chapters, you learned how switch functions can facilitate interconnecting devices on a wired network. Typical business networks make extensive use of wired networks. Physical connections are made between computer systems, phone systems, and other peripheral devices to switches located in the wiring closets.

Managing a wired infrastructure can be challenging. Consider what happens when a worker decides they prefer their computer system in a different location in their office, or when a manager wants to bring a notebook to a meeting room and connect to the network there. In a wired network, you need to move the network connection cable to a new location in the worker's office and make sure there is a network connection available in the meeting room. To avoid these physical changes, wireless networks are becoming more and more common.

In this chapter, you will learn how wireless local area networks (*WLANs*) offer businesses a flexible networking environment. You will learn the different wireless standards available today and the features that each standard offers. You will learn which hardware components are typically necessary in a wireless infrastructure, how WLANs operate, and how to secure them. Finally, you will learn how to configure a wireless access point and a wireless client.

7.1 The Wireless LAN

7.1.1 Why Use Wireless?

Refer to
Figure
in online course

Why have Wireless LANs Become so Popular?

Click the Play button in the figure to view the video.

Business networks today are evolving to support people who are on the move. Employees and employers, students and faculty, government agents and those they serve, sports fans and shoppers, all are mobile and many of them are "connected." Perhaps you have a mobile phone that you route instant messages to when you are away from your computer. This is the vision of mobility-an environment where people can take their connection to the network along with them on the road.

There are many different infrastructures (wired LAN, service provider networks) that allow mobility like this to happen, but in a business environment, the most important is the WLAN.

Productivity is no longer restricted to a fixed work location or a defined time period. People now expect to be connected at any time and place, from the office to the airport or even the home. Traveling employees used to be restricted to pay phones for checking messages and returning a few phone calls between flights. Now employees can check e-mail, voice mail, and the status of products on personal digital assistants (*PDAs*) while at many temporary locations.

At home, many people have changed the way they live and learn. The Internet has become a standard service in many homes, along with TV and phone service. Even the method of accessing the Internet has quickly moved from temporary *modem* dialup service to dedicated DSL or cable service. Home users are seeking many of the same flexible wireless solutions as office workers. For the first time, in 2005, more Wi-Fi-enabled mobile laptops were purchased than fixed-location desktops.

In addition to the flexibility that WLANs offer, another important benefit is reduced costs. For example, with a wireless infrastructure already in place, savings are realized when moving a person within a building, reorganizing a lab, or moving to temporary locations or project sites. On average, the IT cost of moving an employee to a new location within a site is $375 (US dollars).

Another example is when a company moves into a new building that does not have any wired infrastructure. In this case, the savings resulting from using WLANs can be even more noticeable, because the cost of running cables through walls, ceilings, and floors is largely avoided.

Though harder to measure, WLANs can result in better productivity and more relaxed employees, leading to better results for customers and increased profits.

Wireless LANs

Refer to **Figure** in online course

In the previous chapters, you learned about switch technologies and functions. Most current business networks rely on switch-based LANs for day-to-day operation inside the office. However, workers are becoming more mobile and want to maintain access to their business LAN resources from locations other than their desks. Workers in the office want to take their laptops to meetings or to a co-worker's office. When using a laptop in another location, it is inconvenient to rely on a wired connection. In this topic, you will learn about wireless LANs (WLANs) and how they benefit a business. You will also explore the security concerns associated with WLANs.

Portable communications have become an expectation in many countries around the world. You can see portability and mobility in everything from cordless keyboards and headsets, to satellite phones and global positioning systems (GPS). The mix of wireless technologies in different types of networks allows workers to be mobile.

Click on the Wireless LANs button in the figure.

You can see that the WLAN is an extension of the Ethernet LAN. The function of the LAN has become mobile. You are going to learn about WLAN technology and the standards behind the mobility that allow people to continue a meeting, while walking, while in a cab, or while at the airport.

Comparing a WLAN to a LAN

Refer to **Figure** in online course

Wireless LANs share a similar origin with Ethernet LANs. The IEEE has adopted the 802 LAN/*MAN* portfolio of computer network architecture standards. The two dominant 802 working groups are 802.3 Ethernet and *802.11* wireless LAN. However, there are important differences between the two.

WLANs use radio frequencies (*RF*) instead of cables at the *Physical layer* and *MAC* sub-layer of the Data Link layer. In comparison to cable, RF has the following characteristics:

- RF does not have boundaries, such as the limits of a wire in a sheath. The lack of such a boundary allows data frames traveling over the RF media to be available to anyone that can receive the RF signal.

- RF is unprotected from outside signals, whereas cable is in an insulating sheath. Radios operating independently in the same geographic area but using the same or a similar RF can interfere with each other.

- RF transmission is subject to the same challenges inherent in any wave-based technology, such as consumer radio. For example, as you get further away from the source, you may hear stations playing over each other or hear static in the transmission. Eventually you may lose the signal all together. Wired LANs have cables that are of an appropriate length to maintain signal strength.

- RF bands are regulated differently in various countries. The use of WLANs is subject to additional regulations and sets of standards that are not applied to wired LANs.

WLANs connect clients to the network through a wireless access point (AP) instead of an Ethernet switch.

WLANs connect mobile devices that are often battery powered, as opposed to plugged-in LAN devices. Wireless network interface cards (NICs) tend to reduce the battery life of a mobile device.

WLANs support hosts that contend for access on the RF media (*frequency* bands). 802.11 prescribes collision-avoidance instead of collision-detection for media access to proactively avoid collisions within the media.

WLANs use a different frame format than wired Ethernet LANs. WLANs require additional information in the Layer 2 header of the frame.

WLANs raise more privacy issues because radio frequencies can reach outside the facility.

Refer to **Figure** in online course

Introducing Wireless LANs

802.11 wireless LANs extend the 802.3 Ethernet LAN infrastructures to provide additional connectivity options. However, additional components and protocols are used to complete wireless connections.

In an 802.3 Ethernet LAN, each client has a cable that connects the client NIC to a switch. The switch is the point where the client gains access to the network.

Click the WLAN Devices button in the figure.

In a wireless LAN, each client uses a wireless adapter to gain access to the network through a wireless device such as a wireless router or access point.

Click the Clients button in the figure.

The wireless adapter in the client communicates with the wireless router or access point using RF signals. Once connected to the network, wireless clients can access network resources just as if they were wired to the network.

7.1.2 Wireless LAN Standards

Refer to **Figure** in online course

Wireless LAN Standards

802.11 wireless LAN is an IEEE standard that defines how radio frequency (RF) in the unlicensed industrial, scientific, and medical (ISM) frequency bands is used for the Physical layer and the MAC sub-layer of wireless links.

When 802.11 was first released, it prescribed 1 - 2 Mb/s data rates in the 2.4 GHz band. At that time, wired LANs were operating at 10 Mb/s so the new wireless technology was not enthusiastically adopted. Since then, wireless LAN standards have continuously improved with the release of *IEEE 802.11a*, *IEEE 802.11b*, *IEEE 802.11g*, and draft 802.11n.

Typically, the choice of which WLAN standard to use is based on data rates. For instance, 802.11a and g can support up to 54 Mb/s, while 802.11b supports up to a maximum of 11 Mb/s, making 802.11b the "slow" standard, and 802.11 a and g the preferred ones. A fourth WLAN draft,

802.11n, exceeds the currently available data rates. The IEEE 802.11n should be ratified by September 2008. The figure compares the ratified IEEE 802.11a, b, and g standards.

Click the Table button in the figure to see details about each standard.

The data rates of different wireless LAN standards, are affected by something called a *modulation* technique. The two modulation techniques that you will reference in this course are Direct Sequence Spread Spectrum (*DSSS*) and Orthogonal Frequency Division Multiplexing (*OFDM*). You do not need to know how these techniques work for this course, but you should be aware that when a standard uses OFDM, it will have faster data rates. Also, DSSS is simpler than OFDM, so it is less expensive to implement.

802.11a

The IEEE 802.11a adopted the OFDM modulation technique and uses the 5 GHz band.

802.11a devices operating in the 5 GHz band are less likely to experience interference than devices that operate in the 2.4 GHz band because there are fewer consumer devices that use the 5 GHz band. Also, higher frequencies allow for the use of smaller antennas.

There are some important disadvantages to using the 5 GHz band. The first is that higher frequency radio waves are more easily absorbed by obstacles such as walls, making 802.11a susceptible to poor performance due to obstructions. The second is that this higher frequency band has slightly poorer *range* than either 802.11b or g. Also, some countries, including Russia, do not permit the use of the 5 GHz band, which may continue to curtail its deployment.

802.11b and 802.11g

802.11b specified data rates of 1, 2, 5.5, and 11 Mb/s in the 2.4 GHz *ISM* band using DSSS. 802.11g achieves higher data rates in that band by using the OFDM modulation technique. IEEE 802.11g also specifies the use of DSSS for backward compatibility with IEEE 802.11b systems. DSSS data rates of 1, 2, 5.5, and 11 Mb/s are supported, as are OFDM data rates of 6, 9, 12, 18, 24, 48, and 54 Mb/s.

There are advantages to using the 2.4 GHz band. Devices in the 2.4 GHz band will have better range than those in the 5GHz band. Also, transmissions in this band are not as easily obstructed as 802.11a.

There is one important disadvantage to using the 2.4 GHz band. Many consumer devices also use the 2.4 GHz band and cause 802.11b and g devices to be prone to *interference*.

802.11n

The IEEE 802.11n draft standard is intended to improve WLAN data rates and range without requiring additional power or RF band allocation. 802.11n uses multiple radios and antennae at endpoints, each broadcasting on the same frequency to establish multiple streams. The multiple input/multiple output (MIMO) technology splits a high data-rate stream into multiple lower rate streams and broadcasts them simultaneously over the available radios and antennae. This allows for a theoretical maximum data rate of 248 Mb/s using two streams.

The standard is expected to be ratified by September 2008.

Important: RF bands are allocated by the International Telecommunications Union-Radio communication sector (ITU-R). The ITU-R designates the 900 MHz, 2.4 GHz, and 5 GHz frequency bands as unlicensed for ISM communities. Although the ISM bands are globally unlicensed, they are still subject to local regulations. The use of these bands is administered by the FCC in the United States and by the ETSI in Europe. These issues will impact your selection of wireless components in a wireless implementation.

Refer to **Figure** in online course

Wi-Fi Certification

Wi-Fi certification is provided by the *Wi-Fi Alliance* (http://www.wi-fi.org), a global, nonprofit, industry trade association devoted to promoting the growth and acceptance of WLANs. You will better appreciate the importance of Wi-Fi certification if you consider the role of the Wi-Fi Alliance in the context of WLAN standards.

Standards ensure *interoperability* between devices made by different manufacturers. Internationally, the three key organizations influencing WLAN standards are:

- ITU-R
- IEEE
- Wi-Fi Alliance

The ITU-R regulates the allocation of the RF spectrum and satellite orbits. These are described as finite natural resources that are in demand from such consumers as fixed wireless networks, mobile wireless networks, and global positioning systems.

The IEEE developed and maintains the standards for local and metropolitan area networks with the IEEE 802 LAN/MAN family of standards. IEEE 802 is managed by the IEEE 802 LAN/MAN Standards Committee (LMSC), which oversees multiple working groups. The dominant standards in the IEEE 802 family are 802.3 Ethernet, 802.5 Token Ring, and 802.11 Wireless LAN.

Although the IEEE has specified standards for RF modulation devices, it has not specified manufacturing standards, so interpretations of the 802.11 standards by different vendors can cause interoperability problems between their devices.

The Wi-Fi Alliance is an association of vendors whose objective is to improve the interoperability of products that are based on the 802.11 standard by certifying vendors for conformance to industry norms and adherence to standards. Certification includes all three IEEE 802.11 RF technologies, as well as early adoption of pending IEEE drafts, such as 802.11n, and the *WPA* and WPA2 security standards based on *IEEE 802.11i*.

The roles of these three organizations can be summarized as follows:

- ITU-R regulates allocation of RF bands.
- IEEE specifies how RF is modulated to carry information.
- Wi-Fi ensures that vendors make devices that are interoperable.

7.1.3 Wireless Infrastructure Components

Refer to **Figure** in online course

Wireless NICs

You may already use a wireless network at home, in a local coffee shop, or at the school you attend. Have you ever wondered what hardware components are involved in allowing you to wirelessly access the local network or Internet? In this topic, you will learn which components are available to implement WLANs and how each is used in the wireless infrastructure.

To review, the building block components of a WLAN are client stations that connect to access points that, in turn, connect to the network infrastructure. The device that makes a client station capable of sending and receiving RF signals is the wireless NIC.

Like an Ethernet NIC, the wireless NIC, using the modulation technique it is configured to use, encodes a data stream onto an RF signal. Wireless NICs are most often associated with mobile devices, such as laptop computers. In the 1990s, wireless NICs for laptops were cards that slipped into the PCMCIA slot. PCMCIA wireless NICs are still common, but many manufacturers have begun building the wireless NIC right into the laptop. Unlike 802.3 Ethernet interfaces built into PCs, the wireless NIC is not visible, because there is no requirement to connect a cable to it.

Other options have emerged over the years as well. Desktops located in an existing, non-wired facility can have a wireless PCI NIC installed. To quickly set up a PC, mobile or desktop, with a wireless NIC, there are many USB options available as well.

Refer to **Figure** in online course

Wireless Access Points

An access point connects wireless clients (or stations) to the wired LAN. Client devices do not typically communicate directly with each other; they communicate with the AP. In essence, an access point converts the TCP/IP data packets from their 802.11 frame encapsulation format in the air to the 802.3 Ethernet frame format on the wired Ethernet network.

In an infrastructure network, clients must associate with an access point to obtain network services. Association is the process by which a client joins an 802.11 network. It is similar to plugging into a wired LAN. Association is discussed in later topics.

An access point is a Layer 2 device that functions like an 802.3 Ethernet hub. RF is a shared *medium* and access points hear all radio traffic. Just as with 802.3 Ethernet, the devices that want to use the medium contend for it. Unlike Ethernet NICs, though, it is expensive to make wireless NICs that can transmit and receive at the same time, so radio devices do not detect collisions. Instead, WLAN devices are designed to avoid them.

CSMA/CA

Access points oversee a distributed coordination function (DCF) called Carrier Sense Multiple Access with Collision Avoidance (CSMA/CA). This simply means that devices on a WLAN must sense the medium for energy (RF stimulation above a certain threshold) and wait until the medium is free before sending. Because all devices are required to do this, the function of coordinating access to the medium is distributed. If an access point receives data from a client station, it sends an acknowledgement to the client that the data has been received. This acknowledgement keeps the client from assuming that a collision occurred and prevents a data retransmission by the client.

Click the Hidden Nodes button in the figure.

RF signals attenuate. That means that they lose their energy as they move away from their point of origin. Think about driving out of range of a radio station. This signal *attenuation* can be a problem in a WLAN where stations contend for the medium.

Imagine two client stations that both connect to the access point, but are at opposite sides of its reach. If they are at the maximum range to reach the access point, they will not be able to reach each other. So neither of those stations sense the other on the medium, and they may end up transmitting simultaneously. This is known as the hidden node (or station) problem.

One means of resolving the hidden node problem is a CSMA/CA feature called request to send/clear to send (RTS/CTS). RTS/CTS was developed to allow a negotiation between a client and an access point. When RTS/CTS is enabled in a network, access points allocate the medium to the requesting station for as long as is required to complete the transmission. When the transmission is complete, other stations can request the *channel* in a similar fashion. Otherwise, normal collision avoidance function is resumed.

Refer to **Figure** in online course

Wireless Routers

Wireless routers perform the role of access point, Ethernet switch, and router. For example, the Linksys WRT300N used is really three devices in one box. First, there is the wireless access point, which performs the typical functions of an access point. A built-in four-port, full-duplex, 10/100 switch provides connectivity to wired devices. Finally, the router function provides a gateway for connecting to other network infrastructures.

The WRT300N is most commonly used as a small business or residential wireless access device. The expected load on the device is low enough that it should be able to manage the provision of WLAN, 802.3 Ethernet, and connect to an ISP.

7.1.4 Wireless Operation

Refer to **Figure** in online course

Configurable Parameters for Wireless Endpoints

The figure shows the initial screen for wireless configuration on a Linksys wireless router. Several processes should occur to create a connection between client and access point. You have to configure parameters on the access point-and subsequently on your client device-to enable the negotiation of these processes.

Click the Modes button in the figure to view the Wireless Network Mode parameter.

The wireless network mode refers to the WLAN protocols: 802.11a, b, g, or n. Because 802.11g is backward compatible with 802.11b, access points support both standards. Remember that if all the clients connect to an access point with 802.11g, they all enjoy the better data rates provided. When 802.11b clients associate with the access point all the faster clients contending for the channel have to wait on 802.11b clients to clear the channel before transmitting. When a Linksys access point is configured to allow both 802.11b and 802.11g clients, it is operating in mixed mode.

For an access point to support 802.11a as well as 802.11b and g, it must have a second radio to operate in the different RF band.

Click the SSID button in the figure to view a list of SSIDs for a Windows client.

A shared service set identifier (*SSID*) is a unique identifier that client devices use to distinguish between multiple wireless networks in the same vicinity. Several access points on a network can share an SSID. The figure shows an example of SSIDs distinguishing between WLANs, each which can be any alphanumeric, case-sensitive entry from 2 to 32 characters long.

Click the Channel button in the figure to view a graphic of non-overlapping channels.

The IEEE 802.11 standard establishes the channelization scheme for the use of the unlicensed ISM RF bands in WLANs. The 2.4 GHz band is broken down into 11 channels for North America and 13 channels for Europe. These channels have a center frequency separation of only 5 MHz and an overall channel bandwidth (or frequency occupation) of 22 MHz. The 22 MHz channel bandwidth combined with the 5 MHz separation between center frequencies means there is an overlap between successive channels. Best practices for WLANs that require multiple access points are set to use non-overlapping channels. If there are three adjacent access points, use channels 1, 6, and 11. If there are just two, select any two that are five channels apart, such as channels 5 and 10. Many access points can automatically select a channel based on adjacent channel use. Some products continuously monitor the radio space to adjust the channel settings dynamically in response to environmental changes.

Refer to **Figure** in online course

802.11 Topologies

Wireless LANs can accommodate various network topologies. When describing these topologies, the fundamental building block of the IEEE 802.11 WLAN architecture is the *basic service set* (*BSS*). The standard defines a BSS as a group of stations that communicate with each other.

Click the Ad Hoc button in the figure.

Ad hoc Networks

Wireless networks can operate without access points; this is called an ad hoc topology. Client stations which are configured to operate in ad hoc mode configure the wireless parameters between themselves. The IEEE 802.11 standard refers to an ad hoc network as an independent BSS (IBSS).

Click the BSS button in the figure.

Basic Service Sets

Access points provide an infrastructure that adds services and improves the range for clients. A single access point in infrastructure mode manages the wireless parameters and the topology is simply a BSS. The coverage area for both an IBSS and a BSS is the *basic service area* (*BSA*).

Click the ESS button in the figure.

Extended Service Sets

When a single BSS provides insufficient RF coverage, one or more can be joined through a common distribution system into an *extended service set* (*ESS*). In an ESS, one BSS is differentiated from another by the BSS identifier (BSSID), which is the MAC address of the access point serving the BSS. The coverage area is the extended service area (ESA).

Common Distribution System

The common distribution system allows multiple access points in an ESS to appear to be a single BSS. An ESS generally includes a common SSID to allow a user to roam from access point to access point.

Cells represent the coverage area provided by a single channel. An ESS should have 10 to 15 percent overlap between cells in an extended service area. With a 15 percent overlap between cells, an SSID, and non-overlapping channels (one cell on channel 1 and the other on channel 6), roaming capability can be created.

Click the Summary button in the figure to see a comparions of WLAN topologies.

Refer to
Figure
in online course

Client and Access Point Association

A key part of the 802.11 process is discovering a WLAN and subsequently connecting to it. The primary components of this process are as follows:

- *Beacons* - Frames used by the WLAN network to advertise its presence.

- Probes - Frames used by WLAN clients to find their networks.

- Authentication - A process which is an artifact from the original 802.11 standard, but still required by the standard.

- Association - The process for establishing the data link between an access point and a WLAN client.

The primary purpose of the beacon is to allow WLAN clients to learn which networks and access points are available in a given area, thereby allowing them to choose which network and access point to use. Access points may broadcast beacons periodically.

Although beacons may regularly be broadcast by an access point, the frames for probing, authentication, and association are used only during the association (or reassociation) process.

The 802.11 Join Process (Association)

Before an 802.11 client can send data over a WLAN network, it goes through the following three-stage process:

Click the Probe button in the figure.

Stage 1 - 802.11 probing

Clients search for a specific network by sending a probe request out on multiple channels. The probe request specifies the network name (SSID) and bit rates. A typical WLAN client is configured with a desired SSID, so probe requests from the WLAN client contain the SSID of the desired WLAN network.

If the WLAN client is simply trying to discover the available WLAN networks, it can send out a probe request with no SSID, and all access points that are configured to respond to this type of query respond. WLANs with the broadcast SSID feature disabled do not respond.

Click the Authenticate button in the figure.

Stage 2 - 802.11 authentication

802.11 was originally developed with two authentication mechanisms. The first one, called open authentication, is fundamentally a NULL authentication where the client says "authenticate me," and the access point responds with "yes." This is the mechanism used in almost all 802.11 deployments.

A second authentication mechanism is referred to as shared key authentication. This technique is based on a Wired Equivalency Protection (*WEP*) key that is shared between the client and the access point. In this technique, the client sends an authentication request to the access point. The access point then sends a challenge text to the client, who encrypts the message using its shared key, and returns the encrypted text back to the access point. The access point then decrypts the encrypted text using its key and if the decrypted text matches the challenge text, the client and the access point share the same key and the access point authenticates the station. If the messages do not match, the client is not authenticated.

Although shared key authentication needs to be included in client and access point implementations for overall standards compliance, it is not used or recommended. The problem is that the WEP key is normally used to encrypt data during the transmission process. Using this same WEP key in the authentication process provides an attacker with the ability to extract the key by sniffing and comparing the unencrypted challenge text and then the encrypted return message. Once the WEP key is extracted, any encrypted information that is transmitted across the link can be easily decrypted.

Click the Associate button in the figure.

Stage 3 - 802.11 association

This stage finalizes the security and bit rate options, and establishes the data link between the WLAN client and the access point. As part of this stage, the client learns the BSSID, which is the access point MAC address, and the access point maps a logical port known as the association identifier (AID) to the WLAN client. The AID is equivalent to a port on a switch. The association process allows the infrastructure switch to keep track of frames destined for the WLAN client so that they can be forwarded.

Once a WLAN client has *associated* with an access point, traffic is now able to travel back and forth between the two devices.

7.1.5 Planning the Wireless LAN

Planning the Wireless LAN

Implementing a WLAN that takes the best advantage of resources and delivers the best service can require careful planning. WLANs can range from relatively simple installations to very complex and intricate designs. There needs to be a well-documented plan before a wireless network can be

Refer to Figure in online course

implemented. In this topic, we introduce what considerations go into the design and planning of a wireless LAN.

The number of users a WLAN can support is not a straightforward calculation. The number or users depends on the geographical layout of your facility (how many bodies and devices fit in a space), the data rates users expect (because RF is a shared medium and the more users there are the greater the contention for RF), the use of non-overlapping channels by multiple access points in an ESS, and *transmit power* settings (which are limited by local regulation). You will have sufficient wireless support for your clients if you plan your network for proper RF coverage in an ESS. Detailed consideration of how to plan for specific numbers of users is beyond the scope of this course.

Click the Map button in the figure.

When planning the location of access points, you may not be able to simply draw coverage area circles and drop them over a plan. The approximate circular coverage area is important, but there are some additional recommendations.

If access points are to use existing wiring or if there are locations where access points cannot be placed, note these locations on the map.

- Position access points above obstructions.

- Position access points vertically near the ceiling in the center of each coverage area, if possible.

- Position access points in locations where users are expected to be. For example, conference rooms are typically a better location for access points than a hallway.

When these points have been addressed, estimate the expected coverage area of an access point. This value varies depending on the WLAN standard or mix of standards that you are deploying, the nature of the facility, the transmit power that the access point is configured for, and so on. Always consult the specifications for the access point when planning for coverage areas.

Based on your plan, place access points on the floor plan so that coverage circles are overlapping, as illustrated in the following example.

Example Calculation

The open auditorium (a Warehouse/Manufacturing Building Type) shown in the figure is approximately 20,000 square feet.

Network requirements specify that there must be a minimum of 6 Mb/s 802.11b throughput in each BSA, because there is a wireless voice over WLAN implementation overlaid on this network. With access points, 6 Mbps can be achieved in open areas like those on the map, with a coverage area of 5,000 square feet in many environments.

Note: The 5,000 square foot coverage area is for a square. The BSA takes its radius diagonally from the center of this square.

Let us determine where to place the access points.

Click Coverage Area button in the figure.

The facility is 20,000 square feet, therefore dividing 20,000 square feet by a coverage area of 5,000 square feet per access point results in at least four access points required for the auditorium. Next, determine the dimension of the coverage areas and arrange them on the floor plan.

- Because the coverage area is a square with side "Z", the circle that is tangent to its four corners has a radius of 50 feet, as shown in the calculations.

- When the dimensions of the coverage area have been determined, you arrange them in a manner similar to those shown for Align Coverage Areas in the figure. **Click the Align Coverage Areas button in the figure.**

- On your floor plan map, arrange four 50-foot radius coverage circles so that they overlap, as shown in the Plan. **Click the Plan button in the figure.**

Refer to **Figure** in online course

Refer to **Figure** in online course

7.2 Wireless LAN Security

7.2.1 Threats to Wireless Security

Unauthorized Access

Security should be a priority for anyone who uses or administers networks. The difficulties in keeping a wired network secure are amplified with a wireless network. A WLAN is open to anyone within range of an access point and the appropriate credentials to associate to it. With a wireless NIC and knowledge of cracking techniques, an attacker may not have to physically enter the workplace to gain access to a WLAN.

In this first topic of this section, we describe how wireless security threats have evolved. These security concerns are even more significant when dealing with business networks, because the livelihood of the business relies on the protection of its information. Security breaches for a business can have major repercussions, especially if the business maintains financial information associated with its customers.

There are three major categories of threat that lead to unauthorized access:

- War drivers
- Hackers (Crackers)
- Employees

"War driving" originally referred to using a scanning device to find cellular phone numbers to exploit. War driving now also means driving around a neighborhood with a laptop and an 802.11b/g client card looking for an unsecured 802.11b/g system to exploit.

The term hacker originally meant someone who delved deeply into computer systems to understand, and perhaps exploit for creative reasons, the structure and complexity of a system. Today, the terms hacker and cracker have come to mean malicious intruders who enter systems as criminals and steal data or deliberately harm systems.Hackers intent on doing harm are able to exploit weak security measures.

Most wireless devices sold today are WLAN-ready. In other words, the devices have default settings and can be installed and used with little or no configuration by users. Often, end users do not change default settings, leaving client authentication open, or they may only implement standard WEP security. Unfortunately, as mentioned before, shared WEP keys are flawed and consequently easy to attack.

Tools with a legitimate purpose, such as wireless sniffers, allow network engineers to capture data packets for system debugging. These same tools can be used by intruders to exploit security weaknesses.

Rogue Access Points

A rogue access point is an access point placed on a WLAN that is used to interfere with normal network operation. If a rogue access point is configured with the correct security settings, client data could be captured. A rogue access point also could be configured to provide unauthorized users with information such as the MAC addresses of clients (both wireless and wired), or to capture and disguise data packets or, at worst, to gain access to servers and files.

A simple and common version of a rogue access point is one installed by employees without authorization. Employees install access points intended for home use on the enterprise network. These access points typically do not have the necessary security configuration, so the network ends up with a security hole.

Refer to
Figure
in online course

Man-in-the-Middle Attacks

One of the more sophisticated attacks an unauthorized user can make is called a man-in-the-middle (MITM) attack. Attackers select a host as a target and position themselves logically between the target and the router or gateway of the target. In a wired LAN environment, the attacker needs to be able to physically access the LAN to insert a device logically into the topology. With a WLAN, the radio waves emitted by access points can provide the connection.

Radio signals from stations and access points are "hearable" by anyone in a BSS with the proper equipment, such as a laptop with a NIC. Because access points act like Ethernet hubs, each NIC in a BSS hears all the traffic. Device discards any traffic not addressed to it. Attackers can modify the NIC of their laptop with special software so that it accepts all traffic. With this modification, the attacker can carry out wireless MITM attacks, using the laptop NIC acts as an access point.

To carry out this attack, a hacker selects a station as a target and uses packet sniffing software, such as Wireshark, to observe the client station connecting to an access point. The hacker might be able to read and copy the target username, server name, client and server IP address, the ID used to compute the response, and the challenge and associate response, which is passed in clear text between station and access point.

If an attacker is able to compromise an access point, the attacker can potentially compromise all users in the BSS. The attacker can monitor an entire wireless network segment and wreak havoc on any users connected to it.

Defeating an attack like a MITM attack, depends on the sophistication of your WLAN infrastructure and your vigilance in monitoring activity on the network. The process begins with identifying legitimate devices on your WLAN. To do this, you must authenticate users on your WLAN.

When all legitimate users are known, you then monitor the network for devices and traffic that is not supposed to be there. Enterprise WLANs that use state-of-the-art WLAN devices provide administrators with tools that work together as a wireless intrusion prevention system (IPS). These tools include scanners that identify rogue access points and ad hoc networks, and radio resource management (RRM) which monitors the RF band for activity and access point load. An access point that is busier than normal, alerts the administrator of possible unauthorized traffic.

Further explanation of these mitigation techniques is beyond the scope of this course. For more information, refer to the Cisco paper "Addressing Wireless Threats with Integrated Wireless IDS and IPS" available at http://www.cisco.com/en/US/products/ps6521/products_white_paper0900aecd804f155b.shtml.

Refer to
Figure
in online course

Denial of Service

802.11b and g WLANs use the unlicensed 2.4 GHz ISM band. This is the same band used by most wireless consumer products, including baby monitors, cordless phones, and *microwave* ovens. With these devices crowding the RF band, attackers can create *noise* on all the channels in the band with commonly available devices.

Click the DoS 2 button in the figure.

Earlier we discussed how an attacker can turn a NIC into an access point. That trick can also be used to create a DoS attack. The attacker, using a PC as an access point, can flood the BSS with clear-to-send (CTS) messages, which defeat the CSMA/CA function used by the stations. The access points, in turn, flood the BSS with simultaneous traffic, causing a constant stream of collisions.

Another DoS attack that can be launched in a BSS is when an attacker sends a series of disassociate commands that cause all stations in the BSS to disconnect. When the stations are disconnected, they immediately try to reassociate, which creates a burst of traffic. The attacker sends another disassociate command and the cycle repeats itself.

7.2.2 Wireless Security Protocols

Refer to **Figure** in online course

Wireless Protocol Overview

In this topic, you will learn about the features of the common wireless protocols and the level of security each provides.

Two types of authentication were introduced with the original 802.11 standard: open and shared WEP key authentication. While open authentication is really "no authentication," (a client requests authentication and the access point grants it), WEP authentication was supposed to provide privacy to a link, making it like a cable connecting a PC to an Ethernet wall-jack. As was mentioned earlier, shared WEP keys proved to be flawed and something better was required. To counteract shared WEP key weakness, the very first approach by companies was to try techniques such as cloaking SSIDs and filtering MAC addresses. These techniques were also too weak. You will learn more about the weaknesses of these techniques later.

The flaws with WEP shared key encryption were two-fold. First, the algorithm used to encrypt the data was crackable. Second, scalability was a problem. The 32-bit WEP keys were manually managed, so users entered them by hand, often incorrectly, creating calls to technical support desks.

Following the weakness of WEP-based security, there was a period of interim security measures. Vendors such as Cisco, wanting to meet the demand for better security, developed their own systems while simultaneously helping to evolve the 802.11i standard. On the way to 802.11i, the *TKIP* encryption algorithm was created, which was linked to the Wi-Fi Alliance WiFi Protected Access (WPA) security method.

Today, the standard that should be followed in most enterprise networks is the 802.11i standard. This is similar to the Wi-Fi Alliance WPA2 standard. For enterprises, WPA2 includes a connection to a Remote Authentication Dial In User Service (RADIUS) database. RADIUS will be described later in the chapter.

For more about the WEP security weakness, see the paper "Security of the WEP algorithm" available at http://www.isaac.cs.berkeley.edu/isaac/wep-faq.html.

Refer to **Figure** in online course

Authenticating to the Wireless LAN

In an open network, such as a home network, association may be all that is required to grant a client access to devices and services on the WLAN. In networks that have stricter security requirements, an additional authentication or login is required to grant clients such access. This login process is managed by the Extensible Authentication Protocol (*EAP*). EAP is a framework for authenticating network access. IEEE developed the 802.11i standard for WLAN authentication and authorization to use *IEEE 802.1x*.

Click the EAP button in the figure to see the authentication process.

The enterprise WLAN authentication process is summarized as follows:

- The 802.11 association process creates a virtual port for each WLAN client at the access point.

- The access point blocks all data frames, except for 802.1x-based traffic.

- The 802.1x frames carry the EAP authentication packets via the access point to a server that maintains authentication credentials. This server is an Authentication, Authorization, and Accounting (AAA) server running a RADIUS protocol.

- If the EAP authentication is successful, the AAA server sends an EAP success message to the access point, which then allows data traffic from the WLAN client to pass through the virtual port.

- Before opening the virtual port, data link encryption between the WLAN client and the access point is established to ensure that no other WLAN client can access the port that has been established for a given authenticated client.

Before 802.11i (WPA2) or even WPA were in use, some companies tried to secure their WLANs by filtering MAC addresses and not broadcasting SSIDs. Today, it is easy to use software to modify MAC addresses attached to adapters, so the MAC address filtering is easily fooled. It does not mean you should not do it, but if you are using this method, you should back it up with additional security, such as WPA2.

Even if an SSID is not broadcast by an access point, the traffic that passes back and forth between the client and access point eventually reveals the SSID. If an attacker is passively monitoring the RF band, the SSID can be sniffed in one of these transactions, because it is sent in clear text. The ease of discovering SSIDs has led some people to leave SSID broadcasting turned on. If so, that should probably be an organizational decision recorded in the security policy.

The idea that you can secure your WLAN with nothing more than MAC filtering and turning off SSID broadcasts can lead to a completely insecure WLAN. The best way to ensure that end users are supposed to be on the WLAN is to use a security method that incorporates port-based network access control, such as WPA2.

Refer to
Figure
in online course

Encryption

Two enterprise-level encryption mechanisms specified by 802.11i are certified as WPA and WPA2 by the Wi-Fi Alliance: Temporal Key Integrity Protocol (TKIP) and Advanced Encryption Standard (*AES*).

TKIP is the encryption method certified as WPA. It provides support for legacy WLAN equipment by addressing the original flaws associated with the 802.11 WEP encryption method. It makes use of the original encryption algorithm used by WEP.

TKIP has two primary functions:

- It encrypts the Layer 2 payload

- It carries out a message integrity check (*MIC*) in the encrypted packet. This helps ensure against a message being tampered with.

Although TKIP addresses all the known weaknesses of WEP, the AES encryption of WPA2 is the preferred method, because it brings the WLAN encryption standards into alignment with broader IT industry standards and best practices, most notably IEEE 802.11i.

AES has the same functions as TKIP, but it uses additional data from the MAC header that allows destination hosts to recognize if the non-encrypted bits have been tampered with. It also adds a sequence number to the encrypted data header.

When you configure Linksys access points or wireless routers, such as the WRT300N, you may not see WPA or WPA2, instead you may see references to something called pre-shared key (PSK). Various types of PSKs are as follows:

- PSK or PSK2 with TKIP is the same as WPA
- PSK or PSK2 with AES is the same as WPA2
- PSK2, without an encryption method specified, is the same as WPA2

7.2.3 Securing a Wireless LAN

Refer to **Figure** in online course

Controlling Access to the Wireless LAN

The concept of depth means having multiple solutions available. It is like having a security system in your house, but still locking all the doors and windows and asking the neighbors to watch it for you. The security methods you have seen, especially WPA2, are like having a security system. If you want to do something extra to secure access to your WLAN, you can add depth, as shown in the figure, by implementing this three-step approach:

- SSID cloaking - Disable SSID broadcasts from access points
- MAC address filtering - Tables are manually constructed on the access point to allow or disallow clients based on their physical *hardware address*
- WLAN security implementation - WPA or WPA2

An additional consideration for a vigilant network administrator is to configure access points that are near outside walls of buildings to transmit on a lower power setting than other access points closer to the middle of the building. This is to merely reduce the RF signature on the outside of the building where anyone running an application such as Netstumbler (http://www.netstumbler.com), Wireshark, or even Windows XP, can map WLANs.

Neither SSID cloaking nor MAC address filtering are considered a valid means of securing a WLAN for the following reasons:

- MAC addresses are easily spoofed.
- SSIDs are easily discovered even if access points do not broadcast them.

7.3 Configure Wireless LAN Access

7.3.1 Configuring the Wireless Access Point

Refer to **Figure** in online course

Overview of Configuring the Wireless Access Point

In this topic, you will learn how to configure a wireless access point. You will learn how to set the SSID, enable security, configure the channel, and adjust the power settings of a wireless access point. You will also learn how to back up and restore the configuration of a typical wireless access point.

The basic approach to wireless implementation, as with any basic networking, is to configure and test incrementally. Before implementing any wireless devices, verify the existing network and Internet access for the wired hosts. Start the WLAN implementation process with a single access point and a single client, without enabling wireless security. Verify that the wireless client has received a DHCP IP address and can ping the local wired default router and then browse to the external Internet. Finally, configure wireless security with WPA2. Use WEP only if the hardware does not support WPA.

Most access points have been designed to be functional right out of the box with the default settings. It is good practice to change initial, default configurations. Many access points can be configured through a GUI web interface.

With a plan for implementation in mind, wired network connectivity confirmed, and the access point installed, you will now configure it. The following example uses the Linksys WRT300N multifunction device. This device includes an access point.

The steps for configuring the Linksys WRT300N are as follows:

Ensure your PC is connected to the access point via a wired connection, and access the web utility with a web browser. To access the web-based utility of the access point, launch Internet Explorer or Netscape Navigator, and enter the WRT300N default IP address, 192.168.1.1, in the address field. Press the Enter key.

A screen appears prompting you for your username and password. Leave the Username field blank. Enter **admin** in the Password field. These are the default settings for a Linksys WRT300N. If the device has already been configured, the username and password may have been changed. Click **OK** to continue.

For a basic network setup, use the following screens, as shown when you click the **Setup**, **Management**, and **Wireless** buttons in the figure:

- *Setup* - Enter your basic network settings (IP address).

- *Management* - Click the **Administration** tab and then select the **Management** screen. The default password is **admin**. To secure the access point, change the password from its default.

- *Wireless* - Change the default SSID in the **Basic Wireless Settings** tab. Select the level of security in the **Wireless Security** tab and complete the options for the selected security mode.

Make the necessary changes through the utility. When you have finished making changes to a screen, click the **Save Settings** button, or click the **Cancel Changes** button to undo your changes. For information on a tab, click **Help**.

The figure summarizes the implementation steps for an access point.

Refer to
Figure
in online course

Configuring Basic Wireless Settings

The **Basic Setup** screen is the first screen you see when you access the web-based utility. Click the **Wireless** tab and then select the **Basic Wireless Settings** tab.

Basic Wireless Settings

Click the buttons along the bottom of the figure for a view of the GUI for each configuration.

- *Network Mode* - If you have Wireless-N, Wireless-G, and 802.11b devices in your network, keep **Mixed**, the default setting. If you have Wireless-G and 802.11b devices, select **BG-Mixed**. If you have only Wireless-N devices, select **Wireless-N Only**. If you have only Wireless-G devices, select **Wireless-G Only**. If you have only Wireless-B devices, select **Wireless-B Only**. If you want to disable wireless networking, select **Disable**.

- *Network Name (SSID)* - The SSID is the network name shared among all points in a wireless network. The SSID must be identical for all devices in the wireless network. It is case-sensitive and must not exceed 32 characters (use any of the characters on the keyboard). For added security, you should change the default SSID (linksys) to a unique name.

- *SSID Broadcast* - When wireless clients survey the local area for wireless networks to associate with, they detect the SSID broadcast by the access point. To broadcast the SSID, keep **Enabled**, the default setting. If you do not want to broadcast the SSID, select **Disabled**. When you have finished making changes to this screen, click the **Save Settings** button, or click the **Cancel Changes** button to undo your changes. For more information, click Help.

- *Radio Band* - For best performance in a network using Wireless-N, Wireless-G, and Wireless-B devices, keep the default **Auto**. For Wireless-N devices only, select **Wide - 40MHz Channel**. For Wireless-G and Wireless-B networking only, select **Standard - 20MHz Channel**.

- *Wide Channel* - If you selected Wide - 40MHz Channel for the **Radio Band** setting, this setting is available for your primary Wireless-N channel. Select any channel from the drop-down menu.

- *Standard Channel* - Select the channel for Wireless-N, Wireless-G, and Wireless-B networking. If you selected Wide - 40MHz Channel for the **Radio Band** setting, the standard channel is a secondary channel for Wireless-N.

Refer to **Figure** in online course

Configuring Security

Click the Overview button in the figure.

These settings configure the security of your wireless network. There are seven wireless security modes supported by the WRT300N, listed here in the order you see them in the GUI, from weakest to strongest, except for the last option, which is disabled:

- WEP

- PSK-Personal, or WPA-Personal in v0.93.9 *firmware* or newer

- PSK2-Personal, or WPA2-Personal in v0.93.9 firmware or newer

- PSK-Enterprise, or WPA-Enterprise in v0.93.9 firmware or newer

- PSK2-Enterprise, or WPA2-Enterprise in v0.93.9 firmware or newer

- RADIUS

- Disabled

When you see "Personal" in a security mode, no AAA server is used. "Enterprise" in the security mode name means a AAA server and EAP authentication is used.

You have learned that WEP is a flawed security mode. PSK2, which is the same as WPA2 or IEEE 802.11i, is the preferred option for the best security. If WPA2 is the best, you may wonder why there are so many other options. The answer is that many wireless LANs are supporting old wireless devices. Because all client devices that associate to an access point must be running the same security mode that the access point is running, the access point has to be set to support the device running the weakest security mode. All wireless LAN devices manufactured after March 2006 must be able to support WPA2, or in the case of Linksys routers, PSK2, so in time, as devices are upgraded, you will be able to switch your network security mode over to PSK2.

The RADIUS option that is available for a Linksys wireless router allows you to use a RADIUS server in combination with WEP.

Click the buttons along the bottom of the figure for a view of the GUI for each configuration.

To configure security, do the following:

- *Security Mode* - Select the mode you want to use: PSK-Personal, PSK2-Personal, PSK-Enterprise, PSK2-Enterprise, RADIUS, or WEP.

- *Mode Parameters* - Each of the PSK and PSK2 modes have parameters that you can configure. If you select the PSK2-Enterprise security version, you must have a RADIUS server attached to your access point. If you have this configuration, you need to configure the access point to point to the RADIUS server.

- *RADIUS Server IP Address* - Enter the IP address of the RADIUS server.

- *RADIUS Server Port* - Enter the port number used by the RADIUS server. The default is 1812.

- *Encryption* - Select the algorithm you want to use, AES or TKIP. (AES is a stronger encryption method than TKIP.)

- *Pre-shared Key* - Enter the key shared by the router and your other network devices. It must have 8 to 63 characters.

- *Key Renewal* - Enter the key renewal period, which tells the router how often it should change encryption keys.

When you have finished making changes to this screen, click the **Save Settings** button, or click the **Cancel Changes** button to undo your changes.

7.3.2 Configuring a Wireless NIC

Scan for SSIDs

When the access point has been configured, you need to configure the wireless NIC on a client device to allow it to connect to the wireless network. You also should verify that the wireless client has successfully connected to the correct wireless network, especially since there may be many WLANs available with which to connect. We will also introduce some basic troubleshooting steps and identify common problems associated with WLAN connectivity.

If your PC is equipped with a wireless NIC, you should be ready to scan for wireless networks. PCs running Microsoft Windows XP have a built-in wireless networks monitor and client utility. You may have a different utility installed and selected in preference to the native Microsoft Windows XP version.

The steps below are for using the View Wireless Networks feature in Microsoft Windows XP.

Click the numbered steps in the figure to follow the process.

Step 1. On the Microsoft Windows XP toolbar system tray, find the network connection icon that looks similar to the one shown in the figure. Double-click the icon to open the Network Connections dialog box.

Step 2. Click the **View Wireless Networks** button in the dialog box.

Step 3. Observe the wireless networks that your wireless NIC has been able to detect.

If you have a WLAN that is not showing up on the list of networks, you may have disabled SSID broadcast on the access point. If this is the case, you must enter the SSID manually.

Select the Wireless Security Protocol

After having configured your access point to authenticate clients with a strong security type, you must match your client configuration to the access point parameters. The following steps describe how to configure your wireless network security parameters on the client:

Step 1. Double-click the network connections icon in the Microsoft Windows XP system tray.

Step 2. Click the **Properties** button in the Wireless Network Connections Status dialog box.

Step 3. In the **Properties** dialog box, click the **Wireless Networks** tab.

Step 4. In the **Wireless Networks** tab, click the **Add** button. Also, you can save multiple wireless profiles with different security parameters allowing you to quickly connect to the WLANs you may use regularly.

Step 5. In the Wireless Network Properties dialog box, enter the SSID of the WLAN you wish to configure.

Step 6. In the Wireless network key box, select your preferred authentication method from the **Network Authentication** drop-down menu. WPA2 and PSK2 are preferred because of their strength.

Step 7. Select the **Data encryption** method from the drop-down menu. Recall that AES is a stronger cipher than TKIP, but you should match the configuration from your access point here on your PC.

After selecting the encryption method, enter and confirm the **Network key**. Again, this is a value that you have entered into the access point.

Step 8. Click **OK**.

Verify Connectivity to the Wireless LAN

Refer to
Figure
in online course

With configurations set for both the access point and the client, the next step is to confirm connectivity. This is a done by pinging devices in the network.

Open the DOS command prompt window on the PC.

Try to ping a known IP address for a device in the network. In the figure, the IP address is 192.168.1.254. The ping was successful, indicating a successful connection.

Refer to **Packet Tracer Activity** for this chapter

In this activity, you will configure a Linksys wireless router, allowing for remote access from PCs as well as wireless connectivity with WEP security.

Detailed instructions are provided within the activity as well as in the PDF link below.

Activity Instructions (PDF)

7.4 Troubleshooting Simple WLAN Problems

7.4.1 Solve Access Point Radio and Firmware Issues

Refer to
Figure
in online course

A Systematic Approach to WLAN Troubleshooting

Troubleshooting any sort of network problem should follow a systematic approach, working up the TCP/IP stack from the Physical layer to the *Application layer*. This helps to eliminate any issues that you may be able to resolve yourself.

Click the Approach button in the figure.

You should already be familiar with the first three steps of the systematic troubleshooting approach from working with 802.3 Ethernet LANs. They are repeated here in the context of the WLAN:

Step 1 - Eliminate the user PC as the source of the problem.

Try to determine the severity of the problem. If there is no connectivity, check the following:

- Confirm the network configuration on the PC using the `ipconfig` command. Verify that the PC has received an IP address via DHCP or is configured with a static IP address.

- Confirm that the device can connect to the wired network. Connect the device to the wired LAN and ping a known IP address.

- It may be necessary to try a different wireless NIC. If necessary, reload drivers and firmware as appropriate for the client device.

- If the wireless NIC of the client is working, check the security mode and encryption settings on the client. If the security settings do not match, the client cannot get access to the WLAN.

If the PC of the user is operational but is performing poorly, check the following:

- How far is the PC from an access point? Is the PC out of the planned coverage area (BSA).

- Check the channel settings on the client. The client software should detect the appropriate channel as long as the SSID is correct.

- Check for the presence of other devices in the area that operate on the 2.4 GHz band. Examples of other devices are cordless phones, baby monitors, microwave ovens, wireless security systems, and potentially rogue access points. Data from these devices can cause interference in the WLAN and intermittent connection problems between a client and access point.

Step 2 - Confirm the physical status of devices.

- Are all the devices actually in place? Consider a possible physical security issue.

- Is there power to all devices, and are they powered on?

Step 3 - Inspect links.

- Inspect links between cabled devices looking for bad connectors or damaged or missing cables.

- If the physical plant is in place, use the wired LAN to see if you can ping devices including the access point.

If connectivity still fails at this point, perhaps something is wrong with the access point or its configuration.

As you troubleshoot a WLAN, a process of elimination is recommended, working from physical possibilities to application-related ones. When you have reached the point where you have eliminated the user PC as the problem, and also confirmed the physical status of devices, begin investigating the performance of the access point. Check the power status of the access point.

When the access point settings have been confirmed, if the radio continues to fail, try to connect to a different access point. You may try to install new radio drivers and firmware, which is explained next.

> Refer to
> **Figure**
> in online course

Updating the Access Point Firmware

Caution: Do not upgrade the firmware unless you are experiencing problems with the access point or the new firmware has a feature you want to use.

The firmware for a Linksys device, such as the one used in the labs on this course, is upgraded using the web-based utility. Follow these instructions:

Click the Download Firmware button in the figure.

Step 1. Download the firmware from the web. For a Linksys WTR300N, go to http://www. linksys.com.

Click the Select Firmware to Install button in the figure.

Step 2. Extract the firmware file on your computer.

Step 3. Open the web-based utility, and click the **Administration** tab.

Step 4. Select the **Firmware Upgrade** tab.

Step 5. Enter the location of the firmware file, or click the Browse button to find the file.

Click the Run Firmware Upgrade button in the figure.

Step 6. Click the **Start to Upgrade** button and follow the instructions.

7.4.2 Incorrect Channel Settings

Refer to
Figure
in online course

Click the Problem button in the figure.

If users report connectivity issues in the area between access points in an extended service set WLAN, there could be a channel setting issue.

Click the Reason button in the figure.

Most WLANs today operate in the 2.4 GHz band, which can have as many as 14 channels, each occupying 22 MHz of bandwidth. Energy is not spread evenly over the entire 22 MHz, rather the channel is strongest at its center frequency, and the energy diminishes toward the edges of the channel. The concept of the waning energy in a channel is shown by the curved line used to indicate each channel. The high point in the middle of each channel is the point of highest energy. The figure provides a graphical representation of the channels in the 2.4 GHz band.

A full explanation of the way energy is spread across the frequencies in a channel is beyond the scope of this course.

Click the Solution button in the figure.

Interference can occur when there is overlap of channels. It is worse if the channels overlap close to the center frequencies, but even if there is minor overlap, signals interfere with each other. Set the channels at intervals of five channels, such as channel 1, channel 6, and channel 11.

7.4.3 Solve Access Point Radio and Firmware Issues

Refer to
Figure
in online course

Solving RF Interference

Incorrect channel settings are part of the larger group of problems with RF interference. WLAN administrators can control interference caused by channel settings with good planning, including proper channel spacing.

Click the Problem button in the figure.

Other sources of RF interference can be found all around the workplace or in the home. Perhaps you have experienced the snowy disruption of a television signal when someone nearby runs a vacuum cleaner. Such interference can be moderated with good planning. For instance, plan to place microwave ovens away from access points and potential clients. Unfortunately, the entire range of possible RF interference issues cannot be planned for because there are just too many possibilities.

Click the Reason button in the figure.

The problem with devices such as cordless phones, baby monitors, and microwave ovens, is that they are not part of a BSS, so they do not contend for the channel-they just use it. How can you find out which channels in an area are most crowded?

In a small WLAN environment, try setting your WLAN access point to channel 1 or channel 11. Many consumer items, such as cordless phones, operate on channel 6.

Site Surveys

In more crowded environments, a site survey might be needed. Although you do not conduct site surveys as part of this course, you should know that there are two categories of site surveys: manual and utility assisted.

Manual site surveys can include a site evaluation to be followed by a more thorough utility-assisted site survey. A site evaluation involves inspecting the area with the goal of identifying potential issues that could impact the network. Specifically, look for the presence of multiple WLANs, unique building structures, such as open floors and atriums, and high client usage variances, such as those caused by differences in day or night shift staffing levels.

Click the Solution button in the figure.

There are several approaches to doing utility-assisted site surveys. If you do not have access to dedicated site survey tools, such as Airmagnet, you can mount access points on tripods and set them in locations you think are appropriate and in accordance with the projected site plan. With access points mounted, you can then walk around the facility using a site survey meter in the WLAN client utility of your PC, as shown in screenshot 1 in the figure.

Alternatively, sophisticated tools are available that allow you to enter a facility floor plan. You can then begin a recording of the RF characteristics of the site, which are then shown on the floor plan as you move about the facility with your wireless laptop. An example of an Airmagnet site survey output is shown in screenshot 2 in the figure.

Part of the advantage to utility-assisted site surveys is that RF activity on the various channels in the various unlicensed bands (900 MHz, 2.4 GHz, and 5 GHz) is documented, and you are then able to choose channels for your WLAN, or at very least identify areas of high RF activity, and make provisions for them.

7.4.4 Solve Access Point Radio and Firmware Issues

Refer to
Figure
in online course

Identify Problems with Access Point Misplacement

In this topic, you will learn how to identify when an access point is incorrectly placed, and how to correctly place the access point in a small- or medium-sized business.

Click the Problem button in the figure.

You may have experienced a WLAN that just did not seem to perform like it should. Perhaps you keep losing association with an access point, or your data rates are much slower than they should be. You may even have done a quick walk-around the facility to confirm that you could actually see the access points. Having confirmed that they are there, you wonder why you continue to get poor service.

Click the Reason button in the figure.

There are two major deployment issues that may occur with the placement of access points:

- The distance separating access points is too far to allow overlapping coverage.

- The orientation of access point antennae in hallways and corners diminishes coverage.

Click the Solution button in the figure.

Fix access point placement as follows:

Confirm the power settings and operational ranges of access points and place them for a minimum of 10 to 15% cell overlap, as you learned earlier this chapter.

Change the orientation and positioning of access points:

- Position access points above obstructions.

- Position access points vertically near the ceiling in the center of each coverage area, if possible.

- Position access points in locations where users are expected to be. For example, large rooms are typically a better location for access points than a hallway.

The figure explores these issues in a problem, reason, solution sequence.

Click each of the buttons to advance through the graphic.

Some additional specific details concerning access point and antenna placement are as follows:

- Ensure that access points are not mounted closer than 7.9 inches (20 cm) from the body of all persons.

- Do not mount the access point within 3 feet (91.4 cm) of metal obstructions.

- Install the access point away from microwave ovens. Microwave ovens operate on the same frequency as the access point and can cause signal interference.

- Always mount the access point vertically (standing up or hanging down).

- Do not mount the access point outside of buildings.

- Do not mount the access point on building perimeter walls, unless outside coverage is desired.

- When mounting an access point in the corner of a right-angle hallway intersection, mount it at a 45-degree angle to the two hallways. The access point internal antennas are not omnidirectional and cover a larger area when mounted this way.

7.4.5 Problems with Authentication and Encryption

Refer to
Figure
in online course

The WLAN authentication and encryption problems you are most likely to encounter, and that you will be able to solve, are caused by incorrect client settings. If an access point is expecting one type of encryption, and the client offers a different type, the authentication process fails.

Encryption issues involving the creation of dynamic keys and the conversations between an authentication server, such as a RADIUS server, and a client through an access point are beyond the scope of this course.

Remember, all devices connecting to an access point must use the same security type as the one configured on the access point. Therefore, if an access point is configured for WEP, both the type of encryption (WEP) and the shared key must match between the client and the access point. If WPA is being used, the encryption algorithm is TKIP. Similarly, if WPA2 or 802.11i is used, AES is required as the encryption algorithm.

7.5 Chapter Labs

7.5.1 Basic Wireless Configuration

Refer to
Lab Activity
for this chapter

In this lab, you will configure a Linksys WRT300N, port security on a Cisco switch, and static routes on multiple devices. Make note of the procedures involved in connecting to a wireless network because some changes involve disconnecting clients, which may then have to reconnect after making changes to the configuration.

7.5.2 Challenge Wireless Configuration

Refer to **Lab Activity** for this chapter

In this lab, you will learn how to configure a Linksys WRT300N. You will also learn how to configure port security on a Cisco switch, as well as configuring static routes on multiple devices. Make note of the procedures involved in connecting to a wireless network, because some changes involve disconnecting current clients and then reconnecting to the device after configuration changes.

Refer to **Packet Tracer Activity** for this chapter

In this activity, you will configure a Linksys WRT300N, port security on a Cisco switch, and static routes on multiple devices. Make note of the procedures involved in connecting to a wireless network because some changes involve disconnecting clients, which may then have to reconnect after making changes to the configuration.

Detailed instructions are provided within the activity as well as in the PDF link below.

Activity Instructions (PDF)

7.5.3 Troubleshooting Wireless Configuration

Refer to **Lab Activity** for this chapter

In this lab, a basic network and wireless network have been configured improperly. You must find and correct the misconfigurations based on the minimum network specifications provided by your company.

Refer to **Packet Tracer Activity** for this chapter

In this activity, a basic network and wireless network have been configured improperly. You must find and correct the misconfigurations based on the minimum network specifications provided by your company.

Detailed instructions are provided within the activity as well as in the PDF link below.

Activity Instructions (PDF)

Refer to
Figure
in online course

Chapter Summary

In this chapter, we discussed the evolving wireless LAN standards, including IEEE 802.11a, b, g and now, draft n. Newer standards take into account the need to support voice and video and the requisite quality of service.

Refer to
Figure
in online course

A single access point connected to the wired LAN provides a basic service set to client stations that associate to it. Multiple access points that share a service set identifier combine to form an extended service set. Wireless LANs can be detected by any radio-enabled client device and therefore may enable access by attackers that do not have access to a wired-only network.

Methods such as MAC address filtering and SSID masking can be part of a security best practice implementation, but these methods alone are easily overcome by a determined attacker. WPA2 and 802.1x authentication provide very secure wireless LAN access in an enterprise network.

Refer to **Packet Tracer Activity** for this chapter

End users have to configure a wireless NICs on their client stations which communicate with and associate to a wireless access point. Both the access point and wireless NICs must be configured with similar parameters, including SSID, before association is possible. When configuring a wireless LAN, ensure that the devices have the latest firmware so that they can support the most stringent security options. In addition to ensuring compatible configuration of wireless security settings, troubleshooting wireless LANs involves resolving RF problems.

In this final Packet Tracer Skills Integration Challenge activity for the Exploration: LAN Switching and Wireless course, you will apply all the skills you have learned including configuring VLANs and VTP, optimizing STP, enabling inter-VLAN routing and integrating wireless connectivity.

Detailed instructions are provided within the activity as well as in the PDF link below.

Activity Instructions (PDF)

Go to
the online course
to take the quiz.

Chapter Quiz

Take the chapter quiz to test your knowledge.

Your Chapter Notes

active state

A state in which there is no Feasible Successor in the topology table and the local router goes into Active state and queries its neighbors for routing information.

AD

See administrative distance

adjacency

A relationship formed between selected neighboring routers and end nodes for the purpose of exchanging routing information. Adjacency is based upon the use of a common media segment.

administrative distance

Rating of the trustworthiness of a routing information source. Administrative distance often is expressed as a numerical value between 0 and 255. The higher the value, the lower the trustworthiness rating. If a router has multiple routing protocols in it's routing table it will select the route with the lowest administrative distance.

Algorithm

Well-defined rule or process for arriving at a solution to a problem. In networking, algorithms are commonly used to determine the best route for traffic from a particular source to a particular destination.

ALLSPFRouters

A multicast group used in the OSPF routing protocol. The ALLSPFRouters address is 224.0.0.5.

ARP

Address Resolution Protocol. Internet protocol used to map an IP address to a MAC address. Defined in RFC 826.

asymmetric routing

Asymmetric routing is when a path from network 1 to network 2 is different from the path from network 2 to network 1. The paths to network 2 are different than the returning path from Network 2 to network 1.

Asynchronous Transfer Mode (ATM)

Asynchronous Transfer Mode. The international standard for cell relay in which multiple service types (such as voice, video, or data) are conveyed in fixed-length (53-byte) cells. Fixed-length cells allow cell processing to occur in hardware, thereby reducing transit delays. ATM is designed to take advantage of high-speed transmission media, such as E3, SONET, and T3.

automatic summarization

Consolidation of networks and advertised in classful network advertisements. In RIP this causes a single summary route to be advertised to other routers.

Autonomous System (AS)

A collection of networks under a common administration sharing a common routing strategy. Autonomous systems are subdivided by areas. An autonomous system must be assigned a unique 16-bit number by the IANA. Sometimes abbreviated as AS.

Autonomous System Boundary Router (ASBR)

Autonomous system boundary router. An ASBR is located between an OSPF autonomous system and a non-OSPF network. ASBRs run both OSPF and another routing protocol, such as RIP. ASBRs must reside in a nonstub OSPF area.

Backup Designated Router (BDR)

A router that becomes the designated router if the current designated router fails. The BDR is the OSPF router with second highest priority at the time of the last DR election.

Bellman-Ford (algorithm)

Class of routing algorithms that iterate on the number of hops in a route to find a shortest-path spanning tree. Distance vector routing algorithms call for each router to send its entire routing table in each update, but only to its neighbors. Distance vector routing algorithms can be prone to routing loops, but are computationally simpler than link state routing algorithms.

best path

The fastest path to a certain destination. The fastest path being based on the routing protocol's metric.

Border Gateway Routing (BGP)

Border Gateway Protocol. Interdomain routing protocol that replaces EGP. BGP exchanges reachability information with other BGP systems. It is defined by RFC 1163.

boundary router

A router that sits on the edge two discontiguous classful networks. A boundary router can also be known as a router that sits on the edge of two different networks that have different routing protocols. Sometimes the word boundary router is loosely used when discussing OSPF and Autonomous System Boundary Routers.

bounded updates

Updates that are sent only to those routers that need the updated information instead of sending updates to all routers.

cable

Transmission medium of copper wire or optical fiber wrapped in a protective cover.

classful IP addressing

In the early days of IPv4, IP addresses are divided into 5 classes, namely, Class A, Class B, Class C, Class D, and Class E.

classful routing protocols

Routing protocols that use classful ip addressing. They do not use subnet mask information in their routing operation. They automatically assume classful masks.

Classless Inter-Domain Routing (CIDR)

Technique supported by BGP4 and based on route aggregation. CIDR allows routers to group routes together to reduce the quantity of routing information carried by the core routers. With CIDR, several IP networks appear to networks outside the group as a single, larger entity. With CIDR, IP addresses and their subnet masks are written as four octets, separated by periods, followed by a forward slash and a two-digit number that represents the subnet mask.

console port

DTE through which commands are entered into a host.

contiguous

Consistent or adjacent. In terms of contiguous networks, the word contiguous means network blocks that are hierarchical in nature.

Contiguous Address Assignment

Addressing that is not fragmented and follows a hierarchical format allowing for network summarization.

converged

The past tense of converge. When intermediate devices all have the same consistent network topology in their routing tables. This means that they have converged.

convergence

Speed and ability of a group of internetworking devices running a specific routing protocol to agree on the topology of an internetwork after a change in that topology.

cost

An arbitrary value, typically based on hop count, media bandwidth, or other measures, that is assigned by a network administrator and used to compare various paths through an internetwork environment. Routing protocols use cost values to determine the most favorable path to a particular destination: the lower the cost, the better the path.

count to infinity

Problem that can occur in routing algorithms that are slow to converge, in which routers continuously increment the hop count to particular networks. Typically, some arbitrary hop-count limit is imposed to prevent this problem.

Database Description (DBD)

A packet which contains an abbreviated list of the sending router's link-state database and is used by receiving routers to check against the local link-state database. Routers exchange DBDs during the Exchange phase of adjacency creation.

datagrams

Logical grouping of information sent as a network layer unit over a transmission medium without prior establishment of a virtual circuit. IP datagrams are the primary information units in the Internet. The terms cell, frame, message, packet, and segment also are used to describe logical information groupings at various layers of the OSI reference model and in various technology circles.

data-link

Layer 2 of the OSI reference model. Provides reliable transit of data across a physical link. The data-link layer is concerned with physical addressing, network topology, line discipline, error notification, ordered delivery of frames, and flow control. The IEEE divided this layer into two sublayers: the MAC sublayer and the LLC sublayer. Sometimes simply called link layer. Roughly corresponds to the data-link control layer of the SNA model.

Designated Router (DR)

OSPF router that generates LSAs for a multiaccess network and has other special responsibilities in running OSPF. Each multiaccess OSPF network that has at least two attached routers has a designated router that is elected by the OSPF Hello protocol. The designated router enables a reduction in the number of adjacencies required on a multiaccess network, which in turn reduces the amount of routing protocol traffic and the size of the topological database.

Diffusing Update Algorithm (DUAL)

Diffusing Update Algorithm. Convergence algorithm used in Enhanced IGRP that provides loop-free operation at every instant throughout a route computation. Allows routers involved in a topology change to synchronize at the same time, while not involving routers that are unaffected by the change.

discontiguous

Components that are fragmented. For example a discontiguous network comprises of a major network that separates another major network.

discontiguous address assignment

A fragmented network assignment that does not follow a consistent pattern.

discontiguous network

Fragmented network addressing. Networks that do not have a hierarchical scheme. It is impossible to summarize discontiguous networks.

distance vector

see Bellman-Ford (Algorithm)

domain

A portion of the naming hierarchy tree that refers to general groupings of networks based on organization type or geography.

DROthers

DROthers are routers that are not DR or BDR. They are the other routers in the OSPF network.

DSL

Digital subscriber line. Public network technology that delivers high bandwidth over conventional copper wiring at limited distances. There are four types of DSL: ADSL, HDSL, SDSL, and VDSL. All are provisioned via modem pairs, with one modem located at a central office and the other at the customer site. Because most DSL technologies do not use the whole bandwidth of the twisted pair, there is room remaining for a voice channel.

dynamic routing

Routing that adjusts automatically to network topology or traffic changes. Also called adaptive routing.

dynamic routing protocols

Allow network devices to learn routes dynamically. RIP and EIGRP are examples of dynamic routing protocols.

Enhanced IGRP (EIGRP)

Enhanced Interior Gateway Routing Protocol. Advanced version of IGRP developed by Cisco. Provides superior convergence properties and operating efficiency, and combines the advantages of link state protocols with those of distance vector protocols.

equal cost load balancing

When a router utilizes multiple paths with the same administrative distance and cost to a destination.

equal cost metric

A metric that has the same value on multiple paths to the same destination. When multiple paths have equal cost metrics a router can execute equal cost load balancing among those paths.

Ethernet
Baseband LAN specification invented by Xerox Corporation and developed jointly by Xerox, Intel, and Digital Equipment Corporation. Ethernet networks use CSMA/CD and run over a variety of cable types at 10 Mbps. Ethernet is similar to the IEEE 802.3 series of standards.

Feasibility Condition (FC)
If the receiving router has a Feasible Distance to a particular network and it receives an update from a neighbor with a lower advertised distance (Reported Distance) to that network, then there is a Feasibility Condition. Used in EIGRP routing.

Feasible Distance (FD)
The Feasible Distance is the metric of a network advertised by the connected neighbor plus the cost of reaching that neighbor. The path with the lowest metric is added to the routing table and is called FD or feasible distance. Used in EIGRP routing.

Feasible Successor (FS)
A next hop router that leads to a certain destination network. The feasible successor can be thought of as a backup next hop if the primary next hop (successor) goes down. Used in EIGRP routing.

Fiber Distributed Data INterface (FDDI)
Fiber Distributed Data Interface. LAN standard, defined by ANSI X3T9.5, specifying a 100-Mbps token-passing network using fiber-optic cable, with transmission distances of up to 2 km. FDDI uses a dual-ring architecture to provide redundancy.

flapping link
Routing problem where an advertised route between two nodes alternates (flaps) back and forth between two paths due to a network problem that causes intermittent interface failures.

flash
Technology developed by Intel and licensed to other semiconductor companies. Flash memory is nonvolatile storage that can be electrically erased and reprogrammed. Allows software images to be stored, booted, and rewritten as necessary.

Frame Relay
A packet switched data link layer protocol that handles multiple virtual circuits using between connected devices. Frame Relay is more efficient than X.25, the protocol for which it generally is considered a replacement.

gateways
A device on a network that serves as an access point to another network. A default gateway is used by a host when an IP packet's destination address belongs to someplace outside the local subnet. A router is a good example of a default gateway.

high order bits
The 'high order bit' of a binary number is the one that carries the most weight, the one written farthest to the left. High order bits are the 1s in the network mask.

hold time
The maximum time a router waits to receive the next hello packet or routing update. Once the hold time counter expires that route will become unreachable.

hold-down timers
Timers that a route is placed in so that routers neither advertise the route nor accept advertisements about the route for a specific length of time (the holddown period). Holddown is used to flush bad information about a route from all routers in the network. A route typically is placed in holddown when a link in that route fails.

hosts
Computer system on a network. Similar to node, except that host usually implies a computer system, whereas node generally applies to any networked system, including access servers and routers.

hub-and-spoke
A wan topology whereupon various branch offices are connected via a centralized hub or headquarters.

ICMP
Internet Control Message Protocol. Network layer Internet protocol that reports errors and provides other information relevant to IP packet processing. Documented in RFC 792.

IGRP
Interior Gateway Routing Protocol. IGP developed by Cisco to address the issues associated with routing in large, heterogeneous networks.

Interior Gateway Protocols
Internet protocol used to exchange routing information within an autonomous system. Examples of common Internet IGPs include IGRP, OSPF, and RIP.

Intermediate-System-to-Intermediate-System (IS-IS)
Intermediate System-to-Intermediate System protocol (IS-IS) is based on a routing method known as DECnet Phase V routing, in which routers known as intermediate systems exchange data about routing using a single metric to determine the network topology. IS-IS was developed by the International Organization for Standardization (ISO) as part of their Open Systems Interconnection (OSI) model.

Internet Service Provider (ISP)
An ISP is a company that provides access to the Internet to individuals or companies.

IP
Internet Protocol. Network layer protocol in the TCP/IP stack offering a connectionless internetwork service. IP provides features for addressing, type-of-service specification, fragmentation and reassembly, and security. Defined in RFC 791.

IPv6
A network layer protocol for packet-switched internet works. The successor of IPv4 for general use on the Internet.

IPX
Internetwork Packet Exchange. NetWare network layer (Layer 3) protocol used for transferring data from servers to workstations. IPX is similar to IP and XNS.

ISDN
Integrated Services Digital Network. Communication protocol offered by telephone companies that permits telephone networks to carry data, voice, and other source traffic.

LED
Light emitting diode. Semiconductor device that emits light produced by converting electrical energy.

Level 1 Parent route
A first level route in the routing table that has subnets "catalogued" under it. A first level parent route does not contain any next-hop IP address or exit interface information.

Level 1 route
A route with a subnet mask equal to or less than the classful mask of the network address.

Level 2 child route
The subnets that belong to the parent route.

Level 2 route
A subnet is the level 2 route of the parent route.

Link-state
Link-state refers to the status of a link including the interface IP address/subnet mask, type of network, cost of the link, and any neighbor routers on that link.

Link-State Acknowledgement (LSAck)
Link State Acknowledgment Packets are OSPF packet type 5. LSAcks acknowledge receipt of LSA (Links State Advertisement) packets.

Link-State Advertisement (LSA)
Link-state advertisement. Broadcast packet used by link-state protocols that contains information about neighbors and path costs. LSAs are used by the receiving routers to maintain their routing tables.

link-state database
A table used in OSPF that is a representation of the topology of the autonomous system. It is the method by which routers see the state of the links in the autonomous system.

Link-State Packet (LSP)
Broadcast packet used by link-state protocols that contains information about neighbors and path costs. LSPs are used by the receiving routers to maintain their routing tables.

Link-State Request (LSR)

Link State Request packets are OSPF packet type 3. The Link State Request packet is used to request the pieces of the neighbor's database that are more up to date.

link-state router

A router that uses a link-state routing protocol.

link-state routing protocol

A routing protocol in which routers exchange information with one another about the reachability of other networks and the cost or metric to reach the other networks. Link state routers use Dijkstra's algorithm to calculate shortest paths to a destination, and normally update other routers with whom they are connected only when their own routing tables change.

Link-State Update (LSU)

Link State Update packets are OSPF packet type 4. Link State Update packet carries a collection of link state advertisements one hop further from its origin.

load balancing

In routing, the capability of a router to distribute traffic over all its network ports that are the same distance from the destination address. Good load-balancing algorithms use both line speed and reliability information. Load balancing increases the use of network segments, thus increasing effective network bandwidth.

Local Area Networks (LANs)

The term Local Area Network (LAN) refers to a local network, or a group of interconnected local networks that are under the same administrative control. In the early days of networking, LANs were defined as small networks that existed in a single physical location. While LANs can be a single local network installed in a home or small office, the definition of LAN has evolved to include interconnected local networks consisting of many hundreds of hosts, installed in multiple buildings and locations.

loopback

127.0.0.1 is an IP address available on all devices to test to see if the NIC card on that device is functioning. If you send something to 127.0.0.1, it loops back on itself, thereby sending the data to the NIC on that device. If you get a positive response to a ping 127.0.0.1, you know your NIC card is up and running.

loopback address

127.0.0.1 is an IP address available on all devices to test to see if the NIC card on that device is functioning. If you send something to 127.0.0.1, it loops back on itself, thereby sending the data to the NIC on that device. If you get a positive response to a ping 127.0.0.1, you know your NIC card is up and running.

loopback interface

A virtual interface used for management purposes. Unlike a proper loopback interface, this loopback device is not used to talk with itself.

loop-free

Free of loops.

MAC address

Standardized data link layer address that is required for every port or device that connects to a LAN. Other devices in the network use these addresses to locate specific ports in the network and to create and update routing tables and data structures. MAC addresses are 6 bytes long and are controlled by the IEEE.

media

Plural of medium. The various physical environments through which transmission signals pass. Common network media include twisted-pair, coaxial and fiber-optic cable, and the atmosphere (through which microwave, laser, and infrared transmission occurs). Sometimes called physical media.

metrics

Method by which a routing algorithm determines that one route is better than another. This information is stored in routing tables. Metrics include bandwidth, communication cost, delay, hop count, load, MTU, path cost, and reliability. Sometimes referred to simply as a metric.

multiaccess network

Network that allows multiple devices to connect and communicate simultaneously.

Network Address Translator (NAT)

Mechanism for reducing the need for globally unique IP addresses. NAT allows an organization with addresses that are not globally unique to connect to the Internet by translating those addresses into globally routable address space.

neighbor
In OSPF, two routers that have interfaces to a common network. On multiaccess networks, neighbors are discovered dynamically by the OSPF Hello protocol.

Network Interface Card (NIC)
A piece of computer hardware designed to allow computers to communicate over a computer network.

network prefix
Number of bits that are used to define the subnet mask. For example the subnet mask 255.255.0.0 is a /16 prefix.

next-hop
The next point of routing. When routers are not directly connected to the destination network, they will have a neighboring router that provides the next step in routing the data to its destination.

non-broadcast multiaccess (NBMA)
Term describing a multiaccess network that either does not support broadcasting (such as X.25) or in which broadcasting is not feasible (for example, an SMDS broadcast group or an extended Ethernet that is too large).

Non-Volatile RAM (NVRAM)
Non Volatile Random Access Memory. Random access memory that, when the computer shuts down, the contents in NVRAM remain there.

null interface
The null interface provides an alternative method of filtering traffic. You can avoid the overhead involved with using access lists by directing undesired network traffic to the null interface. This interface is always up and can never forward or receive traffic. Think of it as a black hole.

Null0 summary routes
Another mechanism to prevent routing loops. EIGRP always creates a route to the Null0 interface when it summarizes a group of routes. This is because whenever a routing protocol summarizes, the router might receive traffic for any IP address within that summary. Since not all IP addresses are always in use, there is a risk of looping packets in case default routes are used on the router which receives the traffic for the summary route.

Open Shortest Path First (OSPF)
Open Shortest Path First. Link-state, hierarchical IGP routing algorithm proposed as a successor to RIP in the Internet community. OSPF features include least-cost routing, multipath routing, and load balancing. OSPF was derived from an early version of the IS-IS protocol.

Operating System
A software that performs basic tasks such as controlling and allocating memory, prioritizing system requests, controlling input and output devices, facilitating networking, and managing file systems.

OSPF area
A logical set of network segments (CLNS-, DECnet-, or OSPF-based) and their attached devices. Areas usually are connected to other areas via routers, making up a single autonomous system.

packet
Logical grouping of information that includes a header containing control information and (usually) user data. Packets most often are used to refer to network layer units of data. The terms datagram, frame, message, and segment also are used to describe logical information groupings at various layers of the OSI reference model and in various technology circles.

partial update packet
When a router detects a change in a metric it sends a partial update about that specific change to bounded routers instead of sending periodic updates.

passive state
A passive state is a state when the router has identified the successor(s) for a certain destination and it becomes stable. A term used in conjunction with EIGRP.

path vector protocol
A path vector protocol is a routing protocol that marks and shows the path that update information takes as it diffuses through the network. BGP is a user of the kind of protocol because it verifies what autonomous systems the update has passed through to verify loops.

poison reverse
Routing updates that explicitly indicate that a network or a subnet is unreachable, rather than implying that a network is unreachable by not including it in updates. Poison reverse updates are sent to defeat large routing loops.

Power-On Self Test (POST)
Set of hardware diagnostics that runs on a hardware device when that device is powered up.

PPP
Point-to-Point Protocol. Successor to SLIP that provides router-to-router and host-to-network connections over synchronous and asynchronous circuits. Whereas SLIP was designed to work with IP, PPP was designed to work with several network layer protocols, such as IP, IPX, and ARA. PPP also has built-in security mechanisms, such as CHAP and PAP. PPP relies on two protocols: LCP and NCP.

prefix aggregation
Also known as network summarization. A number of IP addresses and IP prefixes can be summarized into a single IP prefix and be announced to other routers only the resulting less specific prefix (aggregated prefix) instead of the more specific IP addresses and prefixes that it covers.

private addressing
An address that is used for internal networks. This address follows RFC 1918 addressing. Not routable on the internet.

privileged EXEC mode
Privileged Exec Mode is the administration mode for the router or switch. This mode by allows you to view router settings that are considered only accessible to the administrator. This mode also allows you to enter global configuration mode. To get into the privileged exec mode you must use the enable command.

protocol-dependent module
A component that is dependent on a certain routed protocol. For example, protocol dependent modules in EIGRP allow it to work with various routed protocols. PDMs allow for EIGRP to keep a topology table for each routed protocol such as IP, IPX RIP, AppleTalk Routing Table Maintenance Protocol (RTMP), and IGRP.

Quality of Service (QoS)
quality of service. Measure of performance for a transmission system that reflects its transmission quality and service availability.

Random Access Memory (RAM)
Volatile memory that can be read and written by a microprocessor.

Read-Only Memory (ROM)
Nonvolatile memory that can be read, but not written, by the microprocessor.

redistribution
Allowing routing information discovered through one routing protocol to be distributed in the update messages of another routing protocol. Sometimes called route redistribution.

redundant paths
Multiple paths to a destination that are usable upon failure of a primary path.

reference bandwidth
The bandwidth referenced by the SPF algorithm when calculating shortest path. In OSPF the reference bandwidth is 10 to the power of 8 divided by the actual interface bandwidth.

reported distance (RD)
Reported distance is the total metric along a path to a destination network as advertised by an upstream neighbor in EIGRP.

Route poisoning
Routing updates that explicitly indicate that a network or subnet is unreachable, rather than implying that a network is unreachable by not including it in updates. Poison reverse updates are sent to defeat large routing loops. The Cisco IGRP implementation uses poison reverse updates.

route summarization
Consolidation of advertised addresses in OSPF and IS-IS. In OSPF, this causes a single summary route to be advertised to other areas by an area border router.

Router
Network layer device that uses one or more metrics to determine the optimal path along which network traffic should be forwarded. Routers forward packets from one network to another based on network layer information.

Occasionally called a gateway (although this definition of gateway is becoming increasingly outdated).

Routing Information Protocol (RIP)

Routing Information Protocol. IGP supplied with UNIX BSD systems. The most common IGP in the Internet. RIP uses hop count as a routing metric.

routing table

A table stored in the memory of a router or some other internetworking device that keeps track of routes to particular network destinations. A router uses this list of networks to determine where to send data.

Routing Table Maintenance Protocol (RTMP)

Routing Table Maintenance Protocol. Apple Computer proprietary routing protocol. RTMP was derived from RIP.

scale

To alter to a certain size according to need. For example a routing protocol is scalable when the router's routing table grows according to the addition of new networks.

serial

Method of data transmission in which the bits of a data character are transmitted sequentially over a single channel.

Setup mode

When a Cisco router boots up and does not find a configuration file in NVRAM it enters setup mode. Setup mode is a dialogue of questions that the administrator must answer in order to configure a basic configuration for router functionality.

shortest path first (SPF)

Routing algorithm that iterates on length of path to determine a shortest-path spanning tree. Commonly used in link-state routing algorithms. Sometimes called Dijkstra's algorithm.

Smart Serial

Cisco Smart Serial interfaces have 26-pin connectors and can automatically detect RS-232, RS-449, RS-530, X.21, or V.35 connectors.

SPF schedule delay

After inputting the command show ip ospf you will see the parameter SPF schedule delay X secs (The X meaning number of seconds). This is the delay time of SPF calculations.

split horizon

Routing technique in which information about routes is prevented from exiting the router interface through which that information was received. Split-horizon updates are useful in preventing routing loops.

static routing

Routing that depends on manually entered routes in the routing table.

successor

The path to a destination. The successor is chosen using DUAL from all of the known paths or feasible successors to the end destination. Used in EIGRP.

Summary Route

Route summarization reduces the number of routes that a router must maintain. It is a method of representing a series of network numbers in a single summary address.

supernet

Aggregation of IP network addresses advertised as a single classless network address. For example, given four Class C IP networks-192.0.8.0, 192.0.9.0, 192.0.10.0, and 192.0.11.0 - each having the intrinsic network mask of 255.255.255.0, one can advertise the address 192.0.8.0 with a subnet mask of 255.255.252.0.

Supernet route

A route that uses an arbitrary address mask, which is shorter than the default classful mask. Used to represent various subnets.

supernetting

Combining several IP network addresses into one IP address. Supernetting reduces the number of entries in a routing table and is done in CIDR addressing as well as internal networks.

Telnet

Standard terminal emulation protocol in the TCP/IP protocol stack. Telnet is used for remote terminal connection, enabling users to log in to remote systems and use resources as if they were connected to a local system. Telnet is defined in RFC 854.

TFTP Server

a server that hosts the TFTP protocol that allows files to be transferred from one computer to another over a network, usually without the use of client authentication (for example, username and password).

Token Ring

Token-passing LAN developed and supported by IBM. Token Ring runs at 4 or 16 Mbps over a ring topology. Similar to IEEE 802.5.

topology database

Also knows as the topology table, the topology database holds the information about the successor, feasible distance, and any feasible successors with their reported distances. Used in EIGRP routing.

topology table

Contains information regarding EIGRP routes received in updates and routes that are locally originated. EIGRP sends and receives routing updates from adjacent routers to which peering relationships (adjacencies) have been formed. The objects in this table are populated on a per-topology table entry (route) basis.

triggered update

A routing update that is triggered by an event in the network.

TTL

Time To Live. Field in an IP header that indicates how long a packet is considered valid.

Type/Length/Value (TLV)

The data portion of the EIGRP packet. All TLVs begin with 16 bit Type field and a 16 bit Length field. There exist different TLV values according to routed protocol. There is, however, a general TLV that describes generic EIGRP parameters such as Sequence (used by Cisco's Reliable Multicast) and EIGRP software version.

Ultimate Route

Also known as a level 1 route, an ultimate route is a route in the routing table that includes a next hop address and an outgoing interface.

unequal cost load balancing

Load balancing that uses multiple paths to the same destination that have different costs or metrics. EIGRP uses unequal load balancing with the "variance" command.

unified communications

A communications system for voice, video and data. The system integrates wired, wireless and mobile devices to create a secure solution for enterprise networks.

Variable Length Subnet Masking (VLSM)

variable-length subnet mask. Capability to specify a different subnet mask for the same network number on different subnets. VLSM can help optimize available address space.

vector

A vector is a quantity characterized by a magnitude (for instance hops in a path) and a direction.

Wide Area Networks (WANs)

Data communications network that serves users across a broad geographic area and often uses transmission devices provided by common carriers. Frame Relay, SMDS, and X.25 are examples of WANs.

wildcard mask

A 32-bit quantity used in conjunction with an IP address to determine which bits in an IP address should be ignored when comparing that address with another IP address. A wildcard mask is specified when setting up access lists.

XNS

Xerox Network Systems. A protocol stack developed by Xerox that contains network protocols that closely resemble IP and TCP. XNS was one of the first protocol stacks used in the first local area network implementations.

CCNA Exploration
learning resources

Cisco Press, the authorized publisher for the Cisco® Networking Academy®, has a variety of learning and preparation tools to help you master the knowledge and prepare successfully for the CCENT™ and CCNA® exams.

From foundational learning to late-stage review, practice, and preparation, the varied print, software, and video products from Cisco Press can help you with learning, mastering, and succeeding!

Companion Guides

Companion Guides provide textbook-style support with additional content from leading Academy instructors.

Network Fundamentals, CCNA Exploration Companion Guide	1-58713-208-7 / 978-1-58713-208-7
Routing Protocols and Concepts, CCNA Exploration Companion Guide	1-58713-206-0 / 978-1-58713-206-3
LAN Switching and Wireless, CCNA Exploration Companion Guide	1-58713-207-9 / 978-1-58713-207-0
Accessing the WAN, CCNA Exploration Companion Guide	1-58713-205-2 / 978-1-58713-205-6

Labs and Study Guides

Labs and Study Guides provide study tools and labs, both from the online curriculum and from leading Academy instructors.

Network Fundamentals, CCNA Exploration Labs and Study Guide	1-58713-203-6 / 978-1-58713-203-2
Routing Protocols and Concepts, CCNA Exploration Labs and Study Guide	1-58713-204-4 / 978-1-58713-204-9
LAN Switching and Wireless, CCNA Exploration Labs and Study	1-58713-202-8 / 978-1-58713-202-5
Accessing the WAN, CCNA Exploration Labs and Study Guide	1-58713-201-X / 978-1-58713-201-8

Other CCNA resources

1-58713-197-8 / 978-1-58713-197-4	31 Days Before your CCNA Exam, Second Edition
1-58720-183-6 / 978-1-58720-183-7	CCNA Official Exam Certification Library, Third Edition
1-58720-193-3 / 978-1-58720-193-6	CCNA Portable Command Guide, Second Edition
1-58720-216-6 / 978-1-58720-216-2	CCNA 640-802 Network Simulator (from Pearson Certification)
1-58720-221-2 / 978-1-58720-221-6	CCNA 640-802 Cert Flash Cards Online

For more information on this and other Cisco Press products, visit www.ciscopress.com /academy

Cisco Press

Learning is Serious Business. **Invest Wisely.**